WHAT I *DiDN'T LEARN* iN BUSiNESS SCHOOL

WHAT I *DiDN'T LEARN* iN BUSiNESS SCHOOL

HOW STRATEGY WORKS in the **REAL WORLD**

JAY B. BARNEY

TRiSH GORMAN CLiFFORD

Harvard Business Review Press
Boston, Massachusetts

Printed in the United States of America

14 13 12 11 10   5 4 3 2 1

No part of this publication may be reproduced, stored in, or introduced into a retrieval system or transmitted, in any form or by any means (electronic, mechanical, photocopying, recording, or otherwise), without the prior permission of the publisher. Requests for permission should be directed to permissions@hbsp.harvard.edu or mailed to Permissions, Harvard Business School Publishing, 60 Harvard Way, Boston, Massachusetts 02163.

Library of Congress Cataloging-in-Publication Data

Barney, Jay B.
    What I didn't learn in business school : how strategy works in the real world / Jay Barney, Trish Gorman Clifford.
        p. cm.
    ISBN 978-1-4221-5763-3 (hardcover : alk. paper)   1. Strategic planning.
2. Decision making.   3. Problem solving.   I. Clifford, Trish Gorman.   II. Title.
    HD30.28.B36835 2010
    658.4'012—dc22

                                                                    2010016499

The paper used in this publication meets the requirements of the American National Standard for Permanence of Paper for Publications and Documents in Libraries and Archives Z39.48-1992.

Jay B. Barney:

This book is dedicated to my wife, Kim; our children, Lindsay, Kristian, and Erin; their spouses, Ryan, Amy, and Dave; and most of all, to our eight grandchildren, Isaac, Dylanie, Audrey, Chloe, Lucas, Lincoln, Royal, and Nolan. They help me remember that no success can compensate for failure in the home.

Trish Gorman Clifford:

I dedicate this book to the Hanrahans and the Gormans: Catherine, Marie, and Austin Hanrahan, who taught me to cope, to appreciate books, to respect history, and to pursue excellence; Robert, Judy, and Peggy Gorman, who taught me that by combining intensity, intelligence, imagination, and integrity, all things are possible. Whatever I didn't learn from them is entirely my own fault.

CONTENTS

PREFACE:
A NOVEL APPROACH

You are about to read a business novel—a story about a recent MBA graduate engaged in helping a large global firm make an important strategic decision. As he struggles to contribute to the strategy development process, our hero, Justin Campbell, discovers the limits of what he did learn in business school, realizes what he could have learned in school but didn't, and—most importantly—unearths some valuable truths about himself.

This book is for:

- High-potential managers charged with developing and implementing strategies under challenging circumstances

- Current business students eager to apply and integrate lessons about what firms can and should do to compete successfully

- Readers interested in how strategic decisions are—and could be—made inside real firms

But why a business novel?

First, we believe that developing and executing strategies effectively requires the application of sophisticated analytical tools. Some of these tools are described and applied in this book. To be effective, these tools must be sensitive to the firm's unique organizational context. The best way to describe the complex and sometimes messy interaction between the analytical and the organizational in the real world is—ironically—through fiction.

Second, strategic decisions go hand in hand with change—change for the firm choosing a new strategy, change for those charged with executing that strategy, even change for those facilitating this process. For this reason, the successful application of rigorous strategic and organizational analysis to determine a firm's path ahead must anticipate the change management processes that enable a firm to travel that path. The novel form makes it possible to examine the implications of strategic choice on organizational, managerial, and even personal change to a greater extent than other approaches.

Finally, strategy work—the work that empowers and enables firms to determine what customers they will serve, which markets they will participate in, and how they will create value—is both intellectually engaging and enjoyable. This novel is our way of bringing strategy lessons to life by sharing the fun and frustrations that are so often a part of strategy making, but that can not be easily conveyed in other kinds of books. Our novel is not a broad-based criticism of modern business education. The title is *What I Didn't Learn in Business School*, not *What Business School Didn't Teach Me*. In fact, Justin—our main character—realizes that he is ultimately responsible for both what he did and did not learn in business school. At one point, he realizes, "It's not that they didn't teach it; I just didn't learn it." On the other hand, he also finds that the "school of hard knocks" is one of the best educators of all.

So, why are we qualified to write a business novel about developing and executing strategy?

Jay Barney, PhD—Jay—is a professor of management and holds the Chase Chair of Strategic Management at the Fisher College of Business at The Ohio State University. The current president of the Strategic Management Society, Jay has published over a hundred articles and books on strategy formulation and implementation—including some of the most highly cited academic articles in the field—and has worked as a strategic consultant with numerous firms.

Patricia Gorman Clifford, PhD—Trish—has worked to understand, develop, and evaluate strategies at hundreds of firms for more than twenty-five years, including stints consulting at the LEK Partnership, with McKinsey & Company, and through her own firm. She teaches strategy to MBAs and executives at the Wharton School of Business, Columbia Business School, and many other corporate and university venues around the world, and writes about and consults to organizations facing complex strategy challenges.

Together, we've written a book that makes the essential tools of strategic and organizational success accessible and practical. Our approach builds on both a thorough knowledge of these tools and a detailed understanding of how they are used in real organizations. As the book unfolds, Justin discovers that strategy making is part science, part art, part intuition, part politics, part analysis, part change management, and part just plain hard work. He also discovers he likes it.

We hope you like it, too. Enjoy!

ACKNOWLEDGMENTS

We have known each other for over fifteen years. During much of that time, we wanted to write something together—something that combined Jay's largely academic career with Trish's academic, consulting, and practice interests. Over the years, we came up with several proposals. Colleagues and publishers were encouraging, but we were never satisfied with our ideas, and nothing developed.

Until Vienna.

At a Strategic Management Society meeting in Vienna, we began talking about why we weren't satisfied with the book ideas we had tossed around. It wasn't, we concluded, that they were bad. Most of them could probably have been turned into reasonable books. But we weren't satisfied with them for at least two reasons.

First, we felt constrained by the industry standard of taking one idea, concept, or framework and exploring its implications for two hundred or so pages. In our real-world strategy experience, a single framework was never powerful enough to be used alone. Indeed, much of the value we brought to our clients, we thought, was our ability to deftly apply several interrelated frameworks to a specific problem or opportunity. To write a "single framework" book would perpetuate the myth that any one framework was enough to do good strategy work.

Second, our practice of strategic management had also taught us that it was important to integrate the analytical and organizational aspects of strategy. An analytically rigorous strategy that can't be implemented by a firm's management team is useless; an organization that successfully implements an analytically flawed strategy is often expediting its own demise. We wanted to write something that addressed how strategic choices are made in a richly nuanced organizational context, with imperfect information, and under realistic constraints.

The story we wanted to tell—using multiple frameworks that integrated analytical and organizational reasoning—was nothing like most other business books. As we passed this idea around, we were told, more than once, that the key to writing a good business book was to have a single message about a single idea, the essence of which could be communicated in the book's title. When we proposed a more integrated approach, we were asked, "But what is the central message of your book? What is the one key takeaway?"

Our central message was that strategy was too complex, and too important, to be boiled down to a buzzword.

To tell our story, we needed to—literally—tell a story. We concluded that the best way to reflect both the diversity and the complexity of real world strategy was to write not a business book, but a business novel. As our characters experienced the process of strategy making, they would encounter both analytical and behavioral issues. A novel would allow us to present many popular strategy tools in an accessible way and would also enable us to unpack the organizational and managerial dimensions of developing and evaluating strategies.

A number of people have helped us to appreciate and articulate the messages in our story.

Jay's early academic colleagues at UCLA, including Bill McKelvey, Bill Ouchi, and Dick Rumelt, continue to have an impact on his thinking, as do his more recent colleagues—Barry Baysinger, Bert Cannella, Javier Gimeno, Mike Hitt, and Bob Hoskisson when we were all at Texas A&M; and Sharon Alvarez, Jay Anand, Kate Conner, Jay Dial, David Greenberger, Sharon James, Konstantina Kiousis, Michael Leiblein, Anil Makhija, Mona Makhija, Steve Mangum, Jeff Reuer, and Alice Stewart when we were all at Ohio State. Jay's MBA and PhD students at all these institutions—many of whom have gone on to have successful careers in their own right—have also had an important impact on his thinking.

Trish's influences from consulting include Bill Barnett, Kevin Coyne, Nathaniel Foote, John Hagel, Stephen Hall, Sallie Honeychurch, Marc Kozin, Jim Lawrence, Toby Lenk, Lenny Mendonca, George Stalk, and Patrick Viguerie. Her cherished clients are too numerous to mention, but Cindy Monroe, Prisca Peyer-Ehrbar, and Mary Weber have been especially inspirational. She would like to thank Rich Bettis, Hugh Courtney, Jane Farran, Therese Flaherty, Jay Galbraith, Pankaj Ghemawat,

Bob Hansen, Sue Helper, Mike Hitt, Michael Jacobides, Mike Lubatkin, Anita McGahan, Rita McGrath, Peter Ring, Dan Schendel, Gabriel Szulanski, and the other gifted academics who have honored her with their collegiality.

Early discussions about this book with Steve Piersenti were both illuminating and challenging. Melinda Merino was undaunted by the novelty of our approach and was an astute and effective champion of our concept. We thank Harvard Business Review Press and especially Kathleen Carr, who expertly shepherded us through the publication process. We benefited greatly from the editing skills of Sarah Weaver and Allison Peter, the production editor, and the design talents of Joel Holland and Stephani Finks—and could not have wished for a more supportive team. And while Jay and Trish like to think we did most of the work on our own, it is likely this book would never have been completed without the talent, commitment, and good humor of Kathy Zwanziger.

A CHARACTER LIST

In order of appearance ...

Justin Campbell: Justin is beginning a new job as an associate at an international management consulting firm. He is from Willow Springs, Texas, majored in mathematics at the University of Texas at Austin, worked as a systems engineer at a high-tech firm, and most recently graduated from a highly respected MBA program.

Vivek Chatterjee: Vivek is a native of India with a PhD in chemical engineering from the University of California at Berkeley. Also an associate at the consulting firm, Vivek has two years of consulting experience.

Gordon Lee: Gordon grew up in Connecticut, studied mathematics and economics at Yale, and worked on Wall Street for two years before earning an MBA from Harvard. He has been with the consulting firm for several years.

Ken McCombs: Ken is a senior director at the consulting firm who develops and maintains relationships with several client organizations. A California native and Stanford MBA with extensive venture capital experience, Ken has been with the consulting firm for over twenty years.

Livia Chambers: Livia graduated from Northwestern University, received a law degree from the University of Chicago, and practiced law briefly. Livia will manage Justin's engagement on a day-to-day basis. She is six years into her consulting career.

Carl Switzer: Carl has been the board chair, CEO, and president of HGS for the past four years. Carl joined HGS in the R&D function over thirty years ago, after receiving a PhD in chemical engineering from the University of California at Berkeley.

Scott Beckett: Scott is the vice president and general manager of the oil and gas products division at HGS. This is the largest and most profitable division in the firm. He has over thirty years experience in the oil and gas industry.

Bob Hutchins: Bob is the vice president and general manager of the packaging division at HGS. Bob's background is in sales. His division is smaller and less profitable than the oil and gas products division.

Shirley Rickert: Shirley is the chief financial officer at HGS. She received her MBA at Wharton and had twenty years of experience in corporate finance prior to becoming CFO at HGS two years ago.

Walter Albright: Walter is the vice president of research and development at HGS. With a PhD in chemical engineering from Purdue and twenty years of experience in R&D at other specialty chemical firms, he joined HGS in his current role five years ago.

Bill Dixon: Bill's formal position is in corporate human resources, although he acts more as a special assistant to the CEO. A former plant manager in one of HGS's Mexican facilities, he was reassigned to corporate headquarters three years ago.

Jackie Condon: Jackie is Justin's girlfriend. They met while he was studying for his MBA and she was studying for a master's degree in clinical psychology. She is currently a PhD student in clinical psychology at UCLA.

Jerry Tucker: Jerry works in the R&D group at HGS and is generally credited for inventing the new technology the strategy team is evaluating, code-named "Plastiwear." He has a PhD in chemical engineering from Case Western Reserve University.

Leonard Kibrick: Leonard also works in the R&D group at HGS. His current assignment is to lead a team of scientists investigating alternative uses of Plastiwear and related technologies. His PhD is in chemical engineering from MIT.

A LITTLE TURBULENCE

I hate turbulence.

I know—as a road warrior, I'm supposed to be able to ignore the bumps, continue to work, and enjoy my drink, all the while maintaining a look of calm indifference to the turbulence rattling the plane around me. Test pilots call it "maintaining an even strain," even during the worst emergencies. As a kid in Texas, I called it "going with the flow."

But, still, I hate turbulence.

I've read the reports. I know that airframes almost never fail, that the wings of a 747 can flex thirty-six feet before they break, that the most dangerous parts of a flight are takeoff and landing, not midair turbulence. I know these things, but this knowledge doesn't comfort me. I still feel queasy—not airsick, but uneasy—when a plane begins to bounce, like I'm not really in control.

As I flew into Chicago that night for my first meeting with my first client as a bona fide consultant, I thought the turbulence was particularly bad. And it shouldn't have been. As far as I could see, the night was cloudless. The lights of small cities dotted the dark Midwest plain as far as the horizon, car lights heading to what I took to be the downtowns of each of these hamlets.

These towns reminded me of my own small-town upbringing in Willow Springs, Texas—about fifty miles west of Austin. I was in the top 10 percent of my graduating class, so I was automatically admitted to the University of Texas at Austin. If the admissions people in Austin had known there were only a hundred seniors in my high school, many with neither ambition nor English, maybe they wouldn't have been so impressed with my record. It didn't matter; I was in and on my way.

Ironically, my path to that airplane that night had been relatively smooth. At UT, I played my two favorite instruments—the violin and mathematics. I discovered two things about college—I liked it and I was good at it. After graduation, I landed a systems designer job at a computer firm in Austin. Those three years were great, but a steady diet of computer code made it clear that a strictly technical track wasn't for me. So, I took the GMAT.

Armed with my grades, my high-tech experience, and a 750, I was admitted to an elite MBA program. One year of core business school classes—marketing, accounting, organizational behavior, strategy—and one year specializing in finance (does anyone *not* study finance in B school?), and I scored interviews on Wall Street and in consulting, with three offers to weigh.

The money on Wall Street was impressive, but the work seemed too much like the technical stuff I'd done at my first job—crank the right number, send in a report.

At business school I'd developed a taste for solving real business problems. We called it "cracking the case," and I was one of the best in my class. I wanted to work with real companies facing real problems—not develop complex spreadsheets analyzing financial swaps. So, I took the best consulting offer I had and looked forward to the challenge. Each year I'd move either up or out. But, for now, I was definitely up *and* out—of Willow Springs.

And that led to this bumpy flight. I'd finished a week of orientation at the firm, a combination of sessions reviewing basic business concepts and requisite briefings on HR policies, expense reporting, and the like. Now I was on my way to my first assignment—HGS, a specialty chemical company headquartered in Chicago. The briefings that had been e-mailed to me Friday summarized the history of HGS. It was founded by Hal Gardon and two of his sons at the turn of the twentieth century in Southern California. Modestly successful through the 1920s, it almost went bankrupt during the Depression, but recovered during

World War II. After the war, the company went public, changed its name to HGS Chemicals, and began diversifying into a range of specialty chemical products. It currently had over $20 billion in sales, plants in fifteen countries, and distributed products to almost every country in the world. Its two largest divisions sold chemical products to the packaging and oil and gas industries. Last year, the firm spent over $500 million on research and development and generated a net income of over $750 million. Its stock price was hovering around $22 per share, which gave it a market value of around $17 billion. Over the previous five years, its share price had been as high as $32 and as low as $18. According to my briefing materials, most analysts thought HGS was a solid, but not spectacular, specialty chemical firm—one whose growth seemed to have stalled in the last few years.

We had been asked to help HGS evaluate options for a new chemical technology they had developed and patented. HGS was exploring the potential of this technology as a fabric, code-named "Plastiwear." It had many attractive features—wrinkle free, soft to the touch, and easy to cut and sew—more like a high-quality cotton cloth than something plastic. Indeed, its main limitation was that HGS scientists could produce it only in white.

Also important was the opportunity to demonstrate our value-add to this high-potential client. If we impressed them with our efforts on this first engagement, we'd be positioned to build a client relationship that could lead to significant additional work.

Client relationship building wasn't my priority, though. The word among my office mates was that my primary job on this first assignment would be to analyze data and develop some kick-ass PowerPoint slides. But I had also heard that the senior director on this project, Ken McCombs, would increase my responsibility as soon as I proved I was up to it.

Like me, Ken was born in a small town—although his was just west of Fresno, in California's central valley. Ken studied economics at Stanford. After graduation, he worked at a Palo Alto–based venture capital firm. An MBA, also from Stanford, a few more years in VC—he was probably already well off when he turned to consulting nearly twenty years ago. After just five years—on the fast track—Ken made partner and had since become a leader in the Chicago office and across the firm. He was married, with two grown children.

So, would I be able to gain Ken's confidence? Was I really up to the task at hand? That nagging sense of insecurity made it more difficult than usual to ignore the turbulence.

It wouldn't have been so bad if I didn't have work to do. Then I could've pretended to be deep in thought, eyes tightly closed, instead of struggling with the papers in my lap. I needed to get a handle on the information about HGS summarized on those pages. I'd printed everything out and reviewed it twice already, but wanted to take some additional notes—quite a challenge in the current situation.

Suddenly it struck me as odd that I should be worried about whether or not a bunch of strangers on an airplane thought I was "maintaining an even strain." It would be one thing if Ken or other members of the team were there with me. But I was the only team member on the flight. So, what did it matter if these strangers knew about my fear of turbulence?

Well, sometimes we need the silent support of strangers. Especially when we're uncertain about who we are and what we're doing, any support is welcome. At least, that's what my girlfriend, Jackie, would say. And she should know. She was a PhD student in clinical psychology at UCLA.

So I maintained an even strain.

Just as suddenly as they'd appeared, the bumps disappeared. There is nothing quite as smooth as a smooth flight after turbulence—like gliding down the face of a perfect ocean wave or floating through two feet of champagne powder. And so it was that night. Severe turbulence followed by champagne powder smoothness.

Finally, we landed, and the pilot's reassuring Southern drawl came over the intercom: "Welcome to Chicago, ladies and gentlemen. Glad you chose to fly with us tonight. Hope to see you again soon."

Geez. He didn't even acknowledge the lousy ride! As I stood up and collected my belongings, it struck me that maybe my smooth-air flying was behind me, that maybe I was going to have to get used to flying in turbulence. That shouldn't be hard. I've read all the reports. I know that airframes almost never fail, that the wings of a 747 can flex thirty-six feet before they break, that the most dangerous parts of a flight are takeoff and landing . . .

But still, I hate turbulence.

REFLECTION QUESTIONS

1. Is Justin ready for his new job? Why or why not?

2. What advice would you most like to give Justin now?

— 1 —

A SIMPLE PROBLEM

Consulting starts early. At least it did on that first day, with a team kick-off meeting at 7:30 a.m. Held in a conference room on the seventy-second floor of the HGS building in downtown Chicago, I suppose the purpose of this meeting was to get to know other members of the consulting team and to share our initial thoughts about the client. I was also looking forward to the breakfast I assumed would be waiting in the room for us.

I arrived at the meeting room twenty minutes early. Nothing like creating a good first impression, I thought to myself. But, in truth, I was too excited to stay at the hotel any longer. I'd been waiting for this morning for over two years, and it was finally here. I planned to flip through my notes on HGS, review the backgrounds of the other members of the consulting team, and be ready to jump right in. My uncertainties from last night were more than matched by my enthusiasm this morning.

I opened the meeting room door. The room wasn't unusual—twenty feet long and fifteen feet wide, with a large wooden table and ten matching chairs around it, a whiteboard at the front, and subtle gray wallpaper, highlighted by a piece of abstract art that to me looked like an orange slash attacking a black and red slash. However, one wall of the conference room was floor-to-ceiling glass and provided a spectacular view of Chicago. Even from the doorway, I was struck by the beauty and complexity of the city below.

And then I noticed Vivek. Or a person I took to be Vivek. I recognized him from his online profile.

"Hi, Justin. My name is Vivek Chatterjee."

I walked over to Vivek and reached out to shake his hand. He stood as I approached.

"Nice to meet you, Vivek. I'm Justin Campbell."

"Your first assignment, right? You must be excited. I know I was when I started."

I wondered if he still got excited about starting a new project. Why else would he be so early?

I explained my early arrival. "I thought I'd take a couple minutes to review my notes on HGS—before the meeting starts, I mean."

"I see. I was doing the same."

I sat down across from Vivek and began rereading my notes on HGS. An uncomfortable silence descended on the room. I tried to read, but my thoughts drifted to what I knew about Vivek from his profile. Born in India, he had received his PhD in chemical engineering from the University of California at Berkeley. He joined the firm two years ago and worked on a wide range of projects. In fact, as far as I could tell, this was the first project where his chemical engineering expertise might actually be relevant. My thoughts were interrupted by a question.

"So, Justin, what do you think the most critical issues are likely to be with this client?"

"I don't know. In fact, it seems to me that this is actually a pretty simple situation—they've got this new technology, we need to identify and value its uses, then we're done—right?"

"Well, it may be somewhat more complicated . . ."

At that moment the door opened, and Gordon Lee stepped in. Five feet ten inches tall, thin, with dark brown hair cut long on the sides and combed back from the front in an elegant wave, Gordon's background was what in Texas we would call "pure silver spoon"—he grew up in some fancy Connecticut suburb, attended a famous prep school (where the Kennedys send their kids, I think), earned a degree in economics and math at Yale, spent two years on Wall Street, then went for a Harvard MBA. He had been with the firm for a few years now.

Gordon seemed to recognize Vivek. "Hi, Vivek." Their handshake seemed genuinely warm. Turning to me, Gordon's demeanor became more formal, almost stiff. He offered his hand, and I shook it. A firm handshake, but not what I'd call friendly.

"And you must be Justin. Glad to have you on board. You studying up on HGS?"

"Thought it might be a good idea."

"We'll soon see."

At that moment, my stomach growled. Everyone was too polite to say anything, but I suddenly realized that there wasn't any food in the room. My assumption about breakfast being provided was wrong. My first day on the job, and I would spend the morning hungry.

"Has either of you seen Ken or Livia?" Vivek wondered aloud.

As if on cue, Ken McCombs and Livia Chambers came through the conference room door. I had heard about Ken and seen his picture, but he was much more impressive in person. He entered the meeting room with the casual confidence of someone who's been there before. Just over six feet tall, with a ruddy complexion and fading freckles across his forehead, Ken strode like the athlete I'd heard he used to be. His dark blue suit was tailored to accentuate his broad shoulders and hide his now expanding waist line. His look was completed with a white shirt— stiff with starch and newly ironed—and a maroon tie with only the barest hint of a pattern.

"Good morning, gentlemen." As Ken approached the table to sit down, I noticed his hair. I imagine it used to be red. Now mostly gray and thinning on top, it was surprisingly unruly, like he had carefully combed it, but the wind had undone all his good work. The result was incongruous—part Wall Street tycoon, part absent-minded professor.

"Sorry I'm a couple minutes late. For those who haven't met her yet, this is Livia Chambers. Livia will be serving as the engagement manager on this project." Ken reached up to smooth his hair, but it only partly complied.

"Good morning, Vivek, Justin," Livia nodded toward us as she took her place near the front of the table, next to Ken. "I know Gordon, of course."

Livia was impressive in her own right. A tall woman with shoulder-length wavy brown hair, she was dressed in a tailored dark blue suit set off by a colorful necklace and matching earrings. Her pale skin suggested she hadn't seen much sun lately, but her movements were both graceful and athletic. Her background was even more impressive—fluent in four languages, she had graduated from Northwestern and then attended the University of Chicago Law School. After a few years at a Chicago law firm, she had been hired as a consultant in the HGS Chicago office about six years ago.

"Great," Ken said, taking over the meeting. "Now that the introductions are out of the way, let's get to work."

"So, Justin." Ken began the substantive part of the meeting with a question directed toward me. "Based on what you know so far, what do you suspect the toughest problem facing HGS is?"

I tried to sound modest, but this engagement didn't seem that complicated to me. "It seems to me that our job is to figure out the different ways this fabric can be used and how valuable it will be in these alternative uses. Actually, when I read the brief, I wondered why we were called in on such a simple problem. It sounds like something any group of well-trained MBAs could do. In fact, I was on a case competition team that had to crack a very similar case in less than twenty-four hours."

"Well, perhaps," Ken interrupted, and paused for what seemed like a long moment. "But I think it's clear that HGS needs our input. They already know at least one use of this fabric. In fact, we can all be part of their market research this morning. Tell me, did any of you notice my shirt this morning?"

Gordon, Vivek, and I looked at each other, but deferred to Livia. She answered first.

"That's a great-looking shirt. It fits you well, looks like it was just ironed, and has a great collar."

"Well," Ken replied, satisfied with his little experiment, "it's made out of Plastiwear. To me, it feels as good as some of the $400 shirts I usually have made. And they say it wears forever, never stains, never needs ironing. HGS estimates that the fabric for this shirt will cost only about

$15 at scale and that they can sell these shirts off the rack at $60 or $70, with custom tailored shirts selling at $150 or $160."

I hoped my jaw didn't drop too far when Ken mentioned his $400 white shirts!

Now Gordon spoke up. "I'm confused. If they have already decided to start making shirts, and if the economics are so promising, why are we here? Are we going to focus on marketing and operations challenges?"

"Good question, Gordon," Livia responded. She seemed to know a great deal about HGS and Plastiwear. "I think once you are fully briefed, our central challenge will be apparent. For example, do you know when they invented this fabric?"

"I assumed it was a fairly new development," replied Gordon.

"Actually, they invented it over three years ago. And they made their first prototype white shirt eighteen months ago. And for eighteen months, HGS has been sitting on this technology, unable to decide what to do."

Gordon and I were both surprised to hear this. I spoke first. "I don't get it. Seems like a reasonable product. They have patent protection on the technology for another seventeen years or so. People want high-quality shirts. The economics leave room for attractive profits. So, why aren't they moving ahead?"

Ken responded, "That, Justin, is why we are involved."

A thought suddenly struck me. "You know, maybe the reason they can't decide is that they don't agree about the assumptions used to model the shirt opportunity. I remember a case study in my MBA program where the entire point was that differences in assumptions could lead to very different conclusions."

Livia shot a look at Ken before responding. "That is a possibility. But why do you suppose different HGS managers would have such widely different assumptions about the future of a single new product? Where did the different assumptions come from in your case study?"

"Well, the professor just assigned us to different groups and then gave each group different assumptions about things like costs and demand to work from in building our cash flow models."

"So, differences in assumptions in your case were artificial," Gordon observed.

"That's right." I felt like a fool having raised this obviously artificial example. I didn't blame my professor—he was making a legitimate point. I blamed myself for learning the wrong lesson. Geez. Of course different assumptions lead to different outcomes. The real question is, where do those differences come from in the first place? Just as I was realizing my mistake, Ken put it into words.

"Well, we're going to have to find out if different individuals in HGS have different assumptions about the future of Plastiwear," Ken deadpanned, "and, assuming they do, who assigned them." As the team chuckled, I tried to join in.

"Any other key issues?" Ken asked.

Livia replied, "I think it might make sense to talk about how interested different members of the HGS leadership team are likely to be in Plastiwear, and how influential these people are likely to be in any decisions that get made. We need to develop a plan to get the critical people on board with any actions we recommend." As she talked, she went to the whiteboard and drew a simple graph, with interest (high versus low) on the vertical axis and influence (high versus low) on the horizontal axis.

I was confused. "Isn't our task just to do the best analysis of Plastiwear that we can, and then let that analysis speak for itself? I mean, if we really crack this case, then the right thing to do with Plastiwear will be obvious to everyone, right?"

Ken replied, "Well, the quality of our analysis is critical, and we *are* going to nail that, that's true. But Livia and I need to begin to grease the skids for our recommendations—and that means figuring out who the critical stakeholders in HGS are, who can help implement our recommendations, and, even more important, who can stop them from being implemented."

All this talk of influence and "greasing the skids" smacked of organizational politics to me. In my old job, politics was what prevented our best technical designs from being adopted. All the software people in my old firm hated politics, especially since we already knew what the best answers were.

Gordon seemed willing and able to address the issues raised by Livia. "Well," he said, "it seems to me that the heads of the two big product

Team's chart of influence and interest of various players

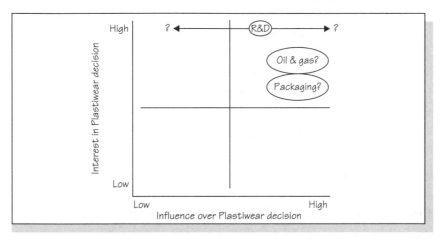

divisions—oil and gas and packaging—are both likely to be interested and influential. Especially Scott Beckett, the head of oil and gas. His division generates the lion's share of revenues and profits for HGS. If he sees capital shifting from his division to a Plastiwear effort, he may be very resistant. He's probably the least interested in changing the status quo."

As Gordon talked, Livia began making notes on the graph on the whiteboard.

Vivek chimed in next. "How about R&D? Who invented Plastiwear—I mean, where in the organization was Plastiwear created? I've never known an inventor who wasn't keenly interested in the fate of their technologies. I don't know how influential they would be in this situation, though."

Ken replied, pointing to the whiteboard, "I don't know either, but let's keep track of who fits where on this matrix, and where we need more information. We must have a good sense of the political landscape long before we make our eventual presentations. Our goal is to use both our analysis and our change management skills to transform those likely to resist our recommendations into supporters."

Everyone else in the room nodded in agreement. I allowed my mind to wander to whether it would make sense to use the arithmetic or geometric mean to calculate the present value of the cash flows associated with Plastiwear shirts.

"Any more issues?" Ken asked.

"Something we may need to be aware of," replied Gordon. "I thought I was going to be done with my last project, but some things are beginning to unravel. I may need to spend a little more time than I expected with that team over the next week."

"Just keep us informed," replied Livia, looking directly at Gordon. "We should be able to work around your schedule as long as we manage expectations well."

With that, my first team meeting as a consultant began to wind down. I found it confusing. I knew I had blown it on the "artificial differences" example, but to me, the whole meeting was light on content and analysis, and heavy on process and politics—keeping track of who's ox is being gored by whom. I thought I'd been hired because of my analytical skills—my grades in finance, my reputation for cracking cases. All this organizational politics stuff—well, it was just distasteful. To me, if we did the right financial analysis, then all this stuff about influence and interest would be irrelevant. Was I wrong?

It was 10:00, and I was getting hungrier by the moment. Just as Ken was bringing the team meeting to a close, there was a knock on the door. Gordon, closest to the door, stood and opened it. There stood a frail-looking woman, around five feet three inches tall, maybe fifty-five years old, with grey hair cut short to her head. She wore a dark blue pleated skirt and a beige blouse. A pair of old-fashioned half-frame reading glasses hung on a chain around her neck, like a librarian from an old movie might wear.

"Excuse me. Is this the strategy consultants' meeting?"

"Yes," Gordon replied. "Please come in."

"Hello. I'm Darla Hood, Dr. Switzer's secretary. Dr. Switzer and the management team will meet you in the conference room down the hall. If you would come with me, I'll take you there." We followed Darla thirty feet down the corridor to another conference room, just like the first, except now a blue slash was attacking a yellow and red slash.

"Dr. Switzer will be right with you. Would you like anything to drink? Coffee or water?" I wanted to at least get some caffeine or liquid in my system, but since everyone else politely demurred, I followed suit, hoping my stomach wouldn't audibly rumble again.

After a couple of minutes, a tall balding man dressed in a gray suit with widely spaced pinstripes, a white shirt, and a blue tie walked into the room. As soon as he entered, Ken moved forward to greet him.

"Hi, Carl!"

"Ken, it's good to see you!" Carl—Carl Switzer, board chair, CEO, and president of HGS—moved rapidly across the room to shake Ken's hand. His movements were quick and fluid—so fast that Ken almost didn't have time to square himself and shake his hand properly. Standing together, it became apparent just how tall Carl was—at least three or four inches taller than Ken's six-foot frame. At about 220 pounds, Carl was physically impressive, despite his balding head. But he had something else about him, a presence. He'd take up a lot of space in any room he entered.

"How's your family doing?" Carl continued.

"Real well. How about yours?"

"Well. We're all planning on getting together at our place on the island next month."

I wasn't sure which island he was talking about. But clearly, Ken and Carl knew each other. This surprised me, since we hadn't worked with HGS before.

"I'll be there next month myself," Ken continued. So, Ken knew what island Carl was talking about, since he had a house there as well. Maybe that's how Ken and Carl knew each other—they were neighbors.

"Great, maybe we can get together and play some tennis."

"I don't know; my ego hasn't recovered from the last time we played."

"Listen to this guy blow smoke. Don't you believe it. Ken is a real athlete—played football at Cal, didn't you?"

"Uh, no, Stanford, and that was a long time ago. But how could you confuse it with a second-rate institution like Cal!" Vivek shifted uncomfortably. As a Berkeley grad, Vivek was required to put down Stanford, just as Ken, as a Stanford grad, was required to put down Berkeley. As a Texas grad, I thought the rivalry between Berkeley and Stanford was a mere sideshow—not as irrelevant as Harvard and Yale, but close!

Ken continued. "Don't worry, Vivek; Carl is a Berkeley graduate just like you. Undergrad and PhD in chemical engineering, I believe."

"That's right. Graduated over thirty years ago. Started as a researcher in the R&D group here at HGS."

I did some quick calculations. That would make Carl about sixty years old. Given his age, he probably served in the military. That meant that he had four or five years before he retired. He had already been CEO for four years, so he was halfway through his tenure. I recalled a business school case where a retiring CEO was feeling pressure to do something big as his biological clock was ticking fast. Was that part of why we were here now?

Just then, another person arrived at the door.

"Hi, Carl. Is this the strategy meeting?"

Carl answered, "Yes, it is, Scott, come in. Gentlemen, lady," Carl nodded toward Livia, acknowledging the only woman in the room, "let me introduce Scott Beckett, VP of oil and gas products. Scott, have you met Ken McCombs? He is heading up this little conspiracy."

Ken reached out and shook Beckett's hand. "Scott, it's nice to see you again. Please, come in and take a seat. We'll get started after everyone arrives."

I was surprised that Ken had met Beckett before, although I didn't know in what capacity. As I was thinking about what that might mean, the other members of HGS's top management team arrived. Carl greeted each enthusiastically.

"Ah, here they are now. Let me introduce Bob Hutchins, VP of the packaging division; Shirley Rickert, our CFO; and Walter Albright, VP of R&D. Ken, would you introduce your team?"

"Glad to," Ken replied. While he quickly introduced our team, I put faces to the names I had read about in the HGS briefing materials: Scott Beckett, VP of the oil and gas products division, a thirty-year veteran of the oil industry, most of it in HGS. He headed up the largest and most profitable business unit in HGS. Robert, or Bob, Hutchins, VP of the packaging division, at forty-two was the leader of the other major business unit in the company. It was smaller and less profitable than the oil and gas division. Shirley Rickert, CFO, Wharton MBA, had twenty years experience in corporate finance, but only two years at HGS. And

Walter Albright, vice president of R&D. Albright had started at HGS five years earlier, after working about twenty years with other specialty chemical firms. His PhD was in chemical engineering from Purdue.

After introductions, Carl continued. "Well, I'm certainly glad you folks are here. I assume you've already been briefed about Plastiwear."

Livia responded for the team. "We know HGS announced this new fabric three years ago and successfully prototyped the first shirts about eighteen months ago. We have already begun to review your internal analyses of Plastiwear: evaluations of the fabric, estimates of its production costs, and so forth. You already know a great deal about this technology and its potential in shirt manufacturing."

"You're right," Carl replied. "But we haven't come to agreement about the strategic importance of this product—or potential product line. There are obviously a host of options we could pursue, and we've been in discussions for some time now. Right now, the only thing I think we agree on is that we'd appreciate an external evaluation of the situation. We're counting on you to help us."

"Thanks, Carl," Livia continued, "we'll do our best." She turned to include the broader management team. "We've already received all the reports that have been done on Plastiwear inside the firm up through about one month ago. Are there any results newer than that?"

"Yes," replied Albright, the VP of R&D, "we just finished another round of tests on Plastiwear shirts."

"Can we get summaries of those reports ASAP?"

"They are being copied as we speak. Our new findings reinforced what we already know: the performance of the material is excellent, but still no progress on color. You can have a Plastiwear shirt in any color you want, as long as it's white." Most of the members of the top management team chuckled quietly. Albright continued, "In fact, I believe that, Ken, you're wearing one of our prototype shirts right now, aren't you?"

"That's right. I think it looks good, and it feels good on."

"Good," Livia continued, refocusing the meeting. "We are currently summarizing your internal analyses and have noted some of the obvious possibilities for moving forward—selling the technology, licensing, fabric manufacture, shirt manufacture, private labeling, some other possible products that might use the technology, and so forth."

"Well, I don't want to spoil anyone's all-nighters," Scott Beckett, from the oil and gas division, said as he looked at Vivek and me, "but I wouldn't waste your time looking at us getting into the shirt business, especially with our own brand. We are a very good specialty chemical firm, and we need to guard our core. Why are we even still discussing the shirt idea? It doesn't have anything to do with our business."

Beckett shifted his gaze to Carl and the other senior managers in the room and then continued. "Listen, we know what we're good at. We should stick to our knitting and keep our focus on what we do best. Core competence is what it's all about. We know how to develop specialty chemical products for the oil and gas and packaging industries. We've been a leader in those industries for years. What has any of this got to do with white shirts?"

Obviously, Beckett had given this speech many times and felt strongly about his point of view. However, as he was talking, it struck me that his use of the concept of core competence pretty much excluded a firm from ever exploring new markets or industries. Is this what "exploiting a core competence" actually means—an inability to change?

My thoughts were interrupted by Albright. "Scott, we've heard all this before. The fact is we've developed something really new here—using your language, a new 'core competence'—with Plastiwear." Albright made quotation marks in the air with his fingers when he said "core competence." He then continued, "If we don't exploit this new technology we'll destroy shareholder value. You've seen the reports—the profit potential for high-end dress shirts is huge. Explain to me why we should forgo these profits, just because fabric doesn't fit into an arbitrary definition of what constitutes our current core competencies. And besides, it's not just about white shirts. Plastiwear has lots of potential uses." Albright was not as eloquent as Beckett, but his passion was as least as great.

Carl interrupted what was obviously a repeat of numerous earlier debates. "Gentlemen, we've been over this ground before. That's why I asked Ken and his team to come here, to help us sort out the best Plastiwear strategies for HGS going forward. I'm sure that, over the next few days, each of you will have an opportunity to share—in detail—your views. Let's hold off on the debate for now. I, for one, am looking forward to hearing their recommendations—and very soon, I might add.

"Besides, I have some new information that may have a direct impact on this effort." Carl paused for effect before continuing quietly, "HGS may be in play."

I knew that was MBA-speak for saying someone was thinking about acquiring HGS. The room was silent.

Carl continued, "On Friday, I received a letter from Allen Hoskins, director of MG Management, a private equity group in New York. It indicated that MG was going to take a substantial stake in HGS and wanted to meet with us in the near future to talk about putting some of their people on the board. While his message didn't say anything about Plastiwear, per se, it did mention our inability to effectively exploit new technologies as one of the main reasons for making their move."

A substantial equity position—this could be a prelude to a takeover. I was about to say so when Gordon beat me to it.

"Do you think this is a prelude to a takeover?"

"Could be. Taking the company private may be the right thing to do. Or not. We simply don't know at this time. I'm keeping an open mind on this. This is why we haven't adopted any poison pills or other takeover defenses. But what I do know is that we have to make a decision and create a solid plan regarding Plastiwear, one way or another. Besides, if Hoskins is interested in us, it's likely that others will be as well."

Shirley Rickert, the CFO, asked the next question. "When do Hoskins and his people want to meet?"

"He suggested next week, but we're looking for ways to buy a little more time. When we meet them we need a clear understanding of Plastiwear's viability, the best ways to exploit it, how it should be manufactured, and so forth. We need a lot of questions answered, and we don't have much time."

Ken then stepped up. "Well, that certainly accelerates the timetable on this engagement. Given the work you guys have done, however, I think we can have some preliminary recommendations to you and your team in, say, eight to ten days. Will that work for you?"

"I'd be grateful, Ken," was Carl's response.

My mind was racing. I knew that this time pressure was going to fall primarily on Vivek's and my shoulders. As junior members of the team, we were the ones who were going to have to dig out the numbers and crank out the analyses. The good news was—like Ken said—HGS had already done a lot of the work. Plus, this had suddenly gone from a straightforward "evaluate the potential of a new technology" MBA kind of project to a potential "save the company" situation. That made all the stakes higher, and I found that exciting.

"Well," Livia stood up, "sounds like we need to get started. Carl, can we work with your assistant, Darla, to set up interviews?"

"Absolutely. She'll see you when you leave here, and I believe she's already got a team room waiting."

"Great," replied Livia.

Carl then turned his attention to Ken. "One other thing. I'd like to add an HGS manager to your team."

"Great," was Ken's response. "In fact, we were hoping you would."

Carl continued, now talking to everyone in the room. "I've asked Bill Dixon to work with Ken's team. I think most of you know Bill." Most of Carl's top management team nodded in recognition. "For your benefit, Ken, Bill has been around this company almost as long as I have. He used to run a plant for us in Mexico but had some health problems. He's been back here in Chicago for three years now. Formally, he has some responsibilities in HR, but he really plays the role of a special assistant to the CEO. Any tough jobs I don't want to do, I call Bill. Bill will help you guys get the lay of the land, help you get in touch with people beyond those in this room you need to talk to. I think he'll also help you understand the culture at HGS. All right then." It seemed that Carl was bringing the meeting to a close. "I think we all understand what is at stake here. HGS is poised to make an important strategic move. I know with everyone's input and insights, we will agree on the best direction, speed, and timing of that move. Let's get to work!"

As I was getting up to leave the room, Carl added one more comment. "Ken and Livia, could you stay here a bit longer? There are some matters I want to discuss with you."

"No problem," was all I heard as I left the room.

REFLECTION QUESTIONS

1. So far, it looks like a Plastiwear shirt would cost around $15 and sell for over $60. What else do you need to know to evaluate the potential of Plastiwear?

2. How might Carl's age and tenure as CEO at HGS influence his approach to Plastiwear opportunities?

3. Why might MG Management be interested in buying HGS?

4. The strategy team needs to gauge the interest and influence of different stakeholders inside HGS with regard to Plastiwear. How might they accomplish this?

5. Why might different managers inside HGS have different assumptions about the potential of Plastiwear?

6. What is the most important thing Justin brings to the strategy team, and what can he do to contribute immediately?

— 2 —

A NEW SHIRT

It was 6 a.m., the morning after my first day at HGS. I had finally returned to my hotel room at 2 a.m. A few ten-minute increments of extra sleep won out over my commitment to morning exercise. Now, I was up, getting ready to continue the work from last night—I mean, from this morning. I also needed to be ready for my first interview, with Shirley Rickert, HGS's CFO, later that afternoon. But right now what I needed most was coffee—black and strong. It was already brewing on the hotel credenza, thanks to the coffee essentials provided to guests.

Work on the HGS project had begun almost as soon as our meeting with the top management team ended. Darla Hood showed Vivek, Gordon, and me to the team room on the seventieth floor. While we organized the room—three computers, a couple of bookshelves, a phone line for conference calls—Darla brought us our IDs.

The physical work of organizing our workspace was surprisingly relaxing, especially after the morning meetings. It also gave Gordon, Vivek, and me time to reflect on what we'd heard.

Gordon was confident. "I'm not surprised by the offer. Someone was bound to notice. The company's stock is trading within sight of its five-year low; its top management team isn't moving to market with its new technology. I suspect there are other opportunities languishing around here as well."

"But why a private equity firm?" Vivek wondered. "If HGS isn't realizing the potential of a new chemical technology, wouldn't a strategic acquirer—like another specialty chemical company—be the logical choice?"

"Who knows?" Gordon answered. "As Carl mentioned, other firms may also be interested. But private equity does like firms with unexploited technologies. They can sell or license these real fast, pay themselves a dividend, and rapidly recoup their investment."

"Is this going to change the nature of our work?" I asked.

"Probably not," replied Gordon. "Really, our task and the interests of the private equity firm are aligned here—we both want to find the highest-value uses of this Plastiwear stuff. We might have different time horizons—they probably want this done yesterday. But besides that, our efforts are consistent."

"Maybe we can call their team and get their analyses," I joked. "Save us some time, for sure."

Gordon grimaced so I quickly shifted back to no-nonsense mode: "There is another big difference. If HGS implements a Plastiwear strategy, Carl and his top management team will still be here. If the private equity firm does, there's a good chance that many of the managers we met with this morning won't have jobs at HGS anymore."

We were just about done setting up the team room when there was a knock on the door.

"Hello, anyone there?"

"Yes, yes, come in," Vivek responded and moved quickly to open the door.

On the other side of the door was a man in his early fifties, about five feet eight inches tall, stocky, with unruly salt-and-pepper hair. He wore baggy gray pants, a worn blue blazer, a blue button-down shirt, and a red tie, not entirely tightened up around his neck. My first impression was that this was a guy who doesn't care how he looks—or maybe, a guy who doesn't have to. His ensemble—if it could be called that—was completed with black shoes that likely hadn't been polished since they were purchased.

"Hi, I'm Bill Dixon. Carl asked me to come down and visit with you folks."

Bill entered the room with his hand extended and a smile on his face. Vivek was closest and introduced himself.

"Hello, I am Vivek Chatterjee. And these are my colleagues Justin Campbell and Gordon Lee."

Bill turned to Vivek, quickly withdrew his hand from the handshake, brought the palms of his hands together, and bowed slightly.

"Namaskar."

Vivek did the same and responded, "Namaskar."

Bill's greeting to Gordon and me was more conventional. "And Mr. Campbell, Mr. Lee, it's a pleasure to meet you as well." His handshake was warm and friendly.

Bill looked around at the team room. "Well, you folks are getting right to work, aren't you? Not the most attractive conference room in the building, but it will meet our needs. So, what's on your agenda for the rest of the day?"

I pulled over a chair, but Bill didn't sit down.

Gordon explained that our first task was to finish analyzing the work that HGS had already done on Plastiwear and the shirt industry, along with some material we dug up on the men's apparel industry. We were just about to divide these reports into two piles—one for me and one for Vivek—when Bill arrived.

"Excellent," was Bill's comment. "I'm familiar with most of these reports already, but it'll be good to get an independent read from you. I have some prior commitments that will keep me busy today, but I'll be able to give you more time after that."

"Well, our work plan draft is out the window since the deadline changed," Gordon explained. "Carl told us about the situation with MG Management this morning." Bill nodded and Gordon continued, "Justin and I are scheduled to interview Shirley Rickert and Scott Beckett tomorrow. You and Vivek, assuming you're available, have meetings scheduled with some corporate marketing people starting tomorrow afternoon."

Bill pulled out his BlackBerry and looked at his schedule. "Why don't you e-mail me a new cut at the work plan and schedule, including any other interviews you've planned. I'll respond with my suggestions."

"Of course. Sounds great," Gordon replied. "I assume you'll work in your own office, but we're hoping you spend enough time here with us so that we can benefit from your experience." Bill put his BlackBerry back in his pocket and looked around the room. After what seemed like a long silence, he smiled again. "Excellent. Well, gentlemen, this should be fun. Here is my card, with all my contact numbers and my e-mail. Vivek, I will meet you, where—here?—tomorrow at what time?"

"How about noon? Then we can get a quick lunch and go to our interviews."

"Excellent. OK, gentlemen, I'll see you later. I'm looking forward to this effort."

And with that, Bill Dixon—our man on the inside—was gone.

I wanted to talk to the others about Bill's role on the team, but Gordon needed to leave. After a quick huddle about our highest priorities, Gordon was gone, and Vivek and I withdrew into our thicket of paper and files.

That was yesterday afternoon. And ever since, I'd been reading and summarizing HGS reports. I'll say this about HGS—they didn't spare any trees when it came to evaluating Plastiwear. My high-priority reading stack alone was over ten inches tall—mostly double-sided—and new e-mails with files attached were coming in from Livia every few minutes! Lots of analysis and still no final decision. Was this a classic case of paralysis by analysis—where managers keep cranking numbers to avoid making a decision? If so, what were these guys afraid of? Or maybe it wasn't fear, but lack of motivation or incorrect incentives? Suddenly I wished I had paid more attention in my OB class.

I found the technical backup for HGS's patent application interesting. It emphasized Plastiwear's unique chemical structure and the valuable properties of Plastiwear fiber and fabric. The patent office agreed that Plastiwear was an original invention and granted HGS a patent in due course. The remaining reports evaluated the market potential of Plastiwear in a variety of markets, although most of this work focused on men's white dress shirts.

I thought about my own shirts as I waited for the coffee to perk. I had brought three on this trip—two white and one blue. I had originally expected to go home after a couple of days, but our new schedule made that impossible. I sent two of the shirts to the cleaners last night and so found myself, this morning, wearing my last clean shirt. It was important for me to look good today since I would be doing interviews with Gordon. It was bad enough to be the rookie, but I didn't want to *look* like the rookie.

It seemed to take forever, but the coffee was finally ready. Now I could get started on my work. I eagerly grabbed my cup and sipped. It was hot, but the deep familiar flavor was comforting. I also knew that the caffeine I was ingesting would give me the kick I needed.

Walking back to my computer, I guess I was paying more attention to drinking than walking. My right foot hit the corner of the bed and I stumbled. Catching my balance, I avoided falling, but splashed scalding hot coffee on the desk, my laptop, and all over me. Putting my cup down, I quickly ran to the bathroom for towels to soak up the spilled coffee. Most of the reports escaped serious damage, and I managed to dry off the computer before it short-circuited.

Only then did I look at my shirt. My last clean shirt. There, on the front right panel, was a coffee stain. Roughly three inches in diameter. The fact that it was shaped like the state of Texas wasn't the least bit comforting. Quickly taking my shirt off, I laid it on the bed and ran to the bathroom for a washcloth and soap. Maybe I could get the stain out before it set. Three minutes of scrubbing made it clear—Texas was not going away. I could hear the jokes already.

So, here I was. My first client interviews, with coffee spilled all over my shirt, and no others in the closet. What were my options?

Option one—maybe no one would notice. One more look at the shirt dashed that hope.

Option two—cleaners. Quickly, I called the concierge. After just a few rings, a voice answered.

"Good morning, Mr. Campbell, this is the concierge. How can I help you?"

"Good morning. Listen, I need to have a shirt cleaned—quickly. It has a coffee stain and I need it today."

"I will be happy to send someone up to collect your shirt and we can get it cleaned. We can have it back to you by three this afternoon."

"Three o'clock? I have a meeting at one; three o'clock won't do."

"I'm sorry, sir."

"Do you have other suggestions?"

"Well, sir, you could purchase a shirt."

"Yes, good. Are there any men's clothing stores around here?"

"Yes, sir, several." The concierge then ticked off several men's stores within a short distance of the hotel. "I can provide directions, if needed. Of course, sir, none of these stores open before ten."

"Well, I can work here until they open."

"Very well, sir. Anything else I can help you with?"

"No, thank you." Maybe this would work out OK. Rather than going to the team room early this morning, I would just work in my room until 9:45 and then go buy a shirt. I would wear the new shirt, give the old one to the concierge to be cleaned, and everything would be fine. On second thought, maybe I better get two new shirts, just in case there is a problem with the cleaning.

I pulled on the coffee-stained shirt, threw my wet towels into the tub, and got things arranged at the desk so I could get to work. And then it struck me, like a bolt of lightning: I had never bought a new white dress shirt before.

I know. It's a little embarrassing. Here I am, twenty-seven years old, a highly educated, sophisticated business professional, staying in a fancy hotel, getting paid the big bucks, and I'd never bought a dress shirt before.

Now, don't get me wrong; I've bought plenty of shirts. T-shirts. With several different slogans—you know, "Hook 'em Horns" and "Aggies Go Home." Even a couple of nice polo shirts with the dead alligators on the front, and some casual button-downs—"business casual" was the standard dress at my old job. But I had never bought dress shirts like those I needed now.

My mom had been the shopper. My whole life. She did the same for my father and my brothers as well. Recently, my girlfriend Jackie bought me a blue dress shirt—one of the shirts I had brought with me on this trip, in fact. But, so far, I had never purchased a white dress shirt for myself. And truthfully, I had no idea where to start. What makes a "good white shirt" good?

It was too early to call my mom, and I wasn't really sure Jackie knew that much about buying shirts. For sure, none of us had ever purchased $400 shirts, like Ken's.

A few minutes on the Internet left me amazed by what I didn't know about buying shirts. One Web site that specialized in customized dress shirts listed all the choices I would have to make if I bought one from them: fifteen types of collars—everything from "classic straight" to "English wide spread" to "narrow contour"; nine types of cuffs—one-button and two-button, rounded corners, square corners, French cuffs; four kinds of pockets; four types of pleats on the back—plain, inverted, side, and box; and four different fronts. And this didn't include fabrics. Or colors. Or patterns.

In choosing fabrics, several factors needed to be considered—one- versus two-ply, fabric weave, thread count, yarn size, and length of cotton. I had no idea what any of this stuff meant. It turns out that one- or two-ply refers to whether a fabric is woven with a single fiber (one-ply) or two fibers twisted together (two-ply). As far as I could tell, two-ply fabrics are smoother and stronger than one-ply fabrics. In terms of weave, the Web site described poplin, broadcloth, twill, herringbone chevron twill, chambray, royal oxford, pinpoint, and dobby. From what the site said, it seemed likely that a pinpoint weave would give me the most classic look. Thread counts—the number of threads per inch, I suppose—vary dramatically and apparently determine what I would describe as the density of a fabric, how thick it is. Lower-quality shirts have thread counts in the 50s to the 80s. Good shirts are in the 100 to 110 range. The best shirts—or at least the most expensive—have thread counts from 120 through 160.

And then there was the cotton. Yarn size measures the thinness of the cotton—something to do with the number of hanks (840 yards) in a pound of cotton. Low-quality cotton—like the stuff in blue jeans—has a yarn count in the teens, while the best cotton fabric has a yarn count in the 200s. Finally, the length of the cotton refers to how long the cotton ball is before it is harvested. The longer the length—this type of cotton is called extra-long staple or ELS cotton—the smoother and softer the fabric. The three ELS cottons generally available seemed to be Egyptian, Seal Island, and pima.

So, based on my online crash course, I decided that I needed to buy a white shirt with a traditional spread collar, two-button cuff with square corners, rounded pocket, box pleat back, plain front, made out of pinpoint two-ply fabric with a thread count greater than 110, a yarn count near 200 or so, made out of ELS cotton. Oh, yes, and I wanted it to fit. I worked on summarizing more of the HGS documents until it was almost ten o'clock, and then set out on my shirt-buying mission.

My first stop was a well-known men's clothing store, one with over a thousand shops in the United States. Growing up, this was the fanciest men's clothing brand I knew, so I thought it would be a good place to start. It looked like I was the first customer of the morning.

"Good morning. May I help you?" asked one of the two salesmen in the store. The salesman looked resplendent, decked out in a suit and tie that, I presumed, were from this very store. The suit was gray flannel, the shirt white, the tie a sea-green pattern.

"Well, as you can see, I need a new shirt." I pointed to the coffee stain.

"Yes, I can see we'll have to find you something immediately. Why don't you look around while I get the measuring tape."

He directed me to a wall of shirts—white, blue, French blue, some patterns, but mostly solids. After just a few seconds, he was back at my side.

"By the way, my name is Jay. Jay Palermo." He reached out his hand to shake mine.

"Nice to meet you. I'm Justin Campbell."

"In town for business, Mr. Campbell?"

I nodded. "I'll be here the next week or two, I guess. Didn't realize the trip would be so long, so I'll probably need more shirts than I planned on."

"Well, we have many excellent shirts to choose from. Here, let me measure you."

The measuring process was thorough—around the neck, chest, and waist, from the top of the shoulder to the wrist.

"Obviously, since you are going to have to buy an off-the-shelf shirt today, some of these measurements are unnecessary. But if you ever decide to special-order some shirts, we'll have them on file at all our stores around the world."

"Thanks."

"So, tell me, what kind of shirt were you thinking of?"

"Well, I would like a white shirt . . ." I paused as I pulled out the list of criteria I had written down earlier. "I would like a two-ply pinpoint all-cotton shirt with a thread count of at least 110, made with cotton with a 200-yarn count, and, if possible, made with Egyptian, Sea Island, or pima cotton."

"I see you've done your homework."

"That's what the Internet is for," I replied with some pride.

"Yes, indeed," he agreed, although I had a sense that Mr. Palermo had forgotten more about dress shirts than I would ever know. "Let me show you what we can do today. First, to get the thread count and cotton type you are requesting, you would have to special-order your shirt."

"How long would that take?"

"About five to six weeks."

"Maybe later." I tried to smile.

"Indeed. But this is what I have in our ready-made line." He held out a white shirt for my consideration. "Thread count of 80, two-ply pinpoint, made with Supima cotton—not as silky as the ELS cottons you requested, but a very good fabric. This particular shirt has a traditional spread collar, a two-button square-cut cuff, a rounded pocket, box pleat in the back, and plain front."

"What would the 120 thread count fabric look like?"

"Here, let me show you." The salesman put down the shirt he had been showing me and brought me to a table where several small books about the size of CDs were stacked. He searched through the stack briefly and pulled out one of the books. Opening the book, he explained, "Here are examples of the fabric you described to me. This particular fabric"—he pointed to one of the samples in the book—"is made out of Egyptian cotton, a thread count of 140, two-ply, of course, pinpoint. Go ahead and see how you like it."

I touched—no, I caressed the fabric in the book. It was noticeably softer than the 80 thread count shirt I could buy today. "Boy, that is nice. I didn't really know there was this much difference between fabrics."

"Yes, this is beautiful, isn't it? A custom-made shirt with this fabric would last you for years."

"How much would that cost?"

"That is our top-of-the-line shirt. It would cost you $387, plus tax."

I had discovered a $400 shirt!

"Well . . . maybe in the future I'll be ordering some of these. In the meantime . . . " I looked back over to the ready-made shirt rack.

"Very well, sir. How many would you like?"

"I think two."

"Fine. That will be $174 plus tax."

As we went back over to the counter to pay for what now felt like completely inadequate—although still pretty expensive—shirts, my mind went back to breakfast, just yesterday, when Ken had favorably compared his Plastiwear shirt to one of his $400 shirts. As I charged my ready-made shirts, I couldn't help but wonder if it would really be possible to buy a shirt that felt and looked like a $400 shirt off the rack for $60, custom-made for $150.

If Plastiwear felt and wore as well as that top-end shirt, one thing was completely clear—I wanted to buy a Plastiwear shirt. In fact, I wanted to invest in Plastiwear!

After seventeen hours reading reports about Plastiwear and shirts, I was really looking forward to my first meeting with a living breathing HGS manager. Gordon and I were scheduled to interview Shirley Rickert this afternoon.

I was hoping Shirley would help me solve a mystery. Six of the reports I read had calculated the present value of the cash flows that Plastiwear white shirts would generate—just like I learned to do in business school. And as far as I could tell, each of these calculations was done correctly—they all projected cash flow net of investment and discounted it back to the present. And yet, these six reports generated different results. And not small differences: two concluded that this opportunity would *generate* almost $1 billion in present value; two concluded it would *destroy* almost $1 billion in present value; and two concluded it would about break even for HGS—a positive present value of $100,000 for one of the reports, a negative present value of $60,000 for the other.

This wasn't supposed to happen. What I'd learned in school was that careful application of principles from finance would create a clear picture of a project's future cash flows, which then could be appropriately discounted. Some small differences in analyses might emerge—but the $2 billion swing in these reports was way beyond the variance I expected, especially since this wasn't exactly a high-tech venture or volatile industry being analyzed.

I'd spent several hours listing differences among these calculations, trying to understand why they'd generated such wildly different conclusions. One clear difference had to do with their projected cash flows. The optimistic calculations estimated that building a Plastiwear plant would cost less than $3.5 million. It looked like these two calculations assumed that some excess capacity in the packaging division could be redeployed to begin making Plastiwear. The pessimistic calculations estimated a cost of over $28 million to build a new plant, including $3 million for environmental protection. Also, the optimistic calculations relied primarily on trade and word-of-mouth advertising to build sales for the new shirts; the pessimistic calculations included advertising and marketing expenses starting at $20 million in the first year and rising to $35 million in year five, at which time they would decrease to $30 million per year, increasing with inflation thereafter. The breakeven reports used cash flow projections midway between these extremes. Even the discount rates these reports used varied. The optimistic calculations used a discount rate of 7.5 percent, equal to HGS's weighted average cost of capital—that is, how much it cost HGS to borrow money and the rate of return it had to promise its investors in order to attract equity investment, weighted by how much debt and equity HGS had. The pessimistic calculations used a discount rate of 24.5 percent and 26 percent, respectively. Again, the breakeven projections used a discount rate that fell between these two extremes—14 percent for one and 15 percent for the other.

Now, one interpretation of this maze of calculations was that HGS had just done a standard sensitivity analysis. With sensitivity analysis, the idea is to try to understand the range of outcomes that an investment might generate. At a minimum, you calculate an optimistic outcome, a middle-of-the-road outcome, and a pessimistic outcome.

Sensitivity analyses—even the simple ones—can give decision makers information about possible outcomes before they make an investment decision. For example, if everything goes right with this investment, will it transform the company? Does it have enough upside potential to create real economic value for the shareholders? And, alternatively, if everything goes wrong with this investment, will it destroy the firm? How much risk is the firm assuming by green-lighting a proposed project?

So, having six different analyses generate a variety of outcomes, ranging from optimistic to pessimistic, by itself, was not a surprise. What surprised me was that these calculations had been done independently of one another—not as part of a larger sensitivity analysis. The guys who generated the optimistic calculations supported the numbers they generated. In fact, one of the optimistic reports included its own sensitivity analysis and concluded that its conservative projection—adding $1 billion of present value to HGS—was the most realistic. In the same way, both of the pessimistic reports included their own sensitivity analyses—one reported as the most reasonable projection the "middle-of-the-road" estimate, the other highlighted the pessimistic estimate.

So, these multiple projections were not the result of a single analyst carefully evaluating the range of possible outcomes associated with this investment; they were the result of six separate analyses, each coming to different conclusions.

I had jotted down some questions to discuss with Gordon, but based on my reading of these reports, I was really looking forward to meeting with Shirley. If anyone could help us to make sense of this mess, it would have to be the CFO. I had agreed to meet Gordon in the team room around noon. I arrived a couple of minutes early. It was empty. No problem. I began to organize my thoughts and ran through some calculations, cross-checking the figures in the reports. A few minutes after twelve, my cell phone rang.

"Hello, Justin Campbell."

"Hi, Justin. It's Gordon. Listen, I'm not going to be able to break away from here for those interviews this afternoon."

"You're not?"

"No. Listen, I'm very sorry about this, but as I mentioned yesterday, this project I've been working on has taken an unexpected turn. I wish I could get someone else to do the work, but I'm really the only one in a position to keep this thing together for this client. So, go ahead with the first interviews." Gordon paused, and I thought I could hear someone talking to him before he continued. "We could reschedule, but given the time crunch we're in at HGS, you should just go ahead."

"These will be the first interviews I've done on this job." I hoped I didn't sound desperate, just truthful.

"Yes, but after getting close to the material, you're in a better position now than I am to do today's interviews. Besides, Ken and Livia both agree, right now there really aren't any other options. Vivek and— what's his name—Bill Dixon, are already at lunch and are scheduled to meet with the marketing folks this afternoon." Gordon took a short breath. "So, you OK with this?"

"Well, I guess if you all agreed already, I'll do the best I can."

"I'm sure you'll do fine." Gordon sounded more rushed than reassuring. "You can get me up to speed later. Make sure you send me your notes. Listen, I've got to run now. I'll talk to you later."

"Bye." And with that, Gordon hung up.

Truthfully, part of me was glad that Gordon wasn't going to be there this afternoon. With Gordon at the interviews, I would be the junior partner—take notes, get coffee, smile at the appropriate times—the Vanna White of the team. Now, these were going to be *my* interviews. If I was lucky, maybe I would crack this case this afternoon. That would start my career at the firm off with a bang. And the truth is—I thought I was up for the challenge. After all my reading, I thought that I knew enough to ask some pretty good questions.

So, that's how I came to be ushered into the CFO's office—wearing my newly purchased white shirt—at 1:00, alone. Shirley's secretary announced me.

"Justin Campbell here to see you, Ms. Rickert."

I entered her office with my hand extended in what I hoped was a confident professional greeting.

"Ms. Rickert, good to see you again."

"Please, Justin. Come in. And please, call me Shirley."

She motioned for me to sit down on a small couch. She sat opposite, in a small chair covered in the same red fabric as the couch, a low black coffee table between us. A small flower arrangement that complemented the colors in the office sat on the table. The whole look was sophisticated, vaguely oriental, yet very comfortable.

"Would you like something to drink?"

"Yes, water would be nice."

"Kathy," Shirley called to the woman outside her door, "will you get the two of us some water?"

A woman I presumed was Kathy came into the room with two bottles of water and gave one to me and the other to Shirley. Our conversation began with some generic banter about business school—how her MBA had changed her life in ways she hadn't anticipated. I took the opportunity to really look at Shirley for the first time. She looked younger than I remembered from our first meeting, with light brown hair parted on the side, just covering her ears. She was wearing black pants and a black jacket. A string of pearls and pearl earrings were her only jewelry. Her conversational style was at once warm and reserved, professional yet cautious. After a few minutes, she checked her watch. "So, will Mr. Lee be joining us?"

"I'm afraid he's been called away on some emergency business." I realized I should have led with this information and hurriedly explained, "He asked me to go ahead and conduct this interview without him."

"Oh." She paused just a tick. "So, how can I help you?"

"Well, I reviewed some impressive analysis on Plastiwear. And not just impressive in terms of volume—although I did measure my reading in inches, not pages."

I thought I caught a smile flicker briefly across Shirley's face. "At HGS we are nothing if not thorough. In fact, sometimes I think we are too thorough."

I set that comment aside, thinking that I might come back to it later, and glanced at my notes. "I did have some questions about the present value analyses that have been done on Plastiwear and the shirt opportunity."

"Bit contradictory, are they?" she asked, as if she already knew how confusing these analyses were.

"Well, at first, I thought that maybe they were defining the bounds of sensitivity analyses. But the more I read, the more it became clear that there is fundamental disagreement about the potential financial impact of Plastiwear on your firm."

"I don't think our disagreement could be any more fundamental."

"So, how do you usually calculate present values at HGS?"

"Oh, our approach is pretty standard. For extensions of current product lines, we use our past experience to estimate what kind of investment will be required—you know, in plant and equipment, distribution, sales and marketing, and all the rest. Then, we go to our current customers to gauge their interest in this new product. This is a little tricky since it's always hard to get an accurate estimate of 'hypothetical sales.' Actual sales tend to lag behind our customer survey estimates, but we factor that in, doing things like latent demand analysis where appropriate. Then, with cost and revenue estimates in place, we project cash flows and discount them back to the current period."

"What discount rate do you use?"

"For product extensions, HGS's cost of capital. Lately between 7 and 8 percent. Then, we do some sensitivity analysis, make sure we're not going to break the company if things turn south on us, and discuss the results in our management meetings."

"Sounds straightforward—like maybe the person who designed this got an MBA in finance from Wharton."

"Oh no," she said, shaking her head. "This process has been in place for at least ten years."

"So, if HGS has been using this process for years, why so much variance for Plastiwear?" I hoped my impatience to get this question answered and move on with the rest of the interview wasn't too obvious.

"Well, with many product extensions, these calculations are very useful. Some people think that Plastiwear is not a product extension—but more of a radical new technology."

"Can't you apply NPV logic for even radical technologies?" I asked.

"Well, to get present value, you need cash flows and discount rates, right?"

"Right."

"For radical new products, cash flows are often tricky to estimate."

"Can't you ask customers about their interest?" I continued.

"That's hard to do when customers don't really have a clear idea about the new technology. Our own scientists don't even have a very good idea about Plastiwear's real potential. And besides, that's only on the revenue side. Estimating the cost of exploiting this technology also requires making sense of ambiguous and incomplete information."

"So it's hard to get good estimates of future cash flows based on questionable revenue and cost estimates. But what about discount rates—there was such a spread in the reports . . ."

"The cost of capital is the opportunity cost of investing in product extensions, and that's the right discount rate," Shirley continued. "If we don't invest in this business, we could invest in our other businesses and earn at least this level of return. But when it comes to Plastiwear, should we use the rate for an extension of our current businesses or the much higher rate for an entirely new business? As you've seen, there are arguments that cut both ways."

"What I was taught is that you should choose a discount rate that reflects the riskiness of the cash flows associated with this investment, not the firm's cost of capital," I added.

"That's right. But, here's the problem. For a really radical innovation, we don't know, for sure, just how risky that cash flow is. If you don't know how risky an investment is, how can you choose an appropriate discount rate?"

"Isn't this where sensitivity analyses come into play—calculating NPV with different cash flow projections and different discount rates?"

"Justin," like a professor losing patience with a slow student, Shirley spoke slowly and carefully, "those kinds of analyses—all they do is quantify your ignorance. They don't tell you which cash flow is accurate and how risky an investment is; they tell you that different combinations of cash flow and risk will generate different NPV outcomes."

"You mean, if different analyses adopt different assumptions, they have to generate different conclusions."

"That's right, Justin." I flashed back to my MBA class.

"So, at HGS, how do you estimate projected cash flows and the discount rate, if the investment is really radical and new?"

"The thing to remember is that present value techniques—even when you are evaluating relatively straightforward investments—are just a way of keeping track of the financial implications of a strategy. NPV is one way we keep score in the game, but it's not the game. NPV is no substitute for having a strategy."

"So, the different numbers that were generated in the reports reflect different strategic analyses?"

"Maybe." Shirley glanced at her BlackBerry and clicked off a reminder. "Maybe the optimists see Plastiwear as an extension of our current businesses."

"Those reports did talk up the advantages of using some excess manufacturing capacity in the packaging division. That sounds like a product extension move."

"Right. And the pessimists all assumed that we would have to build a new plant, deal with attendant environmental issues, and so forth."

"But which of these assumptions about Plastiwear strategy is right?" Now I felt like a frustrated student whose professor won't answer a question.

She looked mildly amused. "Wait. There's something else you must realize about NPV. Sometimes, it can be a powerful tool for objective strategic analysis, but managerial biases can be baked into the analysis—often unintentionally."

"What do you mean?"

"Well, who generated the optimistic present values?"

"Let's see." I quickly flipped through my notes. "The optimistic reports were produced by . . . a team reporting to Walter Albright—vice president of research and development—headed up by his assistant, Jerry Tucker . . ."

Shirley cut in with a wry smile, "Aren't these the people in HGS most directly responsible for the invention of Plastiwear?"

"And the other optimistic report was produced by a team reporting to Robert Hutchins, the leader of the packaging division . . ."

"And the manager in HGS with excess manufacturing capacity that could be put to use to make Plastiwear. Now, Justin, where did the pessimistic reports come from?"

"They both were written by teams reporting to Scott Beckett . . ."

"Yes, the VP of oil and gas. You might expect that he sees Plastiwear as a distraction. You'd also be right if you assumed that any significant capital investment in Plastiwear would likely reduce capital spent on expanding his division."

"So, what you are saying is that these calculations really just mask the personal interests of managers inside HGS?"

"No, I'm not saying that. I am saying this *could* be the case. It might also be the case that each of these teams came to its conclusions by evaluating Plastiwear in purely strategic terms. I don't know which of these explanations, or maybe some other explanation, is true."

"Where did the two middle-of-the-road reports come from?"

"They were generated by my office. To ensure the Plastiwear conversation wasn't dominated by the extremes, I directed a couple of teams to show how Plastiwear would only break even."

"Thus ensuring that all three points of view would be included in the conversation." I nodded in agreement.

"Hopefully. Part of my job as CFO is to 'direct traffic' in these debates, to make sure that all relevant points of view are considered."

"So, you've seen all the background material, including the analyses you helped build. You know the industry and these people. So, on balance, which NPV do you believe?"

Shirley paused before answering. After what seemed an eternity, she squared herself and looked right into my eyes.

"Well, Justin, that is an excellent question. The truth is—I don't know. And more importantly, I don't think it matters."

At that moment, Kathy was at the door.

"Ms. Rickert, your next meeting is about to begin."

"Thank you, Kathy."

Turning to me, Shirley explained, "Kathy always keeps me on schedule." She stood and extended her hand.

"Thank you, Justin, for spending this time with me. If you have any further questions, give me a call."

And with that, Shirley was gone, before I could even formulate a last question for her. I found myself leaving the CFO's office shaking my head in disbelief.

She didn't know. The CFO—presumably the person in HGS who has the best information about the financial implications of Plastiwear—didn't know which of these analyses was right. And, it didn't matter to her that she didn't know. What the heck was going on?

Suddenly, I had this uneasy feeling that much of what I had learned in finance, while not wrong, was largely irrelevant. Actually calculating present value was the easy part, mostly just arithmetic. The hard part was creating a tight logic for generating the projected cash flows and choosing the appropriate range of discount rates—especially when the project in question was radical in nature. And financial analysis really had very little to say about how this was done. Oh, it gave you guidance about what should and should not be included in calculating net cash flows, but was silent about the extent to which these factors were likely to be relevant for a particular project.

Worse yet, Shirley had raised the possibility that these apparently sophisticated analyses were fairly easily swayed by individual biases or corporate politics. Now, instead of being a reliable and tangible basis for choosing a strategy, NPV seemed to be no more than another means for managers to manipulate information to further their careers or protect their interests.

But worst of all, if Shirley—the CFO, the person in the best position to untangle these issues—didn't know which present value analysis I should use, how could I?

REFLECTION QUESTIONS

1. Based on Justin's experience buying a shirt, does your enthusiasm for Plastiwear increase or decrease?

2. Why doesn't Shirley know which NPV analysis is right? Why does she say that it doesn't matter?

3. How interested and influential is Shirley in the Plastiwear decision?

4. Do you agree with Justin that the Plastiwear engagement is actually a pretty simple problem?

5. What other questions should Justin have asked Shirley?

6. How should the strategy team leverage Bill?

— 3 —

A MOVING
TARGET

I had a couple of hours after my meeting with Shirley before my next interview—with Scott Beckett, VP of the oil and gas products division. I used the time to review more reports and to clean up my notes. I was glad that I didn't have to go directly into the meeting with Beckett. He was a division general manager, running the largest and most profitable business unit, and probably the second most powerful person in HGS—after the CEO. I wanted to be really prepared for that interview. And after my meeting with the CFO—well, some of the things I thought I knew for sure weren't exactly wrong, but somehow they felt less concrete and reliable than they had just a few hours ago.

I was finishing up when Vivek and Bill came into the team room. Vivek greeted me.

"Hi, Justin. How are things going?"

"Pretty well. I had an interesting interview with Shirley Rickert, the CFO. I'm just finishing up the notes. I guess you heard that Gordon wasn't able to break away from his other engagement this morning."

Vivek seemed to sense my discomfort. "Oh, I'm sure your interview went well. Can I have a look at your notes?"

"Sure. They aren't quite done—I want to proof them one more time," I said, handing Vivek the copy I had just printed, "but you'll get a pretty clear idea of the interview."

As Vivek scanned the page, Bill asked, "So, what did you think of Shirley?"

"Very nice, very professional, very competent. I was impressed by her overall, but also a bit surprised."

"By what?" Bill seemed genuinely interested.

"Well, you probably know that there are six NPV analyses of Plastiwear floating around. Six analyses, some of which generate really different results. I asked Shirley if she knew which of these analyses were accurate. You know what her answer was?"

"What?"

"She didn't know and it didn't matter."

Bill studied me for a second before replying. "Well, that doesn't surprise me. Shirley's the kind of CFO who tries to facilitate conversations among various factions in the firm. She usually doesn't push a particular point of view, especially on controversial issues, but tries to make sure that all points of view are being heard."

About then, Vivek finished skimming through my draft notes.

"Thanks, Justin. Well written. Sometimes it helps to include the questions you asked in an attachment to your notes. Sounds like you focused in on the NPV work. So, she didn't have an opinion about which analysis was correct?"

"I was just telling Bill."

"Yeah," Bill recapped for Vivek, "Shirley really sees her job as building a consensus, not providing a single 'right' answer."

"Well," I observed, "one thing I figured out very quickly in the meeting was that present value analysis is anything but a clear and objective way to make decisions in a company."

Vivek's observations about present value analysis were more balanced than mine. "It can be a helpful tool. But it can also be abused. You can start with the goal of concluding that a project has a positive present value, and then build a model that generates that conclusion, or you can start with the opposite goal and build a model that reaches a negative conclusion. You don't have infinite flexibility—if you follow accepted norms for constructing net cash flow projections and choosing discount rates—but you always have at least some flexibility. What is next on your agenda?"

"Lunch. Then a meeting with Scott Beckett."

"The oil and gas guy?"

"Yes. He hates Plastiwear. He also managed the two teams that generated the negative present value analyses. I need to find out why he's so down on it."

"Great. Have you structured the questions you'll use with him?"

"I'm just starting to work on them right now. I thought I would organize them into three categories—market size, strategic ownership, and timing of the investment. First: What is the magnitude of the dress shirt opportunity in terms of market size? Second: Which of their assets and attributes make HGS well suited to take a position in this market? And third: Is this the right time to move on this opportunity?" I had pulled these questions from a session held during my orientation week.

Vivek seemed pleased. "Great start. I've used a similar approach, which will make it easier to compare the results of our interviews. And we can also use the same questions to evaluate alternatives to investing in Plastiwear—for example, opportunities for product extensions in the oil and gas division or other innovations."

Vivek then turned his attention to Bill, who looked up from reading through my notes.

"Bill, is there anything helpful you can tell Justin about Beckett?"

"He's no-nonsense," began Bill. "Really understands the ins and outs of the oil and gas business. Ambitious. He probably comes across a bit gruff, but he is deeply committed to both HGS and to the oil and gas division. His people are very loyal—he always looks out for them. A manager's manager. I reported to him when I ran the oil and gas plants in Mexico."

"Thanks for the background." I wondered why Bill hadn't volunteered more, sooner, since he knew the guy so well, but already the two of them were on their feet. "Good. Well, Bill and I are off to interview some more marketing people, in both the oil and gas and the packaging divisions. You'll have our notes later today. By the way, we've already e-mailed our notes from the interviews this morning and posted them in the virtual team room," Vivek remarked off-handedly as he and Bill left the team room.

So far, I had not seen Vivek eat and, given the volume and pace of work he was generating, I had just about concluded that he never slept either. Just what I needed—on my first assignment, I get paired with a consulting "iron man."

That said, the fact that Vivek had validated my approach to organizing questions for Beckett renewed my confidence—a confidence that had taken a hit from my interview with the CFO. In addition, Bill's comments about Shirley suggested that what she told me in the interview was consistent with his experience. That was good news.

Now I had to put the CFO behind me and concentrate on preparing for Beckett. After a couple of hours of additional work over a cold sandwich, I felt like I had a clear agenda for my next interview.

I arrived at Beckett's office a few minutes early. There was no one there to greet me, only an empty chair at what I assumed was his secretary's desk. After a few minutes I peered into the open door of his office. It couldn't have been more different from Shirley's. There was little in the way of comfort. The chairs were solid and heavy, made of metal with black vinyl upholstery—the kind that sticks to your skin on hot and humid days—and the metal desk had seen better days. A whiteboard on wheels stood in the corner, with a few scribbles on it. The walls held plaques for quality and performance awards, but no personal mementos were visible—not even pictures of a spouse or children.

I was tempted to pace the hallway, but redirected my nervous energy to scanning some articles in a trade journal I picked up from a pile of newsletters and periodicals in the common area. Despite having done a couple of oil and gas cases in my MBA program, I soon got the sense that there was a lot I didn't really know about this industry.

After another ten minutes, I thought about calling to check if I was in the right place. Just as I began to dial Darla Hood—Carl Switzer's secretary, who had set up our interviews—Beckett arrived, with his secretary trailing a step or two behind. They were deep in conversation—or more precisely, Beckett was talking and she was nodding and taking notes.

"Martin can get you the numbers, and you can forward them directly to Anne. I don't need to see them. Just make sure we keep a copy for Monday's meeting."

Beckett motioned to me to follow him into the office and gestured toward a chair while he wrapped up his instructions to his assistant. He turned to me and started right in.

"So, if it was your money, would you invest in Plastiwear?"

I was a bit taken aback, but responded, "I'd certainly take a good look at the opportunity. I know I'd rather wear a Plastiwear shirt at an attractive price than pay the same for something less comfortable that didn't last as long."

"Oh, yeah, wearing the shirt." He paused and for the first time looked directly at me. "As a consumer, you have your preferences."

While Beckett had looked pretty put together in our first meeting yesterday—a tailored suit, nice shirt, a perfect tie—today he was more relaxed, like he had gotten his fashion tips from Bill Dixon. Only a step or two above scruffy, his gray pants were a bit baggy, his long-sleeved white shirt well worn, a blue striped tie hanging five inches from his belt. Yesterday, he looked like, oh, I don't know—a CEO in training. Today, he looked like an engineer.

"But," he continued dryly, "we have to consider the situation as manufacturers—not consumers—and from that perspective, this is a very tough play."

"You suggested this in our earlier meeting," I began, but he continued, taking little notice of my comment.

"When evaluating a new product like Plastiwear, I always look at the industry to see whether there is an opportunity for HGS. Some industries are more attractive than others, and sometimes it's hard to decide if—net net—an industry is a good one or not, but the men's dress shirt industry—no question, from the very beginning, I've been convinced it's very unattractive."

I fumbled for words to steer the conversation toward my question list, but wasn't quick enough. Beckett moved to the whiteboard near the window, picked up a marker, and continued.

"We all use five forces for this type of analysis. Start with rivals." To emphasize this point he wrote the word *rivals* on the whiteboard. Suddenly a student, I wrote *rivals* on my notepad as well.

"Rivalry for an HGS entry into men's shirts would be a real problem. It's a fragmented industry with over a hundred players, no one of them dominating more than 3 percent of the market. It's not easy to compete in these types of industries, and the first thing that might come to mind is a roll-up strategy—consolidate the industry by exploiting scale in, say, shirt manufacturing. Maybe we could make a really bold move into this space, buy a few firms, integrate them with our own shirt technology, so that we have some clout. Not practical."

He continued in the same clipped, decisive tone. "Roll-ups work when there are ways to standardize and gain scale. Fashion content makes this industry very resistant to standardization. Even white dress shirts come in hundreds of different style and size combinations, with different fabrics and weaves and other variables."

Agreed. Just browsing the Internet, I was amazed at the complexity of what I had assumed was a simple product. I was going to share my thoughts, but he didn't give me a chance.

"And while there might be some upstream economies of scale in manufacturing the Plastiwear fiber and fabric, there are none in cutting and sewing shirts. That's why so much of this work is sent overseas. You've got one person cutting, maybe, a hundred shirts at once, but assembly can't keep the same pace. Even if you could get some automation—and I don't think that is technically possible—why would you want to make big bets on a particular product or style?"

"What do you mean?" There. My first question.

He looked at me, noticing my attire as he responded. "Obviously, with changes in tastes and fashion, firms that make too large a bet on a particular style, size, or color can easily end up with their cash tied up in unsold inventory. This happens even with common dress shirts—different collars, fabrics, and so forth move in and out of style. One reason the apparel industry remains fragmented, besides the fact that there aren't big scale economies, is that many firms are hesitant to make large investments in any particular cut or style. Unlike consumer electronics, one standard platform won't dominate all our wardrobes anytime soon."

Beckett continued without skipping a beat. "So where is the power to extract profits in this industry? It's a tough play because both the customers and the suppliers have the power." Now he turned to the whiteboard to make his point. "You can't dictate to the customers—the large retailers. They decide what they'll stock, how much they'll pay, and who they'll work with. You also have no leverage with suppliers. The fiber and fabric industry is relatively concentrated, and a small number of players are dictating pricing, supply terms, and delivery schedules. With suppliers who can hold up your production and customers who can take or leave your product, I feel sorry for the poor middleman trying to make a shirt."

At this point, I felt I really needed to join the conversation, but the phone rang, and Beckett picked it up. He conducted some business on another matter without waving me out of the room, so I waited and thought about my next step. I decided to put aside my earlier line of questioning and instead go with his application of the five forces model. Fortunately, I had applied this common model frequently during my MBA program.

As Beckett hung up the phone and prepared to continue his lecture, I jumped in. "At least with a proprietary fabric, you would have a barrier to entry and there would be little threat from new entrants into that segment of the shirt market where Plastiwear could dominate."

"You'd think so, wouldn't you?" Beckett nodded and looked down at his marker. "But you'd be wrong. Patents aren't defensible without deep pockets and vigilant legal teams. I'm not sure we would have the guts needed to stick this strategy out. But for argument's sake, let's assume we can run without direct competition with an iron-clad patent. Many players in plastics, wovens, apparel, and fiber operations are constantly introducing new fabrics and trying new things. We would just be one in the crowd."

"What about branding the shirt, gaining an advantage that way?"

"Did you honestly look at the brand of the fabric when you bought that shirt?" he asked, already sure of my answer.

Shaking my head, I acknowledged his point. "Price and availability had a lot to do with my purchase of this particular shirt. It's not that I ignored the brand on the label, but if this brand of shirt had been too expensive, I wouldn't have bought it. And I definitely don't know the maker of the fabric." I didn't bother to tell him how fresh the purchase experience was in this case.

"Look. I'm not saying no one is willing to pay for a dress shirt made from a branded fabric. But is that market really large enough to justify the investment we would have to make? I don't think so." He continued

Beckett's five forces analysis of the white shirt industry

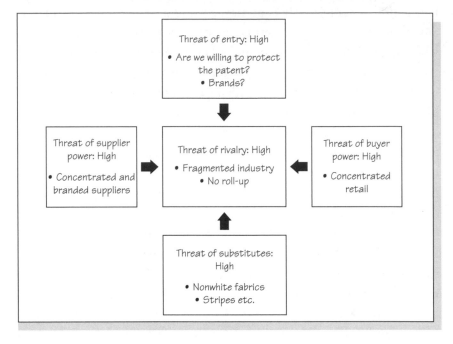

to the rest of the five forces. "There are plenty of substitutes for white shirts, and I don't think we'll suddenly storm that market when people go to work in all sorts of things these days—including plenty of business casual. Here's a crazy idea—maybe a blue shirt, or a striped shirt—could be a substitute for our simple white shirt." At this point, he seemed a bit wound up, but he added some more details to the five forces model on the board silently. His summary: "High rivalry, no barriers to entry, lots of substitutes, powerful buyers, and powerful suppliers. Yeah—sign me up for that industry." The sarcasm dripped off his words.

He continued, "Shirt manufacturing is a dog industry, and we would lose millions if we tried it. Listen, to me this is a classic nonstarter. I'm glad you guys are here, to cut through all the bull crap floating around about Plastiwear so that we can get on with growing our two key businesses." He glanced at his watch and put down his marker. "If you discover anything interesting you'd like to share, contact my assistant and perhaps we can schedule another time together—maybe spend some time talking about some real high-potential strategic investments. Forget Plastiwear."

"Well, thank you very much, Mr. Beckett. This has been very informative." On my pad were blanks next to my three questions: market size, strategic ownership, and timing of the investment. Beckett clearly thought that if an industry was unattractive, the size of the opportunity, its fit with HGS, and its possible timing weren't even worth exploring.

And just as quickly as my interview had begun, it ended, and I found myself back in the hallway.

My meeting with Beckett was enlightening, to say the least. Obviously, he had very strong opinions, and he wasn't shy about sharing them. But I couldn't let that cloud my judgment about his analysis. He did make a compelling case against HGS entering shirts. High rivalry, low barriers to entry that were not easy to fortify, high buyer power, high supplier power, and lots of close substitutes—this was an unattractive industry, no matter how you cut it. If HGS entered and tried to scale up production, protect its patent, and create a brand, I could see how the firm would quickly lose the billion dollars that Beckett's teams projected it would.

That conclusion was disappointing. After all, my own experience buying a white shirt showed me that while I could get a pretty good shirt for around $85, if I wanted a really good shirt—high thread count, high-end cotton, and so forth—I would have to special-order it, and it would cost around $400! If you could get a high-quality shirt at $60, or even $100—and that was what Plastiwear was promising—boy, that looked attractive to me.

But Beckett's analysis seemed airtight. And even though it was negative, it felt good to have such a concrete conclusion to share with the team. And that was what I was going to report in our first team update. Ken had set a 7:00 p.m. meeting time. He would join us on the phone, as would Livia. The rest of the team—including Bill and Gordon—would be there in person. So far, Vivek, Bill, and I were the only ones who had put in any time on this project, so I assumed this meeting was our chance to brief the rest of the team on our conclusions.

I finished my interview with Beckett around 5:00 p.m. That gave me two hours to type up my notes, e-mail them to the rest of the team, and prepare for the team meeting. I also had to respond to the revised work plan Vivek had somehow found time to draft and circulate. But most of all, I had to prepare an airtight case against Plastiwear.

While I had been doing my interviews, Vivek and Bill had been meeting with marketing managers at corporate headquarters and in the two big business units, trying to understand their perspectives on the Plastiwear opportunity. Given Vivek's relative experience, it didn't surprise me that, when the meeting began, Ken and Livia turned to him.

Ken spoke first. His disembodied voice on the telephone reminded me of Charlie on *Charlie's Angels*.

"First, Bill, are you there?"

"Yes, I'm here, Ken."

"Well, Bill, it's nice to meet you, even if it's only over the phone. We consider ourselves fortunate to have you with us on this project. Carl tells me you've already pitched in, helping us in this very tight schedule. We appreciate your help."

"I'll be glad to help however I can."

"Great. Why don't we start with the marketing interviews? Vivek, we've all had a chance to read your notes. Anything you want to add?"

I suddenly realized that I had not read these reports.

"Yes, thanks, Ken." I think Vivek was a little surprised that he was going first, because he was right in the middle of a bite of food when Ken called on him. We had ordered dinner delivered to the team room—our table now stacked high with Chinese food, soft drinks, HGS reports, and printouts from various financial and data collection services.

Regaining his composure, Vivek continued, "I just wanted to emphasize how much the marketing people hate the name 'Plastiwear.' I didn't put this in my notes, but one manager said it sounded like a product right out of *The Jetsons*—you know, the cartoon about the family in the future. And not in a good way."

Several of us chuckled at this reference, although I didn't think Vivek would have ever seen *The Jetsons* growing up in India. I had heard about it, but I'd never actually seen the cartoon.

Gordon agreed. "I also thought it was an unfortunate name. 'Plastiwear'—sounds like something out of an old science-fiction movie. Either that or a line of adult diapers. You can hear the tagline now—'Plastiwear Diapers—When It Counts the Most.'" While this banter went on, I concentrated on the details of my argument against a Plasti-wear investment, a bit impatient about the team spending so much time discussing the name, even in jest.

"Well," replied Livia, who seemed to share my desire to move on, "HGS is a specialty chemical firm, not a marketing company. If we end up recommending that they pursue this opportunity, we can also rec-ommend getting marketing experts involved to come up with a solid branding strategy."

Ken picked up the thread. "Vivek, aside from the unfortunate name, anything else that will add to the synthesis and suggestions in your notes?"

"No. Overall, the marketing managers we interviewed had remark-ably little to say about Plastiwear. They are very much an industrial marketing group and focus almost all their efforts on building the industrial brand. They have no experience and, as far as I can tell, no expertise in retail marketing. If HGS decided to brand Plastiwear shirts, they would have to develop an entirely new skill base—or at least get access to that base from another source, as you've suggested, Livia." Everyone nodded in agreement.

Livia followed up on Vivek's comments. "So, part of this engagement may involve helping HGS either develop or hire some retail marketing expertise or helping them find partners with the appropriate expertise. If we recommend in favor of a retail strategy, that is."

Ken's reply was cautious. "That is always a possibility and might be a way forward. Let's do our homework before we start to think too far into the future or close off any options. What we need now is as objec-tive a read as possible about this opportunity. It seems to me that HGS is framing this as a retail play, and Vivek—it sounds like you didn't have a chance to discuss how some of the B-to-B marketing experience they have at HGS might be relevant to us."

I'm sure that Vivek saw this comment as a mild rebuke. I know I would have.

Ken continued, "So, Vivek, maybe you can think about how we might leverage whatever marketing skills they do have. Also, could you con-tinue to explore which players on the marketing side have the power, or the incentive, to block or accelerate progress on a Plastiwear launch?"

"No problem, Ken. I'll get on those issues right away." I guessed that Vivek would probably be working all night rethinking his approach to marketing and that by tomorrow he would have an entirely new set of ideas. Vivek—consulting "iron man"!

Ken continued, "Bill, did you want to add anything to Vivek's observations?"

"No, I think he summarized the state of marketing in HGS accurately. If we were to try to get into retail, no doubt, we'd have to develop or somehow access some entirely new skills."

Ken then moved the meeting on to me. "Justin, your notes suggest that the VP of oil and gas products is quite pessimistic about Plastiwear and HGS playing in the shirt space."

"Yes, Beckett is extremely pessimistic," I replied.

"Do you have anything to add, over and above your notes?"

"Only to emphasize that I thought his approach—or rather, his team's approach to this problem—was very careful and very thorough."

"And you think the industry attractiveness analysis he used is a good basis for making strategic choices?" asked Livia.

Livia had asked a question I hadn't thought of. In my MBA program, I had learned all about the five forces framework. I had practiced applying it maybe a hundred times, on different cases. But I had never really thought about whether it was a good way to make strategic decisions. I took it for granted—evaluate the attractiveness of an industry and enter only those that were attractive. Oh, there was something in my book about the limits of five forces analysis, but . . .

Suddenly, my response was less confident than I would have liked. "Yes. That's what I learned. Five forces analysis was the starting point for nearly every case we did."

Ken's reply was a bit impatient. "We usually start with that kind of analysis as well. But it's just a preliminary step."

"What do you mean?"

"Well," continued Ken—suddenly not just the senior consultant on the project, but now channeling a demanding professor—"there are a couple of clear limitations of this five forces approach. First of all, how would you characterize the perfect—the most attractive—industry possible, according to the five forces model? For example, how much rivalry would there be?"

"Very little."

"Like, none, right?"

"OK."

"How close would substitutes be in this industry?"

"Not close at all."

"And the other threats?"

"Well, there wouldn't be a threat of entry, no powerful buyers or suppliers."

"Exactly. Now, what kind of industry has the attributes you just listed—no rivalry, no substitutes, no entry, no powerful suppliers or buyers?"

I thought about his question for a second before it became obvious. "That's a monopoly."

"So, what does that mean for using five forces to make strategic choices?"

Again, I had to think quickly, but muddled through. "I guess it means that firms should enter industries that are already monopolies or could be turned into something close to a monopoly."

"And how often is that likely to be a viable option for a firm?"

Yet another question I had not thought of in my MBA program. "I guess, not very often."

"Come on, Justin," continued Ken, "given globalization, the number of industries where a firm can expect to either create or exploit monopoly power is very small. I'm not saying it's impossible. And when we have a client that is operating in a monopoly or oligopoly, sure, five forces logic helps to focus on factors that might make its situation more competitive. But most firms at least have active rivals and viable substitutes."

"I can see that," I replied. "It doesn't seem likely HGS would have a lot of opportunities in any of its businesses, based on five forces logic—given the highly competitive nature of its businesses, I mean."

"That's right. So, what that means is that using five forces to evaluate the attractiveness of an industry doesn't tell us very much about strategic choice. In fact, except in highly unusual circumstances, this type of analysis would recommend not entering most industries, right?"

"Because most of the industries that firms can enter will actually not be all that attractive, at least according to five forces logic," I replied.

"Now you're catching on, Justin. And here's another problem. How easy is it to enter a so-called attractive industry?"

"I'll tell you from my experience, you only want to be in those that are hard to get into. Like that tennis club Ken and Carl belong to," Gordon offered with a wink.

"So," Ken continued, "the cost of entering so-called 'attractive industries' isn't all that attractive."

Ken chuckled, but I wanted to stay on track. I couldn't quite believe what I was hearing. "So," I persisted, "are you saying that five forces analysis is a waste of time?"

"No." Now Gordon was serious. "We almost always start a strategic engagement with five forces and other basic analyses to help identify the competitive and structural challenges in an industry. This list of competitive challenges usually suggests some strategic opportunities that a firm might be able to exploit, or clarifies the sources of some of its problems."

I looked around the table, and Vivek was shaking his head in agreement, while Bill sat quietly, watching with interest as the conversation unfolded in front of him.

Now it was Livia's turn to chime in. "Justin. This is Livia. The five forces framework does a great job helping to identify the competitive threats in an industry. Whatever strategies we develop for Plastiwear will need to address one or more of these threats directly. But using this tool to estimate the overall attractiveness of an industry is usually not that helpful."

Livia continued on a different tack. "Justin, do you know anything about sailing?"

"I've been a couple of times. Why?"

"When I was a child, I just assumed that in order for a sailboat to go, say, east, the wind had to be blowing from the west to the east. I was amazed to learn that, no matter which way the wind blew, a sailboat could always get to where it wanted to go—if it had a skilled sailor at the helm. To me, the five forces are kind of like the wind, the direction that competition within an industry is moving. Strategy is about positioning the firm relative to the prevailing winds in a way to make sure that the firm gets to where it wants to go, no matter what direction the wind is blowing."

"So," Ken said, picking up on Livia's analogy, "it's good to know where the wind is coming from, but our job is to help firms use the wind to reach their profit and other goals. This is the case even if it is blowing directly against a firm, even if all five forces align against being in an industry and make it incredibly unattractive."

"In fact," added Gordon, "some of the most successful firms in the world are successful precisely because they have figured how to use very unfavorable industry winds—high rivalry, high threat of entry, and so forth—to their advantage. Look at Walmart, Southwest Airlines, Nucor Steel, Toyota, Starbucks. These firms have played in some pretty unattractive industries—at least according to a five forces analysis—and still they have been successful."

"In other words," concluded Ken, "while Beckett's five forces analysis of Plastiwear is interesting, it is certainly not definitive. Our job is to identify appropriate ways for our client to compete using Plastiwear, despite these challenges."

"Of course," Livia said, almost to herself, "Beckett might turn out to be right. Men's white shirts may be a nonstarter, no matter what analysis we do."

As the conversation turned to other matters, I considered the two things I had learned so far working at HGS. First, I had learned that net present value analysis tells you nothing about the quality of a firm's proposed strategic activities. Second, I had learned that the attractiveness of an industry, by itself, cannot be used to make good strategic choices. As the team continued with a discussion of the work plan, priorities, and hypotheses, I found it hard to concentrate. I was now in the uncomfortable position of having much of what I thought I knew about strategic analysis—present value and five forces—stripped away from me, and in public as well. What would be my next step? With these gaping holes in my strategy toolkit, how was I going to crack this case?

As our meeting wrapped up, Ken asked each of us if we had any parting comments. When it came my turn, I had nothing to add. Frankly, I was eager to wrap up the call, but Ken wanted to talk more. To me.

"Thanks, everyone. I think we're clear on next steps, but let's stay in close contact on progress toward deliverables. Post and circulate things as you've been doing, but ping me in real time if there is any breaking news. Nice work, Livia, Vivek, Gordon. And thanks again, Bill. Hey, Justin, let's chat this evening, say about 9:00. OK? I'll give you a call on your cell. Shouldn't take long."

"Great," I managed to reply as the meeting concluded.

"Let's chat this evening. I'll give you a call." Those words said everything and nothing, no matter how many times I replayed them in my head. I wondered if it would make sense for me to resign now and take one of the Wall Street offers I had turned down. Better than getting fired by Ken tonight! I knew most consultants didn't stay long, but I hadn't intended to set a record for shortest tenure ever.

I tried to concentrate on the project in the hours after the team meeting, but the same thoughts kept coming to my mind: *"Let's chat . . . shouldn't take long."* What was Ken going to say—*"Well, Justin, obviously, you have failed the firm, failed the client, failed your family—and worst of all, Justin, you've failed yourself. So, you're fired."* That would be a short conversation, for sure. Almost as short as my consulting career.

Waiting for this call was worse than waiting for a dental appointment. At least with the dentist, you're better off after the appointment than before. Later tonight, I wouldn't have a job. Nine o'clock was only an hour away, but it was the longest hour of my life. Every tick of the clock lasted a minute and every minute lasted an hour. Finally, at three minutes after nine, my phone rang.

My heart jumped. But I told myself to let it ring a couple of times—no reason to appear too anxious. Whatever happens, I told myself, keep cool and remain calm.

"Hello, Justin Campbell."

"Hi, Justin. It's Ken. How are things going over there?"

"Well. We just had a couple of reports on the competitive situation in the fabric industry sent over. They are more up to date than what HGS has been working with, although things haven't changed dramatically in three years."

"Good. Those might prove helpful. Listen, Justin, I thought it might be a good idea to talk about how you think things are going. I know we all got thrown a curve ball when the time schedule on this HGS project got shortened to just nine days, especially when Gordon couldn't break out of his client commitments today. That's put more pressure on the team than normal." Ken sounded matter of fact. "Sometimes it's like that, though."

I quickly decided to fess up to my failures. If I pointed out my own weaknesses, maybe Ken would see that I understand my own problems, take mercy on me, and give me another chance. "Well, I do feel like I got off to a rough start."

"What do you mean, Justin?"

"Well, it started when I used that example from my MBA class—on multiple conflicting assumptions about opportunities."

Ken paused, then seemed to connect with what I was saying. "That was a bit naive, but it wasn't a big deal. Sometimes you new MBAs seem to think that doing strategy work is just trying to figure out which case in your program is most like the client. Real-world strategy isn't about cracking the case."

I continued in confessional mode. "Then there was that five forces fiasco."

"The fiasco didn't have to do with your report of the analysis you heard from Beckett, which the team needed to be aware of. In fact, your notes were accurate as far as they went. The issue was that you bought his analysis hook, line, and sinker. You didn't look at his analysis skeptically."

"What fooled me was that he seemed to do a good job on the five forces analysis."

"Two things to keep in mind whenever you see someone apply one of these analytical tools. First, whether it's the five forces framework or present value analysis or whatever, they are just tools. They're like, say, a hammer. You can use a hammer exactly the way it's designed to be used, but instead of building something beautiful or durable, you can build a pile of junk. It's not the tool, it's how the tool is used; it's the skills, interests, and motives of the person using the tool that determine whether the outcome of an analysis is reasonable. That leads to the second thing to remember."

"What's that?"

"When managers present a point of view, assume their point of view reflects some combination of how things actually are and how they want things to be. In your report, you noted, for example, that Beckett said he always opposed the Plastiwear initiative."

"That's what he said."

"As he made clear in our first meeting. Now, one reason he may be opposed to the Plastiwear deal is that he really thinks it is a bad idea—he doesn't buy the economics or he thinks it will hurt the firm. But he must also be considering how this strategic initiative will affect him, his people, and his career. How old is Beckett?"

"Mid-fifties, I think." I paused to check on my guess. "He's fifty-four."

"And how old is Carl, the CEO?"

"He's sixty."

"So, Carl is about five years away from retirement—assuming this unfriendly takeover doesn't happen and unseat him. Beckett's the general manager of the largest, and most profitable, division in HGS. Don't you think his position, experience, and age make him a top contender for CEO when Carl retires?"

"Sounds reasonable."

"Now, if you were Beckett, wouldn't you have a strong incentive to make sure that your division continued to be the largest and most profitable? What is it going to take to continue to grow the oil and gas division?"

"Higher sales, attractive products, maybe some new technologies; I would guess some new manufacturing sites."

"And what does all this take?"

"What do you mean?"

"What will Beckett need to achieve growth?"

"Managerial attention, I guess."

"And capital."

I thought Ken sounded a bit frustrated, so I echoed quickly, "That's right, capital."

"Now if HGS commits to a big investment in Plastiwear, isn't that going to have an impact on the capital available to Beckett and his division?"

"I was taught that if a business unit had a project that could generate positive present value in cash flows, it should be funded."

"Justin, it's time to move beyond MBA-land." Now Ken's frustration was unmistakable. "In the real world, there is a finite amount of capital to spend every year. Demand for this capital is almost always greater than its supply. If HGS makes a big financial commitment elsewhere, then Beckett might not get the capital he thinks he needs to grow his business. He needs to achieve continuous financial improvement in the oil and gas business to keep his current, and possible future, power. "

"So, are you saying that Beckett's analysis was just a way to advance his personal interests?"

"No, nothing that simplistic, but his personal interests color the type and amount of analysis he does. For example, after doing a quick five forces on one industry—men's white shirts—he sees that this industry is unattractive, and so concludes that the firm shouldn't exploit Plasti-wear. Since the first result of his thinking leads to conclusions that are consistent with his preferences, he doesn't push any further—doesn't examine how the threats he's identified in the industry could actually be turned to HGS's advantage, for example. Besides that, he already has a full-time job running his division. He doesn't have a lot of time to do in-depth analyses of Plastiwear applications."

"So, he's predisposed to find a particular answer, and once he finds it, he stops looking."

"Exactly. This is where we, as outsiders, can add value. Our job is to realize that people like Beckett may have stopped thinking about these issues too soon and to push them to think harder about alternatives. I can't count the number of times I've had to work with managers who did analyses that reaffirmed what they already believed, and had to motivate them to start thinking again."

"Was that what I should have done? Ask him hard questions about his analysis, to get him thinking again?"

"Not necessarily. Mostly, at this stage of the project, we're just collect-ing information—getting everyone's point of view out on the table. If there are some obvious weaknesses in his approach, then yes, it makes sense to raise questions and push back. We will do this, but it usually isn't in the first interview. No, Justin, the problem wasn't that you didn't force Beckett to start thinking again."

"So, what was my mistake?"

"Your mistake was that you didn't force *yourself* to start thinking again. You drank his Kool-Aid instead of remaining objective. For example, Becktt's five forces analysis focused on the shirt industry, right?"

"Yes."

"As did his present value analysis—it also focused on returns to HGS if they went into the shirt industry. Right?"

"Yes. So far, most of the analyses I've seen in HGS have focused on men's dress shirts."

"Well, Justin, suppose that instead of going into shirts, HGS used Plastiwear to go into the fibers and fabric industry—selling fibers and fabrics to other firms who then make dress shirts or other products. Becktt didn't do a five forces analysis or conduct a present value analysis on that industry, maybe because he got the answer he wanted from analyzing shirt manufacturing. Maybe there is an opportunity in shirts, maybe it's in the fiber and fabric industry, maybe it's in just doing research and development into fabrics, maybe there is no opportunity here at all. We've barely scratched the surface of thinking about the possibilities. But once you decide which industry you are going to analyze, well, that largely determines the outcome of the five forces analysis. You have the answer when you ask the question. We want to avoid closing down our thinking prematurely."

"Can we use five forces to identify the right industry to study?"

"No," responded Ken. "The five forces framework takes the industry to be analyzed as a given. If you analyze the wrong industry, it really doesn't matter how good the analysis is. Bottom line is we have to explore multiple options along the steps in the value chains that may be opportunities for HGS—especially when we're evaluating a new technology like Plastiwear. Plus, if we close off options too soon, that can create dysfunctional dynamics within our team."

"What do you mean?"

"When you buy into unfounded assumptions or jump to premature conclusions—about what the relevant industry or industries are, about what the right analysis is—you can't provide the objectivity the client needs and deserves. If others on our team do this as well, then conflicts among managers in the client firm are mirrored by conflicts on the strategy team. At that point, unless we're intentionally role-playing, we aren't adding the value we should.

"I hope this gives you some new things to consider," Ken continued, "but I don't mean for you to be too critical of management. That's not a helpful attitude either."

"I got it. Healthy skepticism to remain objective."

"Just one more question for you tonight, Justin. Why do you suppose it was so easy for you to buy into Beckett's analysis?"

"Well, I thought it was rigorous."

"Justin," Ken said, now sounding a bit annoyed. "It was rigorous. Just incomplete, focused on only one of several possible industries, and very likely self-serving. My question to you is—why didn't you see these obvious problems? Why did you drink the Kool-Aid so fast?"

"I don't really know." I reacted honestly, clutching tightly to my last shred of dignity.

"Next time we talk, Justin, you need to know the answer to this question. It's the only way we can make sure you don't get caught up in this same way again. I'd like you to give me a call as you begin to understand what's going on—not just with the client, but inside your head as well. Good night, Justin."

"'Night, Ken."

He hung up.

Well, at least I wasn't fired. And Ken had given me some great insights about strategy and the project here at HGS. But his last question was a hard one. Once the strategy team had described the weaknesses in Beckett's analysis, they were incredibly obvious. Industry attractiveness, by itself, usually doesn't drive strategic choices, since monopolies are so rare and the cost of entering "attractive" industries is generally very high. More important, sometimes a firm can use strategies to turn threats into opportunities, making an unattractive industry attractive—at least to that firm. Even more fundamentally, these kinds of analyses don't tell you which industry to analyze. No matter how rigorously you analyze the wrong industry, you still get the wrong answer—or maybe the right answer to the wrong question. And sometimes industry analysis—like any management tool, I guess—can be used to reaffirm a manager's preexisting preferences rather than to objectively analyze a strategic opportunity.

It's not that five forces analysis is wrong—it just has to be applied appropriately.

But, why hadn't I seen these weaknesses? Had I ignored them during my MBA program as well? Was I just not smart enough to see them? Was I too tired to focus? Those questions echoed in my head well into the night.

REFLECTION QUESTIONS

1. Do you agree with Beckett that "shirt manufacturing is a dog industry, a classic nonstarter"? Why or why not?

2. Justin discovers some important limitations of the five forces model. What are those limitations, and under what conditions does it make sense to use this model?

3. How can the strategy team distinguish between objective information about Plastiwear and information that is colored by the preferences and biases of a particular manager?

4. What other questions should Justin have asked Beckett?

5. If real-world strategy isn't about "cracking the case," what is it about?

6. If you were Justin, what would you say to Ken in your next phone call?

— 4 —

A WORKING
LUNCH

I awoke the next morning at 5:30. I hadn't had any exercise since starting this project, so I forced myself out of bed and down to the hotel gym. Besides, some time on the treadmill would let me think through the last couple of days.

Obviously, sleep had not come easily last night. But ultimately I decided my conversation with Ken was more like a coaching session than a reprimand. In fact, I was willing to bet Ken had had this talk with lots of other junior consultants. This realization provided only hollow comfort—while others might have the same problems, they were still my problems.

I also reviewed what I knew—or rather, what I didn't know—about the project. I knew that HGS's present value calculations were not going to give us our answer. I knew that Beckett's five forces analysis was, at best, overly narrow and probably biased. So, all I really knew was that I didn't really know anything. Great. Not what I expected after so many hours of work.

In fact, the only good news I could see was that—so far—my mistakes had occurred only within the strategy team. I hadn't yet done anything in front of the client that would embarrass me or the firm. I may not have been creating value yet, but at least I wasn't destroying value.

As the electronic screen credited me with two miles of effort, I began to relax. My mind drifted. For the first time since landing in Chicago, I allowed myself to think briefly about my girlfriend, Jackie. This job was so demanding, I didn't even have time to miss her, but she was likely wrapped up in her own work. We'd managed to build the relationship so far in spite of both our busy, often stressful schedules.

I knew Jackie thought I was smart and professional, but I couldn't help but wonder what the other members of the team thought of me. Livia was scheduled to be on-site today. She probably had lots of experience working with new associates, so maybe she wouldn't judge me too harshly. Gordon, on the other hand, probably thought I was a total idiot.

I have to admit, my first impressions of Gordon weren't too positive—Yankee blue blood and all. Maybe it's just my background, but I had an uneasy feeling about him from the very beginning. Where I come from, we don't mind wealthy people—actually, we kind of admire those who make it big—but there is surprisingly little "old money" in a town like Austin. Gordon seems to have come from real old money. Sure, he's bright and well-trained. Not much of the common touch, however.

And then there was Bill, the only member of the team from HGS. He had worked with Vivek so far, and the two of them seemed to be getting along fine. I wondered what he thought of our meeting last night. Was he "spying" on us for the CEO, Carl? Clearly, Bill's loyalty was first to Carl, second to HGS, and only last to the strategy team. Overall, that wasn't much of a problem since the strategy team—as far as I could tell—was committed to improving HGS's competitive position, an outcome that could only help Carl. If we got involved in raucous debates among ourselves, well, that was just part of the process. It was the outcome that mattered. I'm sure Carl knew that, so even if Bill was "spying" on us for Carl, that was fine with me. In fact, maybe Bill could be helpful in getting messages to Carl. We'd hardly have time to pass anything by Carl in this short sprint of an engagement.

As I returned to my room to shower, my mind shifted to that day's agenda. After I quickly reviewed some of the latest studies and data we'd received, Bill and I were going to interview Bob Hutchins, vice president of the packaging division. Vivek was on his own today—Gordon was still tied up elsewhere. The last thing I did last night—I mean this morning—was to e-mail Bill some questions he and I might want to ask Hutchins.

Bob Hutchins, at forty-two, was younger than Scott Beckett. His division was smaller than oil and gas and less profitable as well. Hutchins had said almost nothing in our first meeting, but one of the positive present value analyses of Plastiwear floating around at HGS assumed that it would be manufactured in a packaging division factory that was currently operating at 50 percent capacity. Revenues from Plastiwear sales would probably be partially credited to the packaging division, so based on Shirley's and Ken's logic, I assumed that Hutchins would be in favor of Plastiwear. Really, if Ken was right, Hutchins probably stopped his analysis of Plastiwear as soon as he found a justification for going forward with the investment. I had to remain independent and objective, to make sure that his analysis was not only rigorous, but complete and appropriate.

We were scheduled to meet Hutchins at 9:00 a.m. I walked across the street, flashed my ID at the security desk, and ran into Bill getting coffee outside the team room at 8:30.

"Morning, Justin" was Bill's greeting.

"Morning, Bill. So we're on together today."

"Looks like it."

I tried to draw Bill out as we settled into chairs in the team rooms. "So, how well do you know Bob Hutchins?"

"Not well, really. We've met a few times, but I've never worked in packaging. From what other people tell me, he is a sales-oriented, high-energy guy. But his division's performance has been down for at least a year now."

"Yeah, I heard about the factory running at 50 percent capacity. That's not good."

"He thinks that HGS can manufacture Plastiwear in his factory," Bill replied. "That would fill some capacity—which could make his performance look better."

"Yeah, I think you're right. Did you have a chance to look over the questions I e-mailed?" I handed Bill a hard copy of the questions and continued, "Are you comfortable if I lead off the questioning?"

"Well, I don't read e-mail after 2 a.m., Justin," Bill laughed as he scanned the questions, "but I'll follow your lead and we'll see what we can find out."

We arrived at Hutchins's office on the seventy-second floor about five minutes early. His secretary protected the door to his office like a mother bear protects her cubs, practically snarling back at our greetings.

"Good morning. We have an appointment with Mr. Hutchins." I was trying to be as pleasant as I could. She glanced back at me with suspicion.

"I know. You're early. Sit over there." Without removing her hands from her keyboard, she nodded toward a couch along the wall. "Do you want something?"

"A cup of coffee would be nice," was my reply. I had gotten all my shirts back from the laundry this morning, so I was feeling daring with the coffee.

"Not ready yet."

Bill just waited quietly, looking slightly amused by this exchange.

"Maybe later, then." I tried to be positive and professional.

"Uh huh," was the only response I got.

Four minutes and forty-five seconds later, she looked over at us. "Mr. Hutchins will see you now."

I thanked her as we moved to the office door.

"Hi, I'm Bob Hutchins, VP of packaging. How are you?" He moved out from behind his desk, welcoming us.

He grasped my hand and squeezed—a bit too hard, I thought. Trying to show how tough he was, or was it genuine enthusiasm? Hutchins reminded me of the salesmen I used to see at tech expos—under six feet tall, a bit overweight, brown hair cut short, wearing a French blue shirt with a matching French blue tie, gray pants and black shoes, no jacket. I decided to go with enthusiasm.

"I'm well, thank you." Gesturing toward Bill, I continued. "This is Bill Dixon. You may have met him."

"Oh sure, go way back. How you doing, Bill?" Hutchins shook Bill's hand just as aggressively as he shook mine. He motioned for us to sit in the chairs across from his desk, as he took his seat and continued. "Great, great. Sit down, make yourselves comfortable. This must be kind of exciting for you, Bill—working with the strategy team, meeting with all the senior managers, mergers and acquisitions, technology, all that stuff. It's got to be exciting for both of you. I know it's exciting for me. HGS has been really good to me, and I want to return the favor. And the packaging division—boy, the sky is the limit. Our R&D folks have come up with some great new technologies. Yes, the sky's the limit."

To emphasize his last point, Hutchins slid his hands together in front of him and then shot his right hand into the air, high over his head, like a rocket ship blasting off the earth.

"That does sound exciting," was Bill's observation.

"You bet it is. And that's why we've got to get this Plastiwear product off the ground and running. Plastiwear—have they let you in on all the secrets?"

He didn't wait for a reply before continuing.

"Feels like expensive cotton, cuts well, sews well, can't stain it, lasts forever, makes great shirts. So what if it only comes in white? Heck, white dress shirts are always going to be popular. Classic. Timeless. Right?"

He didn't seem to expect answers to any of his questions.

"So we've got to get into this right now. Ramp it up fast. We don't have time to waste, especially with this takeover thing. We've got to move."

A pattern seemed to be emerging—I was supposed to interview these people, but they talked too much for me to ask any questions. Maybe they think an interview is really an invitation to monologue. He went on, pausing only briefly for a breath.

"But I've been arguing this for some time now. That's why I'm glad you guys are here. Maybe you can get us off dead center. The economics are clear. I had a team do present value studies, and it's easy to see what the right thing to do is."

Finally, an opening. I jumped in. "We saw those reports, but there are other studies that don't agree with your findings."

"Well, that's because they were done wrong. Used the wrong assumptions. They didn't recognize some obvious synergies between Plastiwear and our businesses."

"What synergies?" Bill asked, leaning in toward Hutchins's desk.

"Well, the most obvious one is manufacturing capacity. Right now, we have an opportunity because one of my plants is a little under capacity.

This space would be perfect for manufacturing Plastiwear." He looked from me to Bill and back to me. "Obviously, there are also R&D synergies. After all, our R&D group came up with this stuff."

"I thought R&D was a corporate function. Is there also a packaging R&D group?" I wondered out loud.

"Yes and no. The Plastiwear R&D guys are closely linked with the packaging division. I'm sure that we'll build on Plastiwear to develop new packaging materials in the future. But the bottom line is clear—whatever we do with Plastiwear will require manufacturing capacity, and my division has manufacturing capacity. By sharing the plant, we could reduce overhead costs dramatically—one plant manager instead of two, common accounting, IT, the whole nine yards. We could save lots of money, compared to Plastiwear on its own. That's why our present value analyses were positive and theirs weren't. They didn't see the big picture."

"Can you talk more about the specifics of what you see as the Plastiwear opportunity?" asked Bill.

"Let's take shirts for example. Men's shirts. No doubt. To start we could make the fabric and the shirts right in my factory."

"How much space would that take?" continued Bill.

"That's the beauty of it. The space we have available is perfect. About one-third for making the fabric, the rest for making the shirts."

"What is the fabric-making process like?" I asked, nodding to Bill as it seemed our impromptu tag-team approach was working.

"My background is in sales, not manufacturing. So I don't know all the technical details. But we mix some chemicals in a big vat, then add a reactant and it solidifies. That combination gets squeezed through a mold that creates the fibers. The fibers are then woven into the cloth."

"Do you do this at scale now?" I flipped over my question list, making notes on the back.

"No, no. We run a very small process now to make the fiber. And we outsource the weaving to a small manufacturer. We make less than fifty yards of fabric at a time. But this has allowed us to test the material, try out different weaves and different textures, and our prototypes are gorgeous."

I asked the obvious follow-up question. "What are your plans to test this process at scale?"

"We have discussed it. We know there'll be problems in scaling up, but the process we're using is pretty standard. So, I'm confident we'll be able to do this. Once the fabric is cut, the shirt-assembly process is standard." He motioned again with his whole body, as if he were cutting and sewing, I think. "Just think of large cutting tables and lines of sewing machines."

Bill was smiling, but shaking his head at the same time. "Standard manufacturing. Is there anything proprietary about this process?"

"Not in the process, but definitely in the chemicals and the formulation, Bill. You have to put just the right mix of chemicals into the vat, at the right temperature, with the right active ingredients. That is what makes Plastiwear special and proprietary."

"These vats of chemicals. Isn't there an expensive environmental problem here?" I asked, trying to recall if the estimate I had seen was $3 million or $4 million.

"Another synergy!" Hutchins seemed genuinely happy I'd stumbled on such an intelligent question. "We already have strong environmental controls at our plant. It's a perfect fit, a natural extension of our current business."

I decided to raise an issue voiced by the oil and gas guys. "But your customers are industrial customers. For Plastiwear shirts, your customers would be retail firms."

"You have a point there. There isn't as much synergy downstream, after manufacturing. But upstream—not just in manufacturing, but in chemical sourcing—potential savings there. Lots."

"Plastiwear and your division use similar chemicals in manufacturing?" I hadn't heard this before and was honestly surprised.

"No, but they can be purchased from similar suppliers. If we increase our volume of certain chemicals, we will probably get some volume discounts."

"These savings haven't been locked in yet, have they?" asked Bill.

"Oh, too soon for that. But that doesn't mean there isn't real potential there."

I thought it was time to push back a little harder. "What happens if demand for packaging increases, and you need to increase your manufacturing capacity?"

"Well, that would be a good problem to have. At that point, we would probably have to open a new manufacturing facility and decide whether or not to use it for Plastiwear or for my packaging business. But that probably won't be happening, at least for a couple of years. It's going to take that long for us to bring our next generation of products out of R&D and into the marketplace. By that time, Plastiwear should be well established, and we will probably be adding capacity anyway by then."

Bill took at stab at the heart of Hutchins's analysis. "How would the revenues and profits of Plastiwear be accounted for, within HGS, in your plan?"

"That's another synergy," Hutchins replied. If anything, his enthusiasm seemed to be building. "Since Plastiwear would be sharing our manufacturing location, the revenues and profits it generates could be folded into the profit and loss statements for the packaging division. That way, Plastiwear doesn't have to develop its own accounting organization but can simply piggyback on ours. We could treat it like another product in the portfolio of packaging products in my division. After all, what is a shirt? Really, it's nothing more than packaging for the body!"

Packaging for the body. I thought that might be a stretch for a product extension strategy. "You seem convinced. Why do you suppose others inside HGS are more skeptical about Plastiwear?"

"They just don't see that Plastiwear is a logical extension of our current businesses," Hutchins replied. "There are huge synergies between Plastiwear applications and our other businesses—especially in manufacturing. If you incorporate those synergies into the plan, then Plastiwear is a clear winner. It's even pretty good as a standalone product. So, personally, I don't get their reluctance. Those guys in the oil and gas division are pretty smart, but their lack of confidence is costing us valuable time. Heck, I don't know. I've been doing all the talking here. What do you think? How soon do you think we can get production up and running?"

Hutchins's question was reasonable. To him, it was only a matter of when, not if, HGS should go into Plastiwear. But my conversation with Ken had convinced me that, for the time being, my job was to collect and analyze information, challenging people only if they were making obvious mistakes. Hutchins's logic seemed sound—although sometimes it was hard to spot through his enthusiasm. Hutchins saw Plastiwear as a related diversification move; thus the emphasis on synergies. But I had learned in my MBA program to be wary of synergies—often more hope than substance.

I also remembered Ken's warning about the interests of managers and their potential to impact analyses. At least here, Hutchins's interests were obvious. Plastiwear would fill up his plant, improve his profit and loss statement, and potentially generate new revenues and profits for the packaging division. Maybe Beckett opposed Plastiwear not only because it potentially siphoned investment away from oil and gas—but also because the packaging division might benefit disproportionately from lines of business based on the new technology.

Of course, all of this was speculation. And since related diversification, with associated synergies, is a widely cited justification for going into new businesses, I decided to suspend judgment about Hutchins's arguments. I responded to his question about when to go into Plastiwear production with an honest, but noncommittal, "Oh, we're still in the information-gathering stage."

Hutchins continued talking passionately for some time about HGS, his career, how important packaging was in the economy, and the evils of misguided environmentalists. Bill asked a few questions about other packaging products and seemed familiar with the division's suppliers and customers. While I tried to inject a few questions, I gained no additional insights about Plastiwear, HGS, or the packaging division.

I spent the rest of the morning in the team room writing up my notes and summarizing reports on the fabric industry that we'd requested earlier in the week. Bill disappeared to attend to some other things. I briefly wondered if he was released from other responsibilities to work with us, or if we were something of an overload, when I read an incoming e-mail. DixonW@HGS.com wrote: "Very interesting interview, Justin. Send me your notes and I'll see if I can add anything later this afternoon. I'm off to a lunch meeting with Carl."

Well, at least now I knew for sure he was a spy. Not much of one, however, telling me he was having lunch with his "handler." I also made a mental note to talk to Vivek about Bill's role in his interviews so we were all on the same page.

By 11:30, I was hungry. No one else was in the team room, so I decided to go out to lunch by myself—if for no other reason, to get some fresh air. I'd always heard that Chicago has the best pizza in the world. Yesterday, I had noticed a pizza place down the street, Pantera's Pizza, so I headed there for a quick lunch.

It wasn't too crowded—I barely beat the lunch rush. As I was shown to my table, I was surprised to see who was seated nearby.

"Livia. I didn't expect to find you here." I hadn't seen Livia since our kickoff meeting. Could that have been two days ago?

"Hi, Justin. How's everything?"

"I'm doing fine. How about you?"

"Well, I'm a bit uncomfortable now—that maybe you'll divulge my little secret." She leaned forward, pretending to whisper. "I love this place. I come here for the deep dish pizza almost every time I'm in this part of town." She broke out into a big smile. "It kills my diet, but the Italian sausage is to die for.

"Come join me," she offered. "I just ordered—I've been reviewing the team's notes, but you can give me a live project update." I pulled my chair to Livia's table, and the waiter took my drink order while I perused the menu. Despite her recommendation, I went for the traditional margherita pizza. I didn't want to tell her that Italian sausage makes me burp in an altogether unprofessional way.

"So, Justin, what's the latest theory?"

Livia paused at my quizzical look.

"Go ahead. I think we can discuss the project without making the waiter sign a nondisclosure agreement."

I quickly replayed the highlights of Hutchins's related diversification/synergy story without mentioning any product or company names.

"Ah, Justin, the synergy dream. It usually rears its ugly head on projects like these. You know synergies—often promised, rarely delivered. And, in this case, probably not justified either."

I hadn't come to that conclusion about Hutchins's argument, so I was a bit surprised by the certainty in Livia's voice.

"What do you mean?"

"Well, look at this from the new product point of view. If I were the division general manager of the new product line, I would want to evaluate all my manufacturing options. Maybe I build my own plant, maybe I cooperate with the packaging department and use their plant, maybe I form a joint venture to do my manufacturing for me, maybe I outsource it entirely. But, I don't want to go into this thing assuming that the best way to manufacture my goods is in an existing packaging division plant. This might be great for packaging, but maybe not for me, and maybe not for the firm overall. I would want to keep my options open."

"I can see your point," I nodded hoping she'd continue.

"In fact, in my mind, there have to be pretty compelling reasons to bring activities like manufacturing these new products in-house, to vertically integrate manufacturing."

"What do you mean?"

"Well, think of the advantages of outsourcing. I can get multiple suppliers competing to provide me with the highest-quality service at the lowest price. I can choose to locate manufacturing anywhere in the world—including some places with really low-cost labor. Some other firm has to invest in the plant and equipment required to make this stuff, and that's on its balance sheet. And who knows, maybe if that firm is supplying multiple fiber and fabric companies, it'll be able to re-alize some cost advantage that HGS wouldn't get doing this on its own. And look what happens if I bring this manufacturing in-house."

"What do you mean?"

"Well, I probably pay more for labor, maybe my production costs are higher, I get an expensive overhead load. Excess capacity is already an albatross around packaging's neck. Now you want to hang significant costs on a brand-new product line, right out of the gate."

"Sounds like you'd never manufacture inside the client firm."

"Never say never. But I would only bring it in-house if there were some compelling reason to do so."

The waiter chose this moment to bring our orders. I picked up the first slice. It was everything I had been promised.

"Boy, that's good pizza."

"I told you it was great," replied Livia, as she bit into her own slice.

"So, Livia," I persisted, returning to the topic at hand, "based on your experience, when would you bring a function like manufacturing inside the boundaries of the client firm?"

Livia paused, but I wasn't sure if she was thinking about my question or enjoying her lunch. "Three things would influence my decision: If firms I outsourced to couldn't deliver the quality I needed, if outsourcing put my proprietary technology at risk, if I became dependent on only a single outside supplier. Factors like these would make me think twice about outsourcing."

"You could easily solve the last problem—having only one supplier—by outsourcing to several different firms."

"Alternate suppliers may not be available due to regulations, geography, costs, timing, capability issues, or competitive conflicts. Also, if outsourcing puts your proprietary technology at risk, outsourcing to several suppliers exposes you to a higher risk that you'll lose control of your intellectual property. Obviously, you have to consider the trade-offs. Outsourcing to a single source can allow you to develop a cooperative relationship with that source—look what the Japanese have done with lean manufacturing and preferred suppliers. But if your key supplier has other customers—which is likely in the early days of manufacturing a new product—our client would have much more to lose in this relationship than a hypothetical lone supplier would."

Another bite of pizza and then a brilliant, well-formed question.

"What do you mean?"

Livia responded with the patience of an elementary school teacher working with a kid who'd been absent for half the semester.

"How much would the new line of business be worth if its only supplier decided to stop making this stuff?"

"Not very much."

"And how much is this supplier worth—remember, it probably has several other companies it is manufacturing for—how much is this supplier worth if it decides to stop making our new product line?"

"Its value would drop a little—equal to the value of our contract—but likely less of a drop than we'd suffer."

"So, this single supplier has less to lose than we do. This gives this supplier power in its relationship with us, especially after a formal agreement is struck."

"But, presumably, our client is a much bigger company than this supplier."

"I don't see why overall size would be a factor." Now Livia looked confused. "I guess it might be a factor if our mystery supplier had other supply agreements with the client firm, agreements we could manipulate on price or terms. No matter the relative size, if a fledgling product line is the only thing going on between this supplier and our client, then this supplier has the power in this relationship—in our hypothetical example. That supplier could exploit its power by reducing quality, by demanding higher fees, or by reducing service to us. And we couldn't really do much about it."

"So, multiple suppliers is the way to go."

Livia laughed. "Justin, if only the world were so simple. Multiple suppliers are only an option if the client can maintain control over its technology and if it can find suppliers that can meet its quality and delivery standards. Plus, early on, demand for the product isn't likely to be huge. If manufacturing capacity is divided among several different suppliers, then none of them is going to be able to realize economies of scale, and costs rise."

"Given all these potential problems with outsourcing, why do you think doing manufacturing in-house is such a bad idea?"

"Well, your man in packaging told you that manufacturing the new product uses standard fiber and fabric techniques. Right?"

I nodded with a mouth full of the best food I'd had in days.

"So, in the long run, our client should have no trouble getting several independent suppliers—all of which can produce a high-quality product at low prices. As demand increases and volumes rise, each supplier should be able to drive its costs lower. The only thing in this situation that would make me really nervous about outsourcing is our client's ability to maintain good control of the product's technology."

"So no synergies for packaging? My man in packaging will be so disappointed." I felt more comfortable with Livia by the minute, and hoped she appreciated my dry wit.

"Well, filling up its factory would be good for the packaging division, but it's not at all clear that it would be good for the new products, or for the firm overall. That's why most synergies inside diversified firms are never fully realized—I've seen many times that they're beneficial to one division, but not good enough for all the businesses involved to give them a reason to cooperate."

She paused thoughtfully. "When it comes to cooperating with other businesses within a firm to gain synergies, each of these businesses must think about three things. First, will it be good for their business—will it cut costs or increase revenues? Second, from a cost and quality point of view, can a business realize these advantages on its own, without cooperation? And third, can it realize these advantages by working with an outside provider? Even if cooperation does create value—there's a real synergy there—if a business can realize this value on its own or with outside suppliers, they usually will. It's just easier to take those options rather than trying to cooperate with other businesses inside the firm."

"Couldn't the CEO just mandate this kind of cooperation?"

"He could try. But I've never seen it work, even when incentives are put in place to reinforce the 'mandate.' Sometimes there is intentional stonewalling or a lack of trust. More commonly, misunderstanding, routines, and time pressures combine to frustrate even well-designed efforts to encourage cross-business cooperation."

Livia was finishing up her pizza, but she was definitely on a roll. So I decided to continue our conversation with yet another deep and insightful question.

"What do you mean?" I asked as I picked up my check and calculated the tip.

"Well, we already know that the personal interests of division general managers can conflict, especially when one or more of them see themselves as a potential CEO. But it's more than that. Managers want and deserve to control businesses whose performance they will be evaluated on."

Now we were walking back toward HGS and I tried to summarize, partly so I would remember the conversation and partly in an effort to convince Livia that I wasn't a total moron. "So, the bottom line seems to be, first, that you shouldn't vertically integrate into business functions unless there is a very compelling reason to do so—like if you need to prevent suppliers from taking advantage of you once you outsource to them, or you will lose control of your proprietary technology. And, even when you do vertically integrate, most of the time, it's hard to exploit these functions across divisions to gain synergies. Isn't that kind of a cynical view?"

"Maybe. But I don't think so. I think of it as liberating. In the old days, we used to think organizations had to be big, bulky, vertically integrated, and highly bureaucratic. Now we know we can outsource different business functions, determine whether it is in our mutual interest to cooperate with other divisions, reconstitute our sourcing and production network when it becomes necessary. To me, that's not cynicism. It's flexibility!"

REFLECTION QUESTIONS

1. Why is synergy "often promised, seldom realized"?

2. According to Livia, when should firms outsource a business activity and when should they bring it in-house? Do you agree with her arguments?

3. What challenges would HGS management face if Plastiwear fabric and shirts were manufactured in the half-empty packaging factory?

4. What challenges would HGS management face if Plastiwear fabric and shirts were manufactured by another firm?

5. What other questions should Justin have asked Hutchins?

6. In your view, is Justin working well with the strategy team? Why or why not?

— 5 —

A VALUABLE
CHAIN

My lunch with Livia was both unexpected and enlightening. I felt connected to her, in an odd way—we had shared a lunch at her "secret" restaurant. She seemed nice, with an easy and genuine smile, and for a second, I could see how romances could begin in an intense work setting like this one—two smart, ambitious people thrown together in a high-pressure project, working long hours.

This fantasy evaporated when I reminded myself that, first, I had a girlfriend, and second, at our "secret lunch," Livia and I had talked about synergy and vertical integration—not exactly romantic topics. She obviously wasn't starry-eyed about me.

After lunch, Livia was scheduled to meet with some other HGS managers and I headed back to the team room. When I got off the elevator two floors before she did, all she said was, "Bye, Justin"—with one eye on her BlackBerry.

Back in the team room, I began organizing my thoughts. Livia had made a pretty compelling argument against using the packaging division's space to manufacture Plastiwear and shirts. She reminded me of something my mother used to say—just because you can do something doesn't mean you should do it. My mom used to say this just after I had done something stupid.

Of course, Livia's arguments didn't mean that HGS shouldn't go into the shirt industry, only that there wasn't a compelling reason to use the packaging division's space to do so. What I had learned in my MBA program was that, in the end, HGS's decision to pursue this opportunity—or not—would ultimately depend on whether it could gain and sustain a competitive advantage from doing so. If HGS could gain a sustained advantage from entering this market, our recommendation to move ahead would be strong and clear. If such an advantage was not likely, then HGS should consider selling Plastiwear to a firm better positioned to create a sustained advantage with it. At the least, they should consider licensing the technology to such a firm.

In my MBA program, I had also learned a simple way to evaluate whether or not a strategy was likely to be a source of sustained competitive advantage. It depended on the answer to four questions, something called the VRIO framework.

First, is a strategy valuable? Does it increase a firm's revenues or reduce its costs compared to not pursuing the strategy? Providing value to customers above and beyond what competitors offer is usually the most obvious way to increase a firm's revenues. Eliminating waste from operations or changing the firm's business model to make it more efficient is the quickest route to cost reduction, although location decisions, improvements in quality, and other strategic choices contribute to both top-line and bottom-line value-add. Obviously, strategies that aren't valuable can't be a source of competitive advantage.

Second, does a firm possess unusual skills or other assets that this strategy would utilize? This is the question of rarity—if many firms all have the ability to execute the same strategy, then that strategy will

Justin's notes on the VRIO framework

VALUABLE: Will a strategy increase a firm's revenues/reduce its costs compared to what would be the case if this strategy were not pursued?

RARE: Does a firm possess unusual skills needed to execute a strategy?

IMITABLE: How long will it take other firms to imitate this strategy?

ORGANIZATION: Is a firm efficiently organized to implement a strategy?

- Valuable strategies, by themselves, are only sources of parity.
- Valuable and rare strategies are sources of temporary advantage.
- Valuable, rare, and difficult-to-imitate strategies are sources of sustained advantage.

probably not be a source of advantage. This doesn't mean that valuable, but common, strategies aren't important. Lots of firms have created economic value through valuable but common strategies. Firms shouldn't expect, however, to gain advantages from these strategies—they are only a source of competitive parity, the table stakes that a firm has to ante up to be able to compete.

On the other hand, valuable and rare strategies can be a source of at least a temporary—and sometimes very lucrative—advantage. In fact, numerous firms "make their living" by implementing a series of strategies, each of which is only a source of temporary advantage.

Third, how long will it take other firms to imitate your strategy? Strategies that are hard to imitate—assuming they are also valuable and rare—are more likely to be a source of longer-lasting competitive advantages. If, on the other hand, competitors can begin to imitate a firm's valuable and rare strategy as soon as it becomes public, then that strategy will create only temporary advantages.

I had learned that a firm's strategies can be difficult to imitate for several reasons. Some strategies rely on assets that may be protected by patents. Or maybe the execution of a strategy requires skills that took a particular firm many years to develop. Maybe their execution depends on trusting relationships among a firm's managers, between a firm and its suppliers, or between a firm and its customers which are often difficult and time-consuming for others to replicate. Sometimes it can even be difficult for competing firms to describe exactly why a particular firm has an advantage. Obviously it is hard to imitate what you can't even describe! Whatever the reasons, firms that implement valuable, rare, and costly to imitate strategies will often be able to gain more sustainable advantages.

The fourth question focuses on organization—is a firm organized to execute and protect its sources of advantage? According to my professors, organization—things like a firm's reporting structure, management controls, and incentives—enables firms to realize the full potential of its strategies. But the question of organization often hadn't required an answer, since I found that answering the first three questions in this framework was usually enough to crack a case.

After some more reflection, it struck me that a VRIO analysis of packaging's proposal to manufacture Plastiwear shirts led to the same conclusions that Livia had come to. In particular, even if there was demand for Plastiwear shirts—meaning this manufacturing process might be valuable—there was no reason to believe that HGS had any special shirt-manufacturing skills. In other words, nothing rare in this area.

So, a VRIO analysis suggested that making shirts wasn't likely to be a source of advantage for HGS. What did it say about the other steps in the Plastiwear shirt value chain? Did any of these steps—from doing basic R&D, purchasing raw materials, manufacturing fiber, weaving the fabric, designing the shirt, branding these designs, cutting and assembling shirts, inventory management, distributing the shirts to retail outlets, all the way to selling the shirts to final customers—have the potential to generate sustained advantages?

To examine this possibility, I listed these steps in the Plastiwear value chain down one side of a pad of paper, and the VRIO questions across the top. For each of these stages, I asked just the most important three questions: Are there opportunities here for HGS to increase its revenues and/or decrease its costs? Does HGS have any unusual skills in pursuing these opportunities? Will it take other firms significant time to imitate these strategies?

I then began to fill in the matrix, based on what I had heard in my interviews and what I had read from various industry reports. Some lines were easy to complete—Hutchins had suggested that volume purchasing was an important synergy. No doubt, if volume purchasing was possible—and I didn't know this yet—this would reduce HGS's costs. But it seemed very unlikely that HGS had any unusual skills in this area. I would need to check this out, but my guess was that most reasonably sized specialty chemical firms had volume purchasing programs. This meant that volume purchasing was probably valuable—it reduced costs—but not rare. So, rather than a compelling synergy, as Hutchins hoped, VRIO analysis suggested that volume purchasing was likely to be table stakes for operating in the specialty chemical industry.

I came to similar conclusions about manufacturing the Plastiwear fiber. Again, Hutchins had said that this process was standard; in other words, that HGS wouldn't have to develop any special skills in this activity. If this was true—and I definitely needed to verify this—then even if Plastiwear shirts were in demand, fiber manufacturing would probably

Justin's VRIO analysis of the Plastiwear shirt value chain

Stages in the value chain	Are there opportunities in this stage for HGS to increase revs/decrease costs?	Does HGS have any unusual skills in executing this strategy?	Will it take other firms significant time to imitate this strategy?	Advantage potential?
R&D				
—License Plastiwear	?	Experience with Plastiwear	Maybe—patent + experience	?
—Alternative uses	?	Experience with Plastiwear	Maybe—patent + experience	?
Acquire raw materials				
—Volume purchasing	Probably	Probably not	?	At best, parity
Fiber manufacturing	Probably, yes (if shirt demand exists)	Probably not	—	At best, parity
Fabric weaving	?	?	?	?
Cut and assemble	Probably, yes	Probably not	—	At best, parity
Deliver shirts	Probably, yes	Probably not	—	At best, parity
Retail sales				
—Open retail stores	?	?	?	?
—Internet sales	?	?	?	?

A firm's core competencies are those activities it engages in that (1) create economic value, (2) are rare among competitors, and (3) competitors find difficult or costly to imitate.

not be a source of advantage for HGS. The company would have to get good at it—or outsource it to someone who was good at it—but actually fabricating the fibers would not likely ever be a source of advantage.

While some lines in my matrix were easy to complete, what I really discovered through this analysis was how much I didn't know about Plastiwear. Unanswered questions were all over the page! Even more important, I didn't really have a good sense of the kinds of opportunities that might exist in different stages of the Plastiwear value chain.

For example, most of the work at HGS to this point had focused on going into retail stores to sell shirts. As far as I knew, no one had yet considered selling Plastiwear shirts on the Internet. Also, almost everything I had seen up to this point examined Plastiwear and white shirts. Had anyone considered the possibility of alternative uses for Plastiwear? Maybe aprons for professional chefs?

While, in one way, all these unanswered question were discouraging—I had, after all, been working like a crazy man over the last couple of days—in another way, they were exciting. As I saw it, my job now was to fill in as many of these question marks as possible. That would help me identify those stages in the Plastiwear value chain that had the most potential for creating sustained advantages. If no stages had this potential—well, in that case, I would have a hard time recommending a substantial investment in Plastiwear.

This matrix also helped me understand one of the points Ken had made. Evaluating any isolated stage of the Plastiwear value chain—like whether or not the retail shirt market was attractive—completely misses the point. The retail shirt market may be a critical part of the analysis, but HGS could get into, say, the fiber and fabric business and then sell the fabric to firms that, in turn, made the shirts. And those firms could then sell finished shirts to retail companies to sell to final consumers. Getting into Plastiwear didn't mean, necessarily, getting into the retail shirt market. It should mean getting into those parts of the value chain where HGS could gain and sustain an advantage. If you ask the wrong question, about the wrong industry, it doesn't really matter what the answer is.

Maybe HGS managers focused on the attractiveness of the shirt industry because it was the most obvious way to exploit Plastiwear. Or maybe—like Ken said—it was the kind of opportunity that would lead to decisions closely aligned with the interests of at least some HGS managers. Or maybe HGS just fell too hard for the first product prototype R&D came up with. Whatever the reason, the value chain on my pad helped me see that the decision about whether or not to invest further in Plastiwear did not depend solely on how attractive the retail shirt market was. Instead, it depended on the ability of HGS to exploit its competencies in Plastiwear in different stages in the value chain.

As I thought about competencies, I realized that my matrix also helped make sense of the debate about "core competencies" I recalled from our first client meeting. Systematically looking for defensible, distinctive value was helping me identify HGS's sources of core competence—if it had one—in the Plastiwear shirt business. The more valuable, rare, and difficult to imitate the activities HGS engaged in, the more likely those activities would contribute to a core competence in this business.

I wrote at the bottom of my paper: "A firm's core competencies are those activities it engages in that (1) create economic value, (2) are rare among competitors, and (3) competitors find difficult or costly to imitate." I had a feeling I was leaving something out—but I was definitely onto something!

To me, this was a breakthrough in my thinking. Core competence wasn't just a buzzword to me now. VRIO was no longer just a lecture I'd heard, but a tool I could use to examine real-world strategies.

It had taken several hours of concentrated focus, but for the first time on this engagement, I began to feel like I actually knew what I was doing. I was still a rookie. I still had a lot to learn. Obviously, I didn't exactly know what HGS's distinctive competencies with respect to Plastiwear were yet—or how profitable they might be. But at least I knew the kinds of questions I needed to ask to figure this out. At least I knew what my next move was going to be. All I had to do was figure out the answers to all the questions in my matrix, and I would be able to crack this case.

My phone's ringtone interrupted my thoughts. Hoping to see my girlfriend's number, I glanced at the caller ID. It was Ken. Suddenly, I felt transported back in time to Sunday evening, the flight into Chicago. Five minutes earlier, I had felt champagne powder, with a clear view of my next turns. Now, I felt—well—turbulence!

REFLECTION QUESTIONS

1. Do you agree with Justin's conclusion, "If you ask the wrong question, about the wrong industry, it doesn't really matter what the answer is"?

2. Why is it not sufficient for a strategy to be both valuable and rare?

3. Justin is pleased that his work is progressing well. What suggestions would you give him at this point?

4. Justin's analysis seems to be raising a lot of questions he can't answer. Is this a problem? Why or why not?

5. How should Justin follow up with Livia after their lunch conversation, if at all?

6. What do you think Ken wants to talk to Justin about?

— 6 —

A THOUGHTFUL
WORKOUT

"Hello, Justin Campbell."

"Hi, Justin. This is Ken McCombs. I just got off the phone with Livia. Apparently, you had lunch together today?"

"Yeah. We ran into each other."

"Yes, that's what she said. Listen, I usually would wait until we had a chance to talk in person, but her summary of your discussion raised some red flags for me. Do you have a couple minutes to chat?"

"Red flags? What do you mean?"

Ken began patiently. "I thought we had talked about the mixed motives of managers and the need for objectivity, how managers tend to stop seeking better answers once their analyses support their own preferred outcomes."

"Right."

"So, when Livia told me about your meeting with the VP of packaging, it sounded like you were buying what he was selling. Synergies, diversification, excess capacity?"

"I thought I gave him a fair hearing," I responded warily.

"So, the VP of packaging makes an argument for Plastiwear based on what—synergies? Synergies that improve the performance of his division! Really, Justin." Ken paused. "I didn't expect you'd buy into this argument, hook, line, and sinker."

I tried to respond, to defend myself. "I really didn't buy . . . "

But Ken interrupted. "Justin, you are my eyes and ears on this project. You've got to step back, to develop your own view, not just parrot back what managers are saying."

I decided to try to shift the conversation to some of the insights I had just developed about core competencies and value, rarity, and imitation. "I know. That's what I've been . . . "

Again, Ken interrupted. "Maybe you understand at a theoretical level, but it is time to put those thoughts into action. Be a bit more skeptical. Earlier I asked you why you 'drank the Kool-Aid' so fast on— who was it?"

"Scott Beckett."

"Yeah, Beckett's five forces analysis. Have you thought about that some more—why you seem to accept whatever argument has most recently been presented to you?"

"I've thought about it some, but . . . "

"Well, Justin. It's sadly common. When you don't know what you don't know, you often end up relying on other people's ideas. Coming right out of school, you've probably had some nice, neat problem sets and cases begging to be cracked using the notes from the last lecture. Real-world strategy is nothing like cracking a case. The data you need is never presented to you in a predigested way. Heck—it's hardly ever even available."

Ken paused, then spoke more carefully and evenly. "We often don't even know what the right questions are. No study questions are provided in the real world, Justin. In the end, you need to stop buying into everyone else's arguments and develop your own. It's time to jump in the pool and get wet! Do you understand what I'm saying?"

I was searching for the right words to turn this conversation around, but managed only what I hoped was a convincing, "Yes, I do."

"Good." After delivering his main message, Ken seemed to return to a more mentoring tone. "Now, Justin. A challenging short assignment doesn't give us room for much trial and error. Take advantage of the expertise of the rest of the team, and of Bill Dixon. Especially Bill. We have the analytical skills, but Bill has time on the ground. He knows the players and the issues. Listen, Justin, it's time to step up to the plate. We need an independent, but informed and robust approach to analysis. Got it?"

"Yes, I understand."

"Good."

Then Ken hung up. After a few seconds, I too hung up. We had spoken for less than five minutes. It felt like an hour. I had probably said less than fifty words. There had been so much I wanted to say. I wished we could start again and I could put my thoughts into words.

I know turbulence is not dangerous, that airframes almost never fail, that the wings on a 747 can flex thirty-six feet before they break. But it sure felt like my airframe had just failed and that I had crashed and burned.

What a difference a phone call makes. In under five minutes I went from thinking that I might actually understand what's going on at HSG to then, bam, getting slammed into the ground—I don't have what it takes, I'm not willing to argue an independent point of view, I get sucked into the latest arguments I hear.

After Ken's call, it was clear that I was going to need time to process what he'd said. Although it was close to six, I wasn't hungry, so I headed back to the gym. Although I had worked out that morning, maybe some more strenuous exercise would help.

On the way back to the hotel, the thought occurred to me that Ken had probably given that same lecture to lots of other consultants. Laughing to myself, I wondered if he had written it out ahead of time. Or had he given it so many times he had it memorized? I knew that I had made some fairly common mistakes on this engagement. But so far, I hadn't embarrassed the firm or caused any team disruptions. Really, I hadn't done anything that bad. By the time I got to my room, I'd pretty much convinced myself that this phone call was just part of Ken's standard mentoring routine. I would listen to what he said and take it to heart, of course, but really, I wouldn't need to change much. Things were going along well, and I was sure that pretty soon it would be clear to the whole team how much I was contributing.

As I found my gym clothes and got ready to work out, another thought struck me. What the heck was going on with Livia? Here I am, feeling like we're bonding, while she's stabbing me in the back, telling

Ken that my interview summaries are naive or worse. She completely misrepresented our conversation—a conversation where, as I remember it, I expressed some significant doubts about the synergy argument. Plus, it wasn't really a meeting. She ambushed me at a pizza parlor.

Now that ticked me off. Livia had taken a couple of casual comments out of context and woven a story to Ken that reaffirmed everything Ken was already thinking about me. Was this how Livia got ahead—by shafting others?

I took my anger out on the treadmill, and turned my thoughts to Ken. Why hadn't Ken seen through Livia's manipulation of the facts? Why had he stopped his analysis as soon as he saw results that were consistent with his preconceptions—and with his self-interest? Maybe he had a thing for Livia, maybe that's why he didn't push back when she talked about me. Some communicator, some "mentor." He does all the talking, and I just take it. Next time he starts that crap I'll show him that I can argue against a dominant point of view—even if it's his point of view about me!

After thirty minutes on the treadmill, I switched to a stationary bike—I really wanted to work up a sweat. My anger was starting to subside. I could get angry, but what would that do for me? I could accuse Ken and Livia of having an affair, but that was really far-fetched and in any case, did it really change my situation? And arguing with Ken—that didn't sound like a particularly good idea.

What I really needed to do was figure out specifically what Ken wanted from me. What did Ken actually want me to do—develop my own point of view, figure out what the critical questions were, get the data to answer those questions, work with the rest of the team to test my ideas, analyze the data? I understood, in general terms, what he wanted, and I thought I'd been doing it. Maybe I just needed to show him more of my thinking, send him more e-mails, let him know what I was up to.

So, how could I win Ken over? As I waited for a weight machine to free up, it occurred to me that if I did some dazzling piece of analysis before my next meeting with Ken, that would certainly change his opinion of me.

After weights, I went into the men's locker room, took off my gym clothes, wrapped myself in a towel, and went into the steam room. Sitting there, wearing only a towel, surrounded by steam so thick I could see only a few feet in front of me, I had to admit I was discouraged. The problem was I had heard Ken's message before, in our first phone call. It seemed long ago, but it was barely twenty-four hours.

In this superheated consulting environment, you didn't have much time to change people's opinions. And now, maybe it was already too late. I felt like a drop of sweat hanging on the end of my nose—any moment it would drop off, fall to the floor, and evaporate. That was me. I'd lost Ken's confidence. I probably never had the confidence of any of my other team members. I'd blown a chance I'd never have again—I'd let myself down.

I showered slowly, in no hurry to put my clothes on and head back to work. How could I face my teammates again when I had so clearly failed them? I glanced at my BlackBerry, but didn't want to read more of "iron man" Vivek's notes or give Livia any more ammo to share with Ken. I shoved it into my pocket and decided to delay the inevitable as long as I could by heading down the street from the hotel to a little Chinese restaurant. It was a dive—I wouldn't see any members of the team there. I ordered kung pao chicken, extra spicy. I like food spicy, and tonight I wanted it so spicy it almost hurt to eat it.

With a Diet Dr. Pepper in one hand and extra-spicy kung pao chicken in the other, my spirits began to revive. Yes, Ken had given me quite a talking-to. And, yes, he had probably given that same lecture dozens of times. But that didn't mean he was wrong. Sure, it made me angry, but anger wouldn't be productive in this setting—it rarely is. And I wasn't going to be able to strike some sort of deal with Ken—if I do these things, then you will respect me. I was either going to earn his respect from what I did on the engagement or not. Trying to figure out what Ken would want was an absolutely useless exercise. I had to do what I thought was best.

That was it. What Ken wanted me to do was not to try to guess what he would do, but to do what I thought was best. In fact, just this afternoon, I had begun to make that transition—to go from just trying to answer someone else's questions to developing my own set of questions and tailoring the frameworks to fit the messy reality we faced. I just had to finish what I had already started. Just ask the next question. With the framework I had in place, I did have a plan going forward. I could probably get Gordon and Vivek's input on my work. And Ken and Livia would see it soon enough.

I finished my last bite of chicken around 9:00 p.m. My mouth was burning—in my experience, the dirtier the Chinese food restaurant, the hotter the food. But my mind was clear. And even though I had been up since 5:30 in the morning, I was full of energy and commitment.

What is the next question? That would be my mantra. That is the way I would determine whether HGS had any viable competitive advantage based on Plastiwear. So, instead of going back to the hotel and getting some sleep, I went down the street to HGS's headquarters, up to the seventy-second floor, to the team room. And I started working on answering the next question.

My first interview the next morning was with Jerry Tucker, the chemical engineer who had invented Plastiwear. And I was going to be ready.

I worked until one in the morning. But it was different now. I had renewed confidence and purpose. I knew what questions to ask and why. I used my three categories to continue to generate questions—and answered them when I could. I found myself wishing I'd prepared these before my first three interviews, and before I had scaled a few mountains of reports.

First were questions about the value of Plastiwear: How big was the white shirt market? How competitive? Was the high-end shirt market growing or shrinking? What buying criteria were there besides the fabric—fit and style, for example? What kinds of brands existed in this segment?

Second were questions about how rare Plastiwear-based offerings were. How special was Plastiwear? Were there close substitutes? Did it require special machinery to manufacture the fiber, to weave the fabric, to cut the cloth, to assemble the shirts?

Third were questions about how easy it would be to imitate Plasti-wear. Did HGS have patent protection on the product? Would HGS be willing and able to sue competitors who violated its patents? Also important, could HGS brand Plastiwear? If so, how long would it take and how expensive might it be? Patents aren't the only things that slow down imitation; brands can block, or at least slow, the progress of imitators.

Which outsourcing decisions—manufacturing? cutting? assembly?—risked losing control of HGS's specialized knowledge? How long would it take other firms to "reverse engineer" Plastiwear?

Some of my answers had already emerged. The VP of packaging, for example, had told me that manufacturing Plastiwear required no special machines. And several people had told me that no fabric on the market performed as well as Plastiwear when it came to dress shirts. I didn't know if I believed all these answers—but I tried to note my level of confidence on each answer as I continued to move through the questions. It was like doing a crossword puzzle and noting a possible word, but not writing it in ink, just in case you have to go back and make changes.

This crossword puzzle analogy also made me aware of the connections among the questions I was asking. No single answer fully addressed the question of competitive advantage for HGS based on Plastiwear.

Trying to get exact answers to my individual questions had been an obstacle to seeing the bigger picture, the patterns and trends. Now I understood a bit of Ken's frustration around the way I'd approached the interviews so far. With more confidence in the way I'd developed and organized the questions I was going to ask, I felt that I could take more control of the interviews. Of course, I still needed to be open minded. I was sure I was still going to be surprised by this process. But I had a plan. And I felt good about my plan.

When I got back to my hotel room, I thought I'd better call my girlfriend. It was 1:00 a.m. in Chicago, but only 11:00 p.m. in LA. We had met in graduate school—I was taking a class in organizational psychology because I had to and she was a master's student in industrial organization psychology who was taking the class because she wanted to.

Her name was Jackie Condon. Jackie was short for Jacqueline, but everyone called her Jackie. She wasn't a classic beauty but was attractive in her own way. Her chin was probably narrower than what a Beverly Hills plastic surgeon would have prescribed, and her hair was somewhere between brown, blonde, and red. On a bet, I once pulled single hairs from her head three times and got a different color each time. Her most striking feature was her smile—broad and easy, and she was almost always smiling. And her freckles—like the red in her hair, they refused to fade away.

But what attracted me most to Jackie was that she was so smart. Not in a nerdy "tape on the glasses" kind of way, but she never ceased to amaze me. She quickly understood really complicated ideas and was able to see the implications of those ideas in new settings. She wasn't just smart; she was creative smart. And I liked her a lot.

Our relationship began slowly—the psych students didn't know what to make of the MBA students and we didn't know what to make of them. But when Jackie and I were put into the same group for a project, sparks began to fly. We dated pretty exclusively the rest of that term. After Christmas break, things started getting more serious.

We graduated at the same time. She was accepted into a clinical psych program at UCLA. We figured it didn't really matter whether we both lived in the same city, since I would be on the road most of the time anyway. We made plans to see each other several times during the semester—without any commitment beyond that.

Maintaining the relationship had been harder than I expected. I had called her only once during orientation. But they worked us about sixteen hours a day and I spent the rest of the time hanging out with my new colleagues or asleep. We had talked for over an hour on the Saturday before I came to Chicago, but since arriving here—well, all I did was work. Even now, it was 1 a.m.

But I decided I needed to talk to her about what I had been going through and where I was at now. Not that she would really understand, but she was a great listener. No surprise, given her chosen profession.

"Hello." I heard her voice on the line and, I must admit, my heart leaped in my chest.

"Hi, Jackie, it's me."

"Justin, is that you, Justin? Gee, I hardly recognize your voice. I thought maybe you had died or something."

"I know. I'm sorry. I've been kind of busy."

"Yeah, yeah. So busy you can't call your girlfriend." She was hassling me, but it was in a playful way. I decided to go along.

"No, no. I've called my girlfriend several times. This is the first time I've had a chance to call you."

"Very funny, Justin." I don't think she fully appreciated my humor.

"So, how's class going?"

"Pretty much as I expected. It keeps me tied up. How about you? How's the world-class big-time consulting gig?"

"Well, we work all the time. I guess I expected it to be more like school, but it isn't. No study questions—no hints about the right answers from the TAs." Jackie was an undergraduate TA, so I got the chuckle I was angling for. Then she surprised me.

"You sound discouraged."

Boy, she was good. I had tried to hide my disappointment, but she quickly saw through my subterfuge, even over the telephone.

"Well, it's been a bumpy ride. I said some stupid things in our first team meeting—you know, wet-behind-the-ears kind of stuff. And I'm afraid that I'm not scoring any points with the team leader, a guy named Ken."

"Why do you say that?"

"Well, earlier tonight, he called me on the phone and reamed me pretty good about believing everything the client says, not developing my own point of view, stuff like that."

"How'd you respond?"

"To him? I didn't say much, if anything. He really didn't give me much of a chance. At first, I thought he was just giving me a canned speech. Then I got mad—we've only been working together for a few days, and already he's jumped to all these conclusions about me." I paused to consider how much to share, then plunged on. "Truthfully, I found the whole thing discouraging. Later I realized that I was already doing what he was asking, but I just wasn't quite ready to share my thinking yet. That's what I've been doing tonight, getting more work done so that I can show the team what I've been up to."

"So, have you 'cracked the case'?"

"Well, I'm sure you remember how psyched I'd be to do that in my MBA program—but here, you don't 'crack' these cases. No, what I have now is, I think, a really cool way to organize the questions I need to ask. I didn't have a framework to guide my interviews up to this point, so they were disorganized. Really, the people I interviewed set the agenda, not me. I feel ready to turn that around in the morning."

"Sounds like you have recovered from Ken's phone call."

"Well, I'm recovering."

"Well, I don't want to 'shrink' you, Justin, but it sounds like you are going through a pretty amazing transition."

"What do you mean?"

"It sounds like you're shedding your old identity and taking on a new one. The process you describe is painful—it has all the earmarks of mourning. At least I think I hear signs of an identity shift—or some significant change—as you talk about your interactions with Ken."

"I hadn't thought of it that way. I don't know. So much is going on. I'm very tired. It's pretty late." Suddenly, I felt exhausted, like I couldn't stay awake for another second, like talking to Jackie on the phone for even a couple more minutes would kill me. I found it difficult to breathe, and beads of sweat began to collect on my forehead. My skin felt cold and clammy. I think Jackie heard me struggling to catch my breath.

"Hey, Justin—you OK? Don't take me too literally about this mourning thing!"

"Yeah, I'm OK, I'm OK. I'm sorry." I began to regain some of my composure.

"You scared me there for a second. Listen. Call me again, will you? It sounds like you could use someone to talk to, someone outside the consultants' union. Give me a call and let me get some practice."

When I didn't immediately answer, she dropped her joking tone. "Will you promise to call me?"

"I promise." I wanted to hang up, but also wanted to keep talking. "But, you know, you don't really need much practice."

"Practice makes perfect, Justin."

"You're right. I'll call you tomorrow. Even if we don't have time to talk, I'll call just to say hi."

"Thanks, Justin."

"Hey, Jackie. One other thing. I love you."

"I know, Justin. Good night."

"Good night, Jackie."

REFLECTION QUESTIONS

1. Will the framework Justin developed in this chapter significantly improve his analysis of Plastiwear? Why or why not?

2. Which of Justin's analyses will help him understand who within HGS has the most to win or lose with regard to Plastiwear? How?

3. Justin thinks that this framework will help him take control of his interviews. Do you agree?

4. Jackie compared Justin's behavior to mourning. What might Justin be mourning, and what implications does this have for his ability to contribute to the team's work going forward?

5. To what extent was Ken's feedback to Justin appropriate? How else could he have delivered his message(s) to a new team member?

— 7 —

A SWEEPING VISION

My first interview on Thursday morning was with Jerry Tucker, a senior scientist in HGS's research and development group and the author of the first report ever about Plastiwear. Most of his colleagues credited Tucker with inventing Plastiwear.

The R&D group where Tucker worked was located in a low-rise building in a Chicago suburb. It was close to where Bill lived, so the plan was for me to meet Bill at 8:30 at a coffee shop near the R&D center, where we could prep for our interview over coffee, and still have time to get to the meeting by 9:00. I had planned on it taking thirty minutes to get to the coffee shop. It actually took my cab about forty-five minutes. That gave Bill and me only fifteen minutes to get up to speed.

I entered the coffee shop—they seem to have one on every corner in Chicago—and spotted Bill in the back. He already had his coffee and was eating a muffin. I bought a cup of coffee and an apple turnover, and went to Bill's table.

"Good morning, Justin. Have a nice evening?"

Boy, if he only knew—get a breakthrough in my thinking, get yelled at by my boss, exercise obsessively, tell my girlfriend I love her—what an evening! Of course, I shared none of these things.

"Fine. How about yours?"

"Very relaxing. I also appreciated the commute this morning—this place is only ten minutes from my house."

"Sorry about being late. I thought traffic would be much lighter heading out from downtown."

"This is Chicago. The traffic is heavy, going both ways, all the time. So, what's the plan on this interview?"

I shared with Bill my main interview themes—how could Plastiwear create value, what about it was really unique, and how difficult might it be for others to imitate. His response was satisfying.

"I suppose market size, strategic ownership and timing aren't the right questions for an R&D man," Bill responded approvingly. "Sounds like this approach will work well for today's interviews. We'll see what Jerry has to say about this stuff."

"Do you know him very well?"

"Off and on for twenty years. We aren't bosom buddies or anything, but yes, I'd say I know him."

"Anything I need to know about him before we head over?"

"Well, for most of his career, Jerry was just a run-of-the-mill chemist, doing experiments, solving problems, and so forth. Two years ago—after he was involved in the development of Plastiwear—he started getting into this new age, self-help kind of thing. He's still a great chemist, just a bit over the top sometimes. A good guy. You'll like him. I'm guessing it might be hard to keep him on track with the questions you want to ask."

"Thanks for the heads up." Oh no, I thought, another talker. "Maybe you'd prefer to lead this interview?"

Bill shook his head and stood up, smiling as he looked at his watch and led the way toward the door. The R&D center was not far down the street. Bill had obviously been there many times before. The automatic glass doors opened swiftly and quietly; we entered the reception hall and went directly to the front desk. The reception area was large—large enough for two separate seating areas, a couple of trees, and a desk with a pot of coffee—with high ceilings, at least sixty feet high. It wasn't as fancy as my hotel's lobby, but it was spacious and inviting. In the middle of the hall was a reception desk. The large African American woman behind the desk obviously recognized Bill.

"Dr. Dixon, is that you?" A deep, almost baritone, voice called out to us. She had an accent I found vaguely comforting—not quite Southern, but obviously tinged by some time in the South.

"Hi, Harriet. Yes, it's me."

"Well, Dr. Dixon. It's so good to see you. How've you been?"

"Very well, and how about you?"

"Well, much better now I've seen you. You still stuck workin' downtown with all those suits, Dr. Dixon?"

"Afraid so. Here, let me introduce Justin Campbell. I'm working with him on a special project." With that I came up to the reception desk. Harriet reached out her hand and shook mine.

"Any friend of Dr. Dixon's. It's good to meet you, Dr. Campbell."

"It's Mr., uh, Justin Campbell. No PhD." I tried to sound nonchalant. "And, sorry, I can't operate on you either."

"I'm sorry, Mr. Campbell. Most people here seem to have PhDs of one kind or another. So, I've taken to calling everyone doctor this and doctor that. Sometimes it feels like I'm working in a hospital," she laughed. "I'll get your badge."

As she worked on my badge, she asked, "You're here to see Dr. Tucker, right?"

Bill replied, "Right; could you call him?"

"Sure. And here's your badge, Mr. Campbell."

I looked on the badge. My name was written as "Dr. Justin Campbell, PhD." I decided not to object and sheepishly put it on. I felt a bit like a fraud. But, truth be told, by now even my MBA felt fraudulent.

Along one wall of the reception hall was a row of wooden plaques—maybe forty feet long—one for each patent that had been granted to HGS for work done here. I moved to the end, looking for the Plastiwear plaque, while Bill continued to make small talk with Harriet. Suddenly, a man's voice interrupted my concentration.

"If you're looking for the Plastiwear plaque, it isn't here yet. I'm afraid this shrine is never quite up to date."

I turned around to see someone who I took to be Jerry Tucker. He extended his hand and confirmed my suspicions.

"Hi, Dr. Campbell. I'm Jerry Tucker."

"Hi. Please, just call me Justin."

Bill excused himself from the reception desk and came over.

"Hi, Jerry."

"Hey, Bill. I didn't know you were going to be here."

"Well, it was so convenient I thought I'd tag along. Today I'm the local guide."

"Fabulous. Glad to have you. If you two have been through security, let's go back to my office."

As Tucker led the way, he and Bill began to renew their acquaintance—you know, how's the wife, the kids, the golf game. This was a bit awkward for me since I was excluded from this conversation. However, it did give me a chance to observe the inventor of Plastiwear more closely. Short and nearly bald except for patches of red and gray curly hair on each side of his head, he was thin, but not at all athletic. In fact, his gait combined the wide arm swings that orangutans use to keep their balance with the forward lean of Groucho Marx. He walked like he was in a hurry. His face was pockmarked—probably the result of teenage acne traumas—but when he made eye contact he seemed curious and keenly alert.

"OK. Here's my office."

From our walk, it appeared that most of the R&D group worked in either labs or cubicles. Tucker's office was more private. He had a simple desk, piled high with paper, and a narrow table on the wall next to the desk, similarly stacked two or three feet deep. There was no artwork on Tucker's walls, only a variety of charts and graphs. The date on one of those charts read October 8, 1997.

"I'd apologize for the mess in here, but this is how I work. I can find whatever I need in this office."

I'm a slob myself, so I understood. "Of course. No apology necessary. I'm glad that we have a chance to meet you. The inventor of Plastiwear."

"Yeah. That's what everyone thinks. But you know, it was really a team effort. There were lots of people involved."

"Well, as you probably know, HGS has asked us to help evaluate its potential."

Tucker shot back the question that apparently everyone wanted an answer to. "What have you decided about Plastiwear?"

"Oh, we're still collecting information. That's why I was excited to meet with you, to get some sense of the technical side of Plastiwear."

"Well, ask away."

"Let's start first with the raw materials side of the issue. What are the critical inputs into the manufacture of Plastiwear?"

Tucker seemed uncomfortable. Sweat began to collect on his brow. I thought to myself that maybe there was something fishy about manufacturing this stuff—some environmental issue or a really expensive and unusual chemical component. After a few seconds hesitation, Tucker spoke. He did so with great conviction, almost yelling, with both arms gesturing in the air to make his point.

"Boy, is that the wrong question!"

I was taken aback, to say the least. "What do you mean?"

"I mean, of course we have to buy raw materials to make Plastiwear. But, the critical thing about Plastiwear is that it's going to revolutionize the shirt industry. Then it is going to transform the way clothes of all kinds are made, worn, and cared for. And in the process it is going to fundamentally alter the culture of HGS. In less than five years, this is going to be a totally different company. Transformed."

Bill had warned me about Tucker's "enthusiasm." I tried to settle him down a bit. "Those are bold assertions."

"But it's all possible, if we just capture the vision of what Plastiwear can do."

Now Bill tried to redirect the conversation. "So, do you think that Plastiwear will have the effect of increasing demand for white shirts?"

"The demand for Plastiwear depends only on the imagination of HGS's management. If we—I mean, they—can imagine Plastiwear as the miracle fiber of the twenty-first century, it can happen."

At this point, Tucker stood up and began an apparently well-rehearsed lecture.

"You see, Plastiwear isn't about competing in an existing market—shirts, or fiber, or cloth. Plastiwear's about envisioning a new market, an industry that does not exist today."

The passion I thought I'd seen in prior interviews paled in comparison with Tucker's excitement. "So you think Plastiwear's near-term potential is large?"

"It isn't about what we think. It's about what we believe. Beliefs, passion, and commitment, to see beyond our current assumptions and limitations—that's what will drive Plastiwear. Let yourself imagine selling $20 billion of Plastiwear a year! Can you imagine that!?"

"That would double HGS," I replied.

Tucker was on a roll now. He began pacing, waving his arms as he made his points.

"And why stop at just doubling HGS? The only thing that keeps us from realizing this potential is our own beliefs about Plastiwear, about HGS. If we transform those beliefs, we'll free our minds to explore this technology. That's what I mean when I say that the future of Plastiwear, and the future of HGS, is not in our hands; it's in our minds."

This was a sweeping vision for Plastiwear. But, so far, this interview had been a little light on facts. So, I tried to ground it in some specifics.

"Do you agree that the first market to exploit Plastiwear is shirts? I mean men's dress white shirts?"

"Maybe. But, to me, what's important is not where this journey begins, but where it takes us. How big do we want to be, say, in ten years? And what do we have to do to get there? For example, suppose we build a factory that commits us to having at least $10 billion in Plastiwear sales in ten years—my 'ten in ten' plan. We build that factory now and then fill it up."

Bill tried to tether Tucker's vision to some economic reality. "There is some thought that it might make sense to outsource some aspects of Plastiwear—for example, shirt manufacturing."

"Yes, yes. I've heard that talk. That's based on the old rules of competition. We have to break all those rules, envision a new future to create. If we accept the old rules of competition, we can compete only in the old ways. I'm talking about competing in markets and industries that don't exist yet and competing in ways we have never dared before!"

Now it was my turn. "Could you describe this industry, this market, for me?"

"That's just it. We haven't invented it yet. And if we aren't ambitious enough, we never will!"

Tucker talked as if intensity of delivery somehow compensated for lack of content.

"Look at all the innovative companies in the world," Tucker continued. "You know, Ford with the model T, Starbucks, Southwest Airlines. Those firms were great not because they became incrementally better than their competition. They were great because they made their competition irrelevant! We need to do that with Plastiwear."

"But those companies had identifiable plans, with incremental steps and milestones," I replied.

"Of course, you're right," Tucker looked directly at me, shaking his head with disappointment. "But the key is that they didn't let those plans get in the way of creating a new industry. That's my problem with HGS. We're so used to making modest product extensions; that's how we talk about Plastiwear. We prevent ourselves from seeing opportunities right in front of us. We need to think broadly about what a technology like Plastiwear can do. Think broadly."

With those last two words, Tucker pounded his fist on the table. Admittedly, Tucker's speech lacked detail. A wise-guy professor of mine at Texas had once commented that a paper I wrote had a "paucity of specificity." That was Jerry Tucker, to a tee. But there was something engaging about the man. He did describe a potentially exciting approach to thinking about strategy—sort of a "break-all-the-rules" approach I'd heard some talk about here and there. Maybe anarchy would be energizing. But it still wasn't clear to me what HGS would do tomorrow—besides building a Plastiwear factory big enough to generate $10 billion in sales in ten years. That seemed risky to me. So that's how I replied.

"Practically speaking, the only concrete action step you've described is building a giant factory. Isn't that risky?"

"The real risk is doing nothing. Or not doing enough. We could build a small plant. We could outsource it all. But if we did, the best we could ever be is mediocre. HGS would survive; Plastiwear would maybe generate $250 million in sales, maybe not. But HGS is not fundamentally transformed. Nothing new is created. Just the same old same old."

I was still concerned about his ideas. "But your plans could put a lot of capital, and maybe even HGS's survival, at risk, couldn't they?"

"Is mediocrity really survival? Is it really worth perpetuating? Listen, I know managers would like a mediocre HGS to survive for another fifty years—get their pensions, have a nice secure, simple job. But do our shareholders want that? If that's what they want, they should invest in some dividend-generating government-regulated utilities. We're HGS—a successful specialty chemical company, heavily invested in R&D. We can do better than that. Our shareholders should want us to.

The problem with modern companies is that we really aren't managed for the owners; we're managed to make the lives of the managers comfortable."

Now my finance training came to the fore. "Isn't that what the market for corporate control is for, to enable firm ownership to change hands and ensure that firms do maximize the shareholder wealth?"

"Great question. But, no. Given the costs of an acquisition, only firms doing really poorly will ever get taken over. HGS isn't doing badly. It's just that we're not doing as well as we could. The market for corporate control solves the 'bad firm' problem, not the 'mediocre firm' or the 'not as good as they could be firm.'"

In my mind, I wondered if MG Management's interest in a stake in HGS meant that HGS had changed from a mediocre to a bad firm. Of course, I couldn't discuss this "inside information" with Tucker. Besides, I didn't want the interview to get any further off track.

"So to me," I said, trying to change the subject slightly, "it sounds like you want to use Plastiwear to change HGS."

"That's right. To shift HGS from a placid, mediocre specialty chemical company to an innovative juggernaut."

"And if in the process," I continued, "Plastiwear is a bust and the company loses billions of dollars?"

"That's a risk truly innovative leaders must take. If you aren't willing to risk it all, you can never know true excellence."

Our interview with Jerry Tucker went on like this for another thirty minutes. Bill and I closed the meeting with thank-yous, and Tucker closed with one last exhortation about overcoming the limits of our vision for Plastiwear. On our way out of the building, Harriet came over to Bill and gave him a big hug.

"Now come back here soon, Dr. Dixon. I miss playing with you."

"I will, Harriet. See you soon."

"And you, too, Dr. Campbell. And Dr. Campbell, can I have your badge back, please?"

"Thanks, Harriet," I said as I returned my PhD badge. "I've enjoyed meeting you."

"And I've enjoyed meeting you, too, Dr. Campbell. I hope to see you later, too."

As we walked outside the building, I observed, "She seems very nice."

His reply was simple. "One of the best."

"So, Bill, what'd you think of that interview?"

"Let's go back to that coffee shop, if that's OK. We can talk there."

"Sure."

Once comfortably ensconced at a table, Bill threw out the first question. "So, what'd you think of Jerry?"

"Well, you were right. He doesn't lack enthusiasm. It felt like he had just returned from a retreat with a great motivational speaker—all revved up to do something, just not sure what to do. He certainly has been 'saved' by the 'envision-your-own-future' crowd."

Bill's response was thoughtful, but emphatic. "Personally, I'm skeptical about that whole approach. Books about 'exploring unexplored worlds, creating new markets, sailing in variously colored seas, and setting hairy and audacious goals' are inspirational and everything, but I wonder how helpful they really are. For every one hundred firms that try to create some bold new world, that have audacious goals, I see just one or two actually succeeding. Then, someone studies these successful firms and concludes that having 'audacious goals' leads to success. That's very confused logic."

Bill stirred his coffee and continued. "Listen, invention and innovation are risky, and risk has an upside. The winners get famous and get buildings named after them. But risk has a downside, too. Most innovations fail. If someone tells you that they have a risk-free way to make lots of money, well, they are either lying or breaking the law."

"I've seen a couple of those in the news," I agreed, surprised at Bill's talkativeness and enjoying the conversation. "There was one thing he said that made sense to me. Tucker's idea that companies are managed for the managers, and not for the shareholders, did ring true. Shareholders can diversify their risk easily—through owning a portfolio of stocks. Managers can't do the same for all the investments they make in a company—the risk of being fired, laid off, your firm going bankrupt. So, it's not surprising that managers are more risk-averse than what their shareholders would want."

I continued, virtually quoting a lecture from one of my finance classes. "The board of directors and senior management are supposed to address this problem, to create incentives so managers will choose riskier strategies. But this rarely happens. And when it does, and a firm chooses risky strategies that turn out badly, well, who gets fired—the shareholders? No, the managers. On the other hand, managers who don't take these risks still have jobs, still have careers. Their companies may not be great, but they're not terrible either."

"Well," Bill responded, now somewhat impatient, "these are all great philosophical points. I'm not sure how they apply at HGS. But the real question for today is—did we learn anything from the inventor of Plastiwear?"

"I'd say no. Lots of imagination and hyperbole, not much substance. I hope my next interview, with Walter Albright, will be more fruitful." Albright was vice president of R&D, and Tucker's boss.

"I agree. But we need to hear from all the players." Bill looked like he had more to say, but I wasn't quick enough to probe on who qualified as a "player" in HGS—and why—before he was on his feet. "I'll be working from home the rest of the day. No sense heading downtown now. Let me know if you need me."

"Thanks, Bill."

I finished my coffee and went outside to grab a cab downtown. I used the cab ride to begin summarizing my notes. In the past, I'd found this recap often generated new insights.

Not this time.

I arrived at HGS headquarters, grabbed a premade sandwich in the lobby convenience shop, and headed to the team room. Vivek was there. It looked like he was summarizing notes from his interviews. He looked unusually relaxed—tie loosened, top button on his white shirt undone, black suit coat hung neatly on the coat rack in the corner of the room. His relaxed looks belied his behavior—he was concentrating intensely on what he was typing.

"Vivek! How's it going?"

"Well."

"Me, too. Just had a strange interview with Jerry Tucker—the inventor of Plastiwear. Heavy on the hype, limited on the substance."

"Ah, a visionary. I heard he had those tendencies."

"He does." I thought this might be a good time to bounce some of my new ideas off Vivek. Obviously, my plan to do this in the interview hadn't worked out.

"So, Vivek. What do you think about the Plastiwear opportunity? Have you got time to compare notes on where we're headed?"

"You sound like the managers I've interviewed." He'd now stopped typing and looked directly at me. "If you are serious, I can't tell you what HGS should do, but I am pretty sure what they shouldn't do—make shirts. Beckett may have carried out the wrong analysis, but his conclusion was right. This is an unattractive industry for HGS. But there are plenty of firms that might be willing to sell Plastiwear shirts under their existing brands, as you've seen." He gestured to his notes on the laptop and I realized he was posting everything and assumed I'd read it all. "The consensus we've reached based on our interviews is that there will be plenty of opportunities to partner with firms to sell shirts. Obviously, we'll need to help HGS think about partnering and marketing later, but, assuming the shirts can be made, and assuming there is demand, they should be able to find partners to sell them."

I replied as nonchalantly as I could, realizing Vivek was a few steps ahead of me. "What's funny is that most of the HGS analyses we've seen have focused only on Plastiwear and whether HGS should enter the retail business. Nothing about cutting and shirt assembly, nothing about fiber and fabric manufacturing. Should HGS be in these businesses, or should it just license Plastiwear and collect royalties?"

Vivek responded with a quick nod and spoke quickly and confidently. "To me, it's going to depend on at least three things—demand, potential, and vulnerability of value-add. First, how big is the demand for high-quality, lower-priced shirts. I'm beginning to model this demand now. But, even if this demand is substantial, I'm still not sure an investment in fiber and fabric manufacturing would pay off."

"What do you mean? I thought it was all about the shirts."

He looked at me quizzically. "Don't you think it will also depend on how broad the economic potential of Plastiwear is? If they can use it only for shirts, they won't likely have adequate scale to justify vertically integrating into fibers and fabrics. Maybe they just license the technology to someone else."

"And if that someone else never introduces Plastiwear shirts?" I was baiting Vivek a bit, but he wasn't biting.

"That is, of course, a potential problem—hypothetically. But a licensing contract could be written to give the licensee incentives to make shirts."

"I suppose."

"Finally, I need to know where the real value-added is in this product. Is the real profit opportunity in the fiber, the fabric, or in cutting and assembling end products? And how vulnerable is this value-add? If HGS outsourced production, would another firm be able to appropriate the technology? That's likely where the value is greatest, and whoever controls it captures much of the value of Plastiwear."

I chimed in based on my recent research. "Personally, I'm pretty skeptical about fabric cutting and shirt assembly. Almost everyone in the industry offshores this."

"Yes, but not everyone has a proprietary fabric—or at least the potential for a proprietary fabric. Maybe, to control its intellectual property, to prevent it from being imitated or just flat out stolen, maybe HGS has to control the whole process and even make the shirts."

As Vivek was sharing his analysis, I was struck by how closely it paralleled mine, developed just yesterday. Not only had we both concluded that the retail shirt industry was a no-go for HGS, but our form of reasoning was similar. Vivek wanted to know the market potential for Plastiwear—in shirts and in other uses—so he could understand how valuable it was. He also wanted to know if Plastiwear had some unusual features—he used the term proprietary—and just how vulnerable it was to imitation. If you could get past the differences in terminology, we basically agreed that decisions about Plastiwear would depend on how valuable, rare, and costly to imitate it was.

"I think we're on the same page, Vivek. But I've had a difficult time getting the people I've been interviewing to talk about the details of Plastiwear. It's been mostly about what is best for a particular manager or a portion of the firm, rather than the firm overall."

"People often do try to avoid being pinned down to details." Vivek seemed more than ready to move on.

"Any suggestions?"

"Just keep asking important questions, probing for insights, and synthesizing your findings." Vivek tossed off these instructions, but something in my face must have caused him to stop and change his flippant tone to one of more concern. "You do have a written list of questions, an interview protocol, don't you?"

"I started developing one yesterday." I exaggerated a bit. It wasn't so much an interview protocol as some scribbled notes.

"Well, that will help structure your interview. Make it clear that you need to work through your protocol and then just keep going back to it. I usually send mine ahead to the interviewee, along with a summary report of 'what we know and what we need to know.' But it's more than sticking to the protocol—it's about being prepared to have a conversation with the person you're interviewing. You certainly don't want to waste their time—or your own."

"Iron man" Vivek strikes again! "How do I make sure that I am open to ideas, points of view, that aren't built into the protocol?"

"Well, if an answer surprises you, that's an opportunity to learn. So, at that point, suspend the protocol and have a conversation about that topic."

I was impressed and chagrined. Again. I hadn't taken the interview segment of my new consultant orientation very seriously—thinking I'd be doing analysis and cracking cases, I suppose, rather than listening, sharing, and probing for information. "So," I probed, "surprises are good?"

"It depends on what kind and when. By the end of an engagement, if we are still getting surprised, it's because we have missed something important. Speaking of which, I don't want to miss my next appointment. But I'm concerned you and I are working too much in parallel. Let's meet later and spend some time making sure we avoid redundancies. I've been covering for Gordon, but I'm hoping you can take on a few things he was originally expected to do."

All this additional work didn't seem to worry Vivek too much as he stood up, stretched, adjusted his tie, and put on his coat.

"Good luck with your next interview."

"Thanks, Vivek. And thanks for the advice."

"No problem. See you later."

I tried to remain calm while Vivek left the room. But as soon as he was gone, I shook my head in self-disgust. An interview protocol. Reviewing your agenda with your interviewee. How simple. They had mentioned this and much more in the orientation, but I had assumed Gordon would get the first interview organized and had been flying by the seat of my pants ever since. I had exaggerated the "protocol" that I had developed to Vivek. But as I looked at my watch, I realized that I probably had enough time to take my scribbled notes and organize them into a series of tiered and branching questions that looked something like an interview protocol.

It occurred to me that no amount of structure could have redirected this morning's interview, but I put those thoughts aside and started working furiously.

REFLECTION QUESTIONS

1. Which is a bigger risk—implementing Tucker's "ten in ten" plan or doing nothing with the Plastiwear technology?

2. To what extent is Tucker correct in saying the HGS shareholders want and expect the firm to take risks?

3. What managerial and organizational challenges come to mind when you think about putting Tucker's vision into action?

4. Once Tucker made his position clear, what other questions should Justin have asked him to make the interview more helpful?

5. Why doesn't Bill share Tucker's enthusiasm about setting BHAGs (big hairy audacious goals) and "break(ing) all the rules"?

6. Why didn't Justin get more value out of his orientation training with the consulting firm?

— 8 —

A LONE RANGER

I arrived at Walter Albright's office a couple of minutes early. I had hoped that Gordon would be with me today, but he was still tied up with his other client.

Apparently, Albright was still at lunch. His secretary pointed me to the waiting area. As instructed, I went to the designated spot and—now remembering more of my orientation basics—stood next to what appeared to be a very comfortable couch. We'd been told consultants stood while waiting in order to reinforce the message that they were ready to work and were always aware of the value of the client's time.

Well, I was sure working. Here I was, just four days into my first real client assignment, and I had already made a fool of myself in front of my colleagues several times, been suckered in by the flimsy logic of a couple of vice presidents, had the limitations of my expensive MBA education made glaringly obvious, and been yelled at by my boss—twice.

But, overall, I was feeling pretty good.

Of course, none of that had been 100 percent fun, but I thought I was making progress. And my conversation with Vivek made me feel like I wasn't totally out to lunch. We seemed to at least have some common conclusions about Plastiwear's future; he and I would make a good team if we worked together. My recently organized interview protocol heightened my sense of confidence.

My reverie was interrupted by Albright's secretary.

"Dr. Albright will see you now."

Albright's office on the seventy-second floor was large, almost sixty feet square, and once again dominated by a wall of floor-to-ceiling windows, providing a dazzling perspective on the city. As always, I tried to ignore the view. His desk was pushed to one side and cluttered with just one layer of paper, not the three on Tucker's desk.

Albright himself was about six feet tall, almost entirely bald, with only about two inches of surprisingly black hair on each side of his head—the look of a Samurai warrior in classic black-and-white Japanese films. His round face, framed by wire-rimmed glasses, was smiling, and he motioned for me to sit down. Apparently, he was just finishing a phone call.

"Yeah, Carl. That will work. Uh-huh. OK, great. I'll talk to you later."

After hanging up the receiver, he turned his attention to me.

"Sorry about that. It was Carl Switzer."

Briefly I wondered if Carl was really on the line, or whether Albright was faking it, just trying to show how important he was. Boy, was I becoming cynical.

"So," Albright continued. "Tell me about yourself, Justin Campbell."

"Well, I'm . . . "

"I'm Walter Albright, VP of corporate R&D. So, how are things going so far?"

"Well, it's been a whirlwind, what with the shortened schedule and next week's deadline." That didn't sound too confident, so I quickly added, "But we're beginning to make headway."

"I can imagine," replied Albright. But his eyes said, "I doubt it." "So, we better get started. What can I do for you?"

"Well, I had a couple of questions I thought you could answer."

"Ask away."

Frankly, the interview was already not going very well. In the future, I was going to need some sort of brief bio and engagement summary prepared, up front, to get these things off on a better foot. As I opened my notebook and glanced at my opening questions, I hoped to turn things around.

"First, I wanted to get your sense of the potential size of the Plasti-wear market."

"Great question. Right now, the market we have quantified most fully is men's dress shirts. In North America, that market is about $3 billion. It's fragmented, both in manufacturing and retail distribution, but there are some strong brands in the market. The fiber and fabric market is more consolidated; it also has some important brand names. But I think what people who don't support Plastiwear forget is that white men's shirts, even though it is a reasonably large market, is just one of the uses of Plastiwear. This fabric has a wide variety of applications."

"Any examples?" I was skeptical since, so far, all I had heard about was white shirts.

"Here's one my guys are working on. You know buildings in earthquake zones—California, Japan—I mean big buildings in these places, have to be built with some vibration-dampening systems, like giant shock absorbers that let the building move during an earthquake."

"Yes, I've heard of this." Thank goodness for the Discovery Channel.

"Well, you know then that these systems aren't really shock absorbers. Instead, they're smooth metal plates that rest on each other and shift a bit if an earthquake happens."

I nodded, trying to seem like I was keeping up.

"Well, to make a long story short, in some conditions, the steel on these plates begins to rust. This reduces the ability of the plates to shift, and diminishes the effectiveness of the plates during an earthquake."

"I can see how that could be a problem."

"Well, it turns out that Plastiwear is the perfect lubricant between these plates. It's chemically stable, it's impervious to water and other chemicals, it keeps its structure even when subjected to enormous pressure, and, if installed correctly, it completely prevents rust. In our preliminary tests, it performs better than all the alternatives—better than any petroleum-based options like grease and even better than all current fabric-based solutions."

"How big is that market?"

"A little less than $1 billion per year worldwide, with the majority of growth projected in Asia."

"What about competition?" Now he had my full attention.

"Well, there are some large players in the market, but we think Plasti-wear is a superior technology and maybe we can persuade builders to try Plastiwear with performance guarantees and product demonstrations."

"Do you need regulatory approvals to use Plastiwear in this setting, before you start selling it to builders?" I quickly tried to apply my planned line of questioning to this new opportunity.

"Yes, of course. We'll look into how to get those or whether our clients would procure the permits if and when we get serious about this. But that's only the beginning. You asked about other applications; here's another one." He paused only briefly before continuing. "It turns out if you compress twelve layers of Plastiwear together, it's strong enough to resist puncture by small-caliber bullets. Not big guns or any-thing, but small bullets. Do you know the biggest source of failure with current bulletproof vests?"

I shook my head. "No. That's not a topic I've thought much about."

"People don't wear them when they should. The reason they don't wear them is that they're hot and uncomfortable. Not Plastiwear bullet-resistant shirts. They look good, they're comfortable, and they give you pretty good protection against all but the largest-caliber bullets. We're thinking another market might be bullet-resistant shirts for police, military, or civilian applications."

"That's fascinating. How much research have you done into this market?"

"Not much. But the market for bulletproof jackets is $10 billion in the United States alone, and no one's really cracked the comfort prob-lem. Given the advantages of our fabric in all but the most dangerous areas, I'd guess that the market for bullet-resistant Plastiwear shirts is bigger than that. Of course, one critical factor will be understanding and impressing our target customers—for example, the Department of Defense would be our buyer for military contracts and police depart-ments. We'd have to run performance trials, meet published specs, commit to strict delivery timelines—and even then, the budget may not be there."

"Are there other potential uses?"

"We've come up with dozens so far by just letting the R&D guys fool around—in fuel cells and in winter clothing, to name just two more.

We need to set up an independent division within HGS, invest in them for a couple of years, and give them the task of commercializing Plastiwear ASAP, with full P&L responsibility a couple of years later. Shirts! I wish dress shirts had never surfaced. What a sideshow! Heck, I think that Plastiwear can be justified on the basis of five or six different uses, totally independent of dress shirts."

"Are most of the opportunities upstream, rather than down? It sounds like you see a lot of potential for HGS to profit from Plastiwear-based fibers and fabrics," I ventured.

"Absolutely. Scott is right in one way—no way should we get into the manufacture or retailing of shirts. Of course we shouldn't. But that doesn't mean we shouldn't get into the fiber and fabric business. But not as part of the packaging division, just to fill up its empty plant. That's insane."

"Why?"

"Well, as you've probably figured out by now, HGS is pretty good at product extensions. We've done them for decades in both the oil and gas and the packaging businesses. But Plastiwear is not a product extension—no matter what they say in the packaging department. You can't take Plastiwear and drop it into a product extension organization, a product extension mentality."

"What do you mean?"

"Well, with product extensions, we can forecast future cash flows pretty precisely. We know who the potential customers are—sometimes we have contracts in hand well before new products are introduced. With innovative products, like Plastiwear, we can't do this. Heck, we don't know which of ten or fifteen uses of Plastiwear will have the most potential. We can't ask customers to evaluate these alternatives because, for most of them, customers have never thought of these uses before. Really, until we create this stuff, customers don't really exist."

"So, how are you going to choose among these alternatives?"

"Maybe we don't have to. Maybe we partner with companies that make different Plastiwear-based products. We make the fiber and fabric and supply it to these companies."

"Do you run the risk of losing control of your technology?"

"That's a risk, obviously. But we have strong patents and if we can brand Plastiwear as 'the miracle fabric of the twenty-first century,' we should maintain control."

Recalling my conversation with Livia, I asked, "But why would companies be willing to make products out of Plastiwear if HGS is the only supplier?"

Albright looked at me quizzically, "I guess if we needed to we could give them guarantees in their contracts. But if there are enough profits in the end-product markets, customers, users, and partners will come out of the woodwork. But this won't happen if Plastiwear is managed in an existing HGS division."

"Could you say more?" If the products were really this good, I didn't see why he was so concerned about the location of the Plastiwear group and whom it reported to.

"The problem is that our current employees—in oil and gas and in packaging—are good at running their current businesses, exploiting current technology, controlling costs, hitting quality and delivery targets week after week. That's what they do. Plastiwear is only tangentially linked to those businesses. It would be difficult for these same people to find the time and develop the skills needed to explore the potential of a brand-new technology like Plastiwear."

"Can't they get training in the skills they need to understand Plastiwear better?"

He chuckled. "Justin, I think you know that the management skills required to exploit existing technologies are completely different from those required to explore new technologies. Plastiwear, the technology, is in place. But Plastiwear, the product—we're just beginning to explore that space. We'll need leadership and staff who can take risks, run experiments, and make ongoing judgments about viability and priorities with ambiguous information. They'll need to build enthusiasm, foster creativity, and build new relationships. Frankly, even if our current leaders and best engineers made the time to focus on these potential opportunities, they just aren't cut from that cloth."

I had not anticipated talking so much about the organizational dimensions of Plastiwear, but they were obviously important. Despite this, I decided that I better get back to my interview protocol. "So, are there products or services that are close substitutes for Plastiwear in these different applications? Just how rare and unusual is this fabric?"

"Of course, that varies by application. And our competitive research for each of these applications has just barely begun. I will say this. Plastiwear has some pretty unusual physical characteristics: its ability to retain its molecular structure in different settings—that's where its wrinkle resistance comes from, by the way; its fire resistance, resistance to water—that's where its stain resistance comes from; and its ability to let air and other gases pass through it. This last feature we've only recently been working with. Plastiwear might be a great membrane for certain fuel cells. It might also be very effective for winter clothing—warm, but doesn't trap moisture. Again, we've just scratched the surface with this stuff."

I nodded in interest. No one had communicated the potential of Plastiwear so broadly. I tried to get my bearings and move back to my planned line of questioning. "Suppose these markets are out there. If you start selling Plastiwear, how long before other firms start selling Plastiwear knockoffs, either the same fabric or a similar fabric with a slightly different name?"

"Well, the good news is that we do have a strong patent. But patents are no guarantee against imitation. In specialty chemicals, you can patent stuff down to the molecular level—the specific atoms that combine to create Plastiwear. Other firms can change the formula hoping to imitate Plastiwear, without violating the patent, but changing the molecule usually changes the properties of the product, and sometimes dramatically." Albright's secretary came to the door and tapped her watch. Not aggressively, but her message was clear. Albright waved in acknowledgment and went on. "We know, for example, that if you change a couple parts of our molecule, Plastiwear doesn't coalesce into a fiber, so you can't fabricate it."

I was concerned. "So if you outsourced the production, your supplier firms might have quality problems in fabricating it into the type of fabric I've seen?"

"Well, that's one way to look at it. But we're seeing a new set of opportunities. Now we can explore Plastiwear derivative liquid products."

"You mean things like a spray-on Plastiwear?"

"Absolutely. I have a team working on another patent application now. We like new chemical formulas, as opposed to an end product; it is harder to 'see' what we've been up to and imitate us without violating our patents."

"What do you mean?"

"In a packaging firm where I used to work, we'd invest millions to come up with a new package. As soon we sold it to our customers, competitors would bring out their own similar packaging—or save themselves the trouble if it wasn't a big hit for us. Patents don't protect you from other firms imitating your product's features."

"So by basing your strategy on specialty chemicals, you feel that imitation is less likely to be a problem?"

"No, I'm not that naive. If Plastiwear is as big as I think it's going to be, competitors will find ways to develop products that are similar to it, but don't violate our patents. And even if they do violate our patents, we—HGS—have to be willing to press them hard legally. To me, the key to reducing the threat of imitation is to build a brand name around Plastiwear. By the way, I hate that name—Plastiwear. Sounds like something from a 1950s science fiction movie."

"You can always come up with a better name."

"Couldn't be much worse. Makes Gore-Tex sound good." He grimaced and continued. "But, whatever the name, our branding strategy will be important if it is to become the miracle fabric of the twenty-first century."

"Is there a 'miracle fabric' plan under way?"

"I'm leaving that to the marketing people. I'm not a marketing person, but I can tell you that unless Plastiwear gets out on its own, unless it gets its own leadership and organization—people who are living and dying with this product—we won't make the splash we could. We've got to get the organization right. That's what this private equity thing is all about."

"Do you think the PE folks are serious?"

"Listen, the word about Plastiwear has been on the streets for over eighteen months. Information about its uses is beginning to leak out. The total size of this opportunity—could be huge. And here we are, talking about making shirts and going into retail. If we're acquired, this technology would be licensed to an established fiber and fabric firm so fast it would be breathtaking. Then, its real value would become clear."

I was still thinking about the possibility that Plastiwear could become the miracle fabric of the twenty-first century as Albright continued.

"So either we do it—HGS sets up a Plastiwear division and figures out how to make and market this stuff—or the market will pick up that option for a price. And when that happens, look out." He paused thoughtfully again. "For me, I've about concluded that the only way Plastiwear can realize its potential is if we are taken over and this political standoff gets resolved."

"Standoff?"

He looked surprised at my question. "Surely, it's obvious to your team. What reasonable management team generates six different studies with six different outcomes just valuing Plastiwear in making shirts—like it's the only thing we could make with this stuff? I swear it's like we're exploring one corner of one closet in a forty-room mansion. We'll have to get out of our own way to realize the true potential of Plastiwear."

My meeting with Albright answered a lot of questions, but it raised many more. Albright was convinced that Plastiwear wasn't a one-off technology, good for only one product—white shirts. Plastiwear was potentially a family of technologies in at least two forms—a fiber/fabric and a liquid. And it had a wide range of possible market applications. He was also convinced that HGS could sustain any competitive advantage it got from Plastiwear, but only if the company dedicated the right organizational and financial resources to this effort. And if HGS didn't do it, Albright was sure a private equity firm would.

However, Albright's views were challenging as well. So far, I had spent most of my time on the size and structure of the white shirt market. Just getting a handle on that market was hard enough. Now Albright was talking about construction, bulletproof vests, fuel cells, winter clothing, and who knew what else. How could I get my mind around all these markets? And we only had, really, a few days left until we had to make our recommendations.

Obviously, I was going to have to get really organized if I was going to make sense out of all this. So, right after the interview, I went to the team room. It was empty. I took a blank sheet of paper and down the left side I wrote each of the opportunities that Albright had mentioned. Across the top of the sheet, I listed the categories of information I might need to evaluate Plastiwear's potential in these markets.

Generating these categories took some time. It seemed to me that I'd first want to know the size of each of these markets, and whether and how fast they were growing. Of course, that's tricky when some of these markets don't even exist yet.

As I developed my chart, I went back to my interview notes. Albright believed that Plastiwear had two sources of advantage: it had technical properties that were superior to competing products, and it could be branded as something like "the miracle fabric of the twenty-first century." But in which of the potential applications would these attributes of Plastiwear be valuable, rare, and costly to imitate?

Suppose, for example, that Plastiwear didn't have clear technical advantages over bullet-resistant clothing on the market today. Then the technical features HGS embedded in Plastiwear wouldn't be rare in this application and thus would only be a source of competitive parity—keeping HGS in the race but not winning the race for them. On the other hand, technical attributes might give Plastiwear at least a temporary advantage, a competitive lead that would last—as long as other firms didn't catch up by imitating those product features.

It seemed to me we'd also need to investigate more practical issues about entering new markets and beginning to exploit them. How soon would HGS obtain its first customers? Could these customers help test and prototype new Plastiwear applications? I also wondered about regulatory constraints. I had raised this issue in the earthquake construction example, but it could be a problem in several potential Plastiware applications. And, since the consensus seemed to be that HGS would sell Plastiwear—either the fiber, the fabric, or the liquid form—to customers who would then use it in products, the availability of potential partners downstream or in complementary markets seemed important to me. Partners might also be important upstream, if the decision was

Justin's opportunity analysis matrix for Plastiwear

	Market size?	Growth?	Rarity: HGS advantage?	Imitability: Sustained HGS advantage?	First customers/ timing?	Regulatory constraints?	Possible partners?	Exploit a market extension or explore a radical new technology?
White dress shirts								
Earthquake construction								
Bullet-resistant clothing								
Fuel-cell membranes								
Winter clothing								

made to outsource Plastiwear manufacturing and close cooperation was necessary to ensure quality.

The last element in my new matrix came right out of my interview with Albright, but I thought Tucker would agree. Albright seemed very concerned that HGS—an organization with a proven track record in exploiting existing technologies—could not be expected to explore a brand-new technology like Plastiwear. That's why he thought it was so important that Plastiwear be organized as a separate unit inside HGS. So, it seemed to me that it might make sense to evaluate whether a particular application of Plastiwear was some sort of product extension for HGS, or a more radical innovation—or perhaps both? The answer to this question might have a significant impact on how HGS would organize around Plastiwear—and whether it might actually need to "break some rules" about how HGS typically did business.

I thought these columns were a good starting point. I could always add more categories to my matrix once I made progress filling it in. I hoped answering these questions might help me whittle down the opportunities so I could focus on just the most attractive options and work more efficiently.

I looked at the matrix. The list of possible Plastiwear applications gave me pause. Albright and I hadn't talked about opportunities in any systematic way. In fact, according to my notes, he'd mentioned that Plastiwear might have dozens of applications, but I listed only five. While it was now clear that Plastiwear wasn't just about shirts, I wouldn't be surprised if there were uses for Plastiwear that Albright hadn't even mentioned that would also be worth examining. I added a CYA note on my pad of paper: "Selected examples. Not a comprehensive list."

Before I invested time in understanding these diverse markets, I needed to talk to someone familiar with more of the potential uses of Plastiwear. I should have asked Albright who in R&D was investigating these alternatives. But I hadn't.

I was embarrassed to have to call Albright back and get the names of people to follow up with, but it would be more embarrassing not to have the full story. I was reaching for the phone when I vaguely remembered something I had heard during my orientation—I was supposed to always ask who else I should talk to as I finished an interview. I was also supposed to ask for more information sources when I sent my thank-you note to the people I interviewed. Thank-you notes! I hadn't been sending anything to follow up after the interviews I'd had so far. At least it wasn't too late to shoot off some e-mails.

Putting down the phone, I drafted an e-mail thanking Albright for his time, and asked who I might talk to about alternative uses of Plastiwear. It might have been helpful for Vivek to look over my e-mail before I sent it, but pressed for time, I pressed Send.

The thought struck me—should I have cc'd Ken, or Livia, on this e-mail? Should I have summarized the main points of the interview, or at least played back some of the important things Albright said? As I stewed over thank-you note etiquette, I realized I already had a reply from AlbrightW@HGS.com, who wrote:

"No problem. Enjoyed our chat. The team leader working on Plastiwear applications is Leonard Kibrick. He can give you a rundown on all the work they are doing." Albright included Kibrick's contact information. Impressed by the speed of the response, and relieved that I could once again move forward, I placed a quick phone call to Kibrick's office and booked an hour with him at 2:00 the next afternoon.

I thought about doing more thank-yous, or drafting the interview protocol for the Kibrick meeting, but instead turned to the empty boxes on the page in front of me and got to work.

So now that I had a way to organize the questions, it was time to convert the piles of information I was surrounded by into answers. I quickly reviewed my notes. Let's see, Albright had said that the earthquake construction market was just under $1 billion. So I wrote in the "market size" column and the "earthquake construction" row "$1 billion."

Then I stopped. I had done it again—the thing that Ken warned me about last night. Yes, Albright was convincing. He seemed to be less political than some of the other people I had interviewed. But he had his personal interests as well. He clearly wanted Plastiwear to be given every opportunity to grow. Given that incentive, he might exaggerate the size of potential Plastiwear markets. Maybe he also exaggerated the advantages of Plastiwear over competing technologies. I couldn't trust this $1 billion number, just on Albright's word. For the time being, I wrote an asterisk next to the number and noted Albright as the reference.

To fill in this matrix, I was going to have to get—to the extent I could—independent estimates of market size, growth potential, and so forth. At a minimum, I would have to get some external validation for any numbers provided to me by HGS personnel, or at least I'd have to vet their sources.

So, how could I get this information? I had already used my firm's and HGS's databases to get some information about the apparel and fabric industries. Some of these databases were proprietary to our firm—research conducted by us and some aggregate data from prior studies for prior clients. Others were from publicly available sources. I decided to focus first on collecting information about what I thought would be the market easiest to define, the bullet-resistant shirt market.

Using the firm's proprietary database, I typed "bulletproof vests" in the search box. The reply was not encouraging: "No matches within the specified search parameters." I've always wondered why programmers use language like this—"no matches within the specified search parameters." Sounds like a robot. Why not, oh, I don't know—"No matches, try again" or "No luck, sucker!" Anything but this "geek speak."

I tried a couple of different approaches. Typing in "personal protection" generated a list of studies on the retail market for deodorants, feminine hygiene products, and condoms. Not real close. "Safety clothing" generated some research on construction hats, shoes, and on-the-job safety programs. Closer, but not helpful.

I decided to go in a different direction. Albright had mentioned two specific markets where a bullet-resistant shirt might be attractive—police and military. I chose the police first, and typed "police uniforms." It turns out that there is a trade association for firms that make uniforms, including police uniforms. This trade association had collected a fair amount of data about various aspects of this industry. After paying the data access fees, and making a mental note to expense them later, I found an entire section of its data set on police uniforms. Turns out that one of the key accessories sold along with police uniforms was personal antiballistic armor—that is, bulletproof vests.

This research, done three years ago, showed that demand for bullet-proof vests was constrained by the fact that most armor was uncomfortable and hot to wear, as Albright had mentioned. Given the cost and discomfort, most police departments only equipped those in the force most likely to face deadly gunfire—members of SWAT teams and the like—with bulletproof vests.

Albright was also right in suggesting that a bullet-resistant shirt was a new product category. There wasn't anything out there quite like it. But at least this study gave me a rough feel for the size of the personal antiballistic armor market in police departments in North America.

With my success on police uniforms, I decided to take a similar approach with the military market. Turns out that—according to some U.S. Department of Defense studies—the military uniform market is much larger than the police uniform market. Also, the military (or more precisely, the U.S. military, since I couldn't quickly find data on non-U.S. militaries) orders considerably more bulletproof vests—they call them "flak jackets" and "personal armor"—than the police.

One of the government reports I found showed that the major failure associated with bulletproof vests—just like Albright said—is that people aren't wearing them when they come under fire. This isn't a problem when, say, a group of soldiers goes out on patrol. These guys know they may be under fire, and so they all wear their vests.

The real problem is when they are in places or doing things where it is less likely that they will be in the direct line of fire—at headquarters, in the barracks, at a restaurant. In these settings, they almost never wear the personal armor they're issued—it's too hot, too bulky, too uncomfortable. And so, if there is an unexpected attack—an all-too-frequent occurrence—they are left without protection.

It seemed to me that it was in this context that a bullet-resistant shirt—made out of Plastiwear—might be a nice complement to the bulletproof vests currently used by the military. Those serving in a war zone could wear the shirt all the time. It would always provide some protection. Then, when they actually went into combat, they could put on their vests, and the shirt and vest, working together, could provide even more protection.

Besides that, shirts covered the entire torso and arms, providing more protection than a vest. It also struck me that military pants could be made out of Plastiwear, to give the lower body and legs some protection as well.

As I was getting excited about this market, I suddenly remembered—it only comes in white. It seems very unlikely that the military would be happy about dressing their soldiers in white clothes—head to toe. It might work for the Navy—you know, dress whites and everything. But not only would it look ridiculous, white is not the best choice for camouflage. So, with Plastiwear clothing, soldiers may be protected from small-caliber fire, but they might make better targets.

Maybe HGS could partner with another firm that could create a top layer of colored or camouflage fabric over the Plastiwear. I made some notes under partners and early customers, and continued toggling between reading, researching, and trying to fill in my matrix.

I then began examining the potential of Plastiwear in the fuel-cell and other markets I had listed on my matrix. I followed the same drill—finding some prior research or industry studies that described key attributes of these industries. Whenever possible, I used this information to fill in a blank in the matrix. I also added another column: "critical issues." I did this after I realized that white was not the optimal color for military applications. So "critical issues" became a catchall for things that would have to be resolved for us to be able to confidently evaluate these markets and related strategic options.

A couple of the studies I read identified the person who had been responsible for doing the work, along with contact information. Whenever I could, I e-mailed these people to ask about any additional, more up-to-date work that had been done. I also included questions not addressed in their study—without revealing the technology or the company I was working for, of course. By dinnertime, I had received replies from two of these people. One gave me some very helpful leads on earthquake-damage abatement.

In filling out the matrix, I decided it was important to get some idea of the potential of Plastiwear in these different markets but, at this point, it was also important not to get stuck in any one of them, looking for too precise an answer. After all, I hadn't yet talked to Kibrick to hear about the full set of alternatives. Maybe some of these ideas I was exploring weren't all that promising. And even if they were promising, a decision about pursuing them wasn't going to depend on whether the market was $840 million or $780 million in size.

What I was really after was to get enough information to set some data collection priorities over the next few days, and make some go/no-go decisions next week about the areas of highest potential for Plastiwear.

Time flew by. I ordered dinner in at nine. I had no idea I had been working on this for almost seven hours. I worked as I ate. It almost felt like I was living a business case—there was an answer out there. How big was the market? Where was it growing? Who were the critical players? Was there a low-risk entry strategy? And the databases I was searching seemed to have many of the answers, if I was just clever enough to find them.

It occurred to me that I should call Vivek and get his help filling out the matrix. It was just a passing thought. He had mentioned that he wanted to talk about my interviews, but that could wait. After all, I had developed the matrix. It was important. And it was my analysis. And I was already deep into collecting the information needed to fill it out. And it was late at night—I didn't want to disturb him. And when I was really honest with myself, I wanted to be able to present this completed matrix, together with all my sources, to Ken and the team. I would see Vivek tomorrow. What I really wanted was to be able to give Ken a call tomorrow night, to let him know where I stood.

After gulping down dinner, I threw myself back into the research with renewed energy. The construction market was hard to get information about—the proposed use of Plastiwear in this market was pretty specialized. The potential of Plastiwear for fuel cells was also difficult to judge. It was a small market with serious growth potential. Here, the technical properties of Plastiwear would be critical, so I really focused on questions to ask Kibrick the next afternoon. I refined my interview guide as I worked. Note to self: leave time to clean up and reorganize the protocol before 2:00 tomorrow.

I went back to the hotel at 1:30, but I was up by 6:00 a.m. To save time, I worked in my hotel room in the morning. By lunch, I had filled in about three-fourths of the blanks in my matrix with information or estimates of some sort, and I was definitely looking forward to my meeting with Kibrick.

———————————

I was satisfied and excited, and ready for a change of scenery. I decided to have my lunch and organize my interview protocol back over at HGS, in the team room. As I walked in, there was Vivek typing away on his computer. Livia was there as well, talking to him and referring to some reports laid out between them.

"Hi, Vivek, Livia. How are things going?"

Vivek looked relieved. He talked more quickly than usual. "Wow, Justin, glad to see you. I was worried when you didn't show up to work with me yesterday as I thought we'd agreed."

So, the "iron man" consultant actually wanted—no, needed—more time with me!

He went on before I could reassure him. "I thought maybe you were sick. I was going to call your hotel if we didn't hear from you soon. But we got pretty engrossed in pushing our thinking to the next level"—he pointed to the whiteboard on the far wall of our team room—"and I'm just glad you're here now."

Livia tried to lighten the mood. "I told Vivek maybe you were out sightseeing or trying out more of Chicago's fine restaurants." She smiled with her mouth, but her eyes looked serious. "We've spent the morning analyzing some potential uses of Plastiwear. This is some of what we have so far. There's more in the document Vivek's got going on his laptop, and you've probably already reviewed our early drafts in the virtual team room."

On the whiteboard was a matrix. Down the side of the matrix was a list of potential uses of Plastiwear. Among other things, I saw bullet-resistant clothes, fuel cells, tents, and parachutes. Across the top of the matrix was a list of questions, including: market size, projected growth rate, existing market structure, HGS's advantages, sustainability, critical purchasing criteria.

My heart sank.

REFLECTION QUESTIONS

1. What are three differences between product extensions and innovations that impact strategic decisions?

2. What are three differences between product extensions and innovations that impact organizational decisions?

3. How are the questions in Justin's new matrix (in this chapter) related to the questions in his old matrix (in chapter 5)?

4. Justin wants to sort out strategy first and then think about the organization. Is this a reasonable way to prioritize his work?

5. How can Justin ensure his interviews provide meaningful input to the strategy development process?

6. Justin has just discovered that he has been working in parallel with the rest of the team. What should Livia do now to ensure the success of the project?

— 9 —

A TEAM EFFORT

Vivek and Livia had done—in the morning—what it had taken me all of yesterday afternoon, most of the night, and this morning to do. Equally devastating, they had come up with almost the same organizing tool I had. I thought I was being so clever, so creative.

I was such a rookie.

"What's wrong, Justin?" was Livia's first question. "You look pale."

What could I say—that I hated them for their competence, their efficiency, for blowing my chance to get back in Ken's good graces? What could I say?

"Oh, nothing. Actually, I've been working on something similar to what you've got there."

Vivek was mildly interested. "OK. Let's see what you've got. Maybe you can fill in some of our missing pieces, cross-check our information sources. The more sources the better, although right now, we're most interested in setting priorities about where to conduct further research."

I couldn't even show off that I knew we didn't need great precision right now. Vivek already knew that—of course. I gave Vivek a hard copy of the matrix I had spent the last twenty hours completing.

"Sure, here is what I've got so far."

"When did you start this?" Livia asked.

"Yesterday afternoon, after I interviewed the R&D VP. He was the one who suggested that Plastiwear had uses besides white shirts." Livia opened her mouth to speak, but seemed to reconsider and nodded to Vivek.

Vivek explained. "I've been collecting all the alternatives that have come up in the marketing interviews. They've been scattered throughout the notes I've been posting, but I combined them into a master list and included it in my last e-mail yesterday afternoon. Maybe you haven't seen those notes yet?"

I was embarrassed to say that I was working so hard—by myself—that I hadn't opened Vivek's e-mails or even looked into the VTR—the virtual team room. All I could say was, "No, I haven't read them yet."

Livia again looked ready to say something but only shook her head once hard and returned to her work. Vivek seemed to ignore my mistake. "I haven't talked to the R&D guy in charge of exploring Plastiwear alternatives yet. What's his name?"

"Leonard Kibrick," I quickly responded. At least I could add something to this conversation.

"Yes, Kibrick," replied Vivek. "We need to talk to him to make sure this list of alternatives is sufficiently complete and determine where Plastiwear can be most competitive with current—or emerging— players in these markets."

"Well," I said, relieved that I could bring something substantive to the conversation, "I have an appointment to interview Kibrick in a couple of hours."

"Good," Vivek responded. "Can I join you?"

"Of course. Livia, do you want to come as well?"

"No, I want to get this material ready to share with Ken. Plus, two at an interview is good; three can be a bit overwhelming." Turning her attention back to the whiteboard, Livia asked, "So, Justin, what did you come up with that we can add?"

Quickly, we compared my results with theirs. Sometimes we used the same data source and agreed about the information in the matrix. Sometimes we used different data sources, but still agreed. This gave us more confidence in our conclusions. Other times, we used the same or different data sources and disagreed. When that happened, we put both conclusions in the matrix and circled them with source notes. This way we could come back to these points later.

After an hour or so, all of my information had been integrated into the matrix on the whiteboard. Not all the squares were full, but most of them were. And though we didn't always agree, between the three of us, we knew quite a bit about Plastiwear and its potential uses—at least the ones that had been discussed up to this point. Toward the end of this work, Livia turned to me.

"Thanks for the input, Justin. And you came up with your matrix and these data on your own?"

"Pretty much."

"Well, getting an independent read on these issues is extremely helpful. And I like how your questions complement ours. Vivek and I have each done this kind of work on other projects, and I know he was expecting to include you in some team time working together yesterday. That would have been more efficient, but considering you played Lone Ranger, this is," she paused, "helpful."

"Thank you, thank you very much." I think I actually blushed. Truthfully, these were the first encouraging words I had heard since I started working on this project, and I realized I'd been starving for some positive feedback. Anything. I wished they had come from Ken, but Livia would do. At almost the same instant, I wondered if Livia was really damning me with faint praise. But the look on her face, her body language—both suggested that she was sincere.

Vivek broke into my self-congratulatory haze. "Livia, I was thinking that it might make sense to group these application possibilities into larger categories, like product segments."

"What did you have in mind?" asked Livia.

Vivek replied, "Well, it strikes me that we have at least three kinds of products here—for construction, for clothing, and for recreation. If we think of these segments, with these specific products as examples within those segments, other opportunities might present themselves. So, for example, in the clothing segment, we've got white shirts and bullet-resistant shirts/pants. But what about hunting clothes? In recreation, we've got tents and parachutes, but what about fabric for hang gliders? I think breaking out our analysis at the product segment level will help us spot even more potential uses of Plastiwear."

I had noticed one product that didn't seem to fit into Vivek's typology. "What about fuel cells? They don't seem to fit."

Clearly, Livia had bought into Vivek's idea. "It's OK to have a few orphan products, but I really like this approach, Vivek. Will you and Justin restructure our matrix into segments like these?"

Vivek answered for both of us. "Sure."

Abruptly, Vivek changed the subject. "Shouldn't we be heading out to the R&D center pretty soon? It's about an hour away, isn't it? By taxi? That is where Kibrick is, isn't it?"

Another important question I had forgotten to ask—where was Kibrick's office?

"Oh. Let me check. One second."

Quickly, I found the company phone list online and looked up Kibrick.

"Yes, he's at the R&D center. We better go." And with that, the time I had scheduled to organize the interview protocol for Kibrick was gone.

Vivek and I were able to flag a cab without any difficulty and settled in for the ride out to the R&D center. Truthfully, I wasn't too excited about this trip. I didn't know Vivek very well. I assumed we didn't have much in common. He seemed quiet and introspective—incredibly hard-working, but not someone I'd seek out at a party. I worried the ride would be punctuated by awkward silences. I was wrong.

"So, Justin. What has surprised you the most on this project?"

"I guess the speed. It's now Thursday. We started work on Monday. I think we're making progress—getting started on the matrix was a great leap forward."

"'Great Leap Forward'—the term Chairman Mao used to describe the Communist Party's attempts to centrally control the Chinese economy, attempts that routinely killed millions of Chinese."

"Perhaps not the best term to use, then."

"Perhaps," replied Vivek, with only a trace of sarcasm. "But it has gone fast, faster than normal because of the external pressure." He nodded toward the cab driver, reminding me that we couldn't say anything about the takeover that might be overheard outside the firm. "Anything else?"

"I've enjoyed working with the team. We did lots of team projects in the MBA program, but those were all on cases. This is the real thing. I'm starting to appreciate how much I can rely on this team."

I tried to say this without irony. Last night, I really didn't want to interact with the team, because I wanted to get all the credit for "cracking the case." But if I had kept in better communication with the team yesterday and last night, I could have worked directly with Vivek and Livia, and we probably would have made far more progress than we had to this point. I guess I was coming to appreciate the value of working on this team, but I was a slow learner.

"So, what is your view of the opportunity now?" Vivek seemed intent upon hearing my answer.

"Well, I hope to know more after this next interview. And certainly, we don't have enough information to do full-blown present value analyses on any of these opportunities, including even the white shirt opportunity."

"In my experience, we seldom do."

"That's been interesting, too." I was referring to the fact that the "holy grail" of my MBA education—present value analysis—had remarkably little to add in this new product development process. I had just about concluded that present value analysis was only useful in settings where you really didn't need it, that is, in settings where you already had a good sense of the cash flows that a strategy would generate and how risky those cash flows were. In those settings, calculating NPV was easy and still useful as a financial rather than a strategic tool.

Vivek continued. "So, even without perfect numbers, what do you think about the technology? For example, would you invest your own money? Could you imagine joining our client's firm full time to pursue its next big strategy?"

I thought that was an odd question. I had only been working for the firm for ten days. This was my first engagement. It was clearly premature for me to be thinking about jumping ship for a client organization.

Vivek went on. "You know, that's the litmus test for strategic opportunities. In the face of imperfect information, it often comes down to a combination of what you know and what you feel." He waited expectantly.

"Well, depending on what we learn today, it seems like there are potentially viable opportunities. Right now, I've got my hands full with my new job and I don't have any money to invest." I tried to keep my tone light. "But I'm predisposed to recommend starting small with the new technology set up with its own P&L. After a couple of years and a couple of products, we'd see what the group had come up with. You know, set up the organization and let a thousand flowers blossom."

"A phrase Chairman Mao used to encourage dissidents to share their concerns about the party, after which he killed several hundred thousand of them."

"Geez. I didn't realize how much of Mao had crept into my day-to-day vocabulary."

"It's not a big deal. Modern Chinese history is a hobby of mine. In any case, I agree with your main point. This technology will never get the kind of managerial attention it needs to flourish if it's kept within the current organizational structure. What about manufacturing—the fiber and fabric? Any thoughts on this?"

"I've been spending most of my time the last couple of days thinking about downstream, customer uses, not upstream manufacturing. I'm pretty sure we shouldn't recommend that HGS get into shirt manufacturing."

Vivek looked at me quizzically. "That's a no-brainer. Beckett and the oil and gas people are right about that part of the shirt industry. Even if there was money there, the client doesn't have those skills. But what about fiber and fabric manufacturing? Personally, I think they need to retain control of the intellectual property rights associated with their innovations. If they outsource manufacturing entirely, IP could become a problem."

"Maybe," was my reply. "But on the other hand, if they build a giant factory to make fiber and fabric at scale and none of these opportunities turns out to be profitable, then they are stuck. Especially if the factory is highly customized."

"We don't know if that is going to be the case or not—both the intellectual property rights questions and the special manufacturing requirements questions need to be addressed."

"Yeah," I agreed, "so far, all they've done is manufacture very small amounts of fiber, and the fabric weaving is outsourced. The packaging VP told me that he thought the weaving, cutting, and sewing processes are all very standard, but they have quite limited experience at this point."

"If they really are standard, that argues against vertical integration. But if you outsource everything, then you might run into quality control and IP problems."

I thought this gave me an opportunity to kid Vivek a little bit, maybe even make him laugh. I had yet to see him laugh. "Yeah, the IP problems would be particularly bad if HGS outsourced its manufacturing to India." Vivek didn't even crack a smile.

"IP in India is reasonably secure; it's less secure in China."

"So, Vivek, why do our conversations always come back to China?"

I couldn't believe it—Vivek actually chuckled. Not a full-blown laugh, but close. Just for a second.

"Seriously," Vivek was back on task, "on the one hand, they should vertically integrate into fiber and fabric manufacturing in order to protect their intellectual property. On the other hand, what if distinctive value just isn't there on this technology? What would our client do with an underutilized fiber and fabric manufacturing plant? That risk seems to argue against in-house manufacturing."

Vivek continued his analysis. "The extent to which manufacturing this fiber and fabric requires special technology seems to cut both ways. On the one hand, if it is highly specialized technology, then the firm might opt to retain control of it. Suppliers may not have the skills to handle it, and you may not want to risk their learning too much. However, if you put a big investment into this technology, and the marketplace isn't receptive, you have an empty factory with special equipment no one else wants." Vivek shrugged his shoulders and went on. "If, on the other hand, the technology is fairly standard, then you could outsource manufacturing to any number of firms with relatively low risk. But in this setting, the risk if you invest yourself is also lower, because any unused capacity should be easily repurposed or sold. The real question isn't about outsourcing; it is about the nature of the technology—whether it is firm-specific or not."

Vivek's analysis was almost too quick for me to follow and he spoke rapidly in a low voice as the cab rattled along. I did remember something from my MBA. In the face of high fixed costs and uncertain demand, joint ventures, especially with an option to increase your stake if the product in question does really well, are often attractive entry vehicles. You manage the downside risk while maintaining a claim on the upside. So, that was my suggestion.

"What about a joint venture with, say, a Mexican fiber and fabrics firm? HGS already has several partners in Mexico. Bill spent part of his career as a plant manager down there, so maybe he could help us identify potential partners. The firm could monitor quality, retain control of its intellectual property, limit its capital investment in the plant, and benefit from the manufacturing expertise of its partner. The ideal partner will also already have strong customer relationships relevant to high-priority target markets."

"A JV has potential, but choosing the right partner is everything. You're right, Bill's input could be very important here. Good idea."

With this, our conversation shifted to more personal matters. Somehow, we got on the topic of cricket. Turns out that Vivek and I had something in common. He was once a very good cricket player, and I once saw a cricket bat. Vivek was trying to explain the intricacies of the game to me, and I was asking him how any sporting activity could go on for several days, and then end with a draw, when we arrived at the R&D center.

As I was getting out of the cab—Vivek paid—I couldn't quite let go of this joint venture idea. Maybe that would be a way to let HGS pursue Plastiwear, but with a well-defined and limited downside risk. Given the amount of uncertainty HGS faced with Plastiwear, a joint venture would give them flexibility—keep the JV small if it turned out that Plastiwear wasn't a huge hit; increase your investments, even acquire your JV partner, if Plastiwear was a big hit. It seemed to me—if HGS could manage it—that some kind of alliance would create strategic options and flexibility for HGS, and the cost of getting access to these options was just the cost of forming and managing this joint venture. So—a JV gives you options at a relatively small and fixed cost.

As Vivek and I approached the front door of the R&D center, it struck me that Vivek and I had just experienced the advantages of a joint venture. I wondered if HGS ever would.

REFLECTION QUESTIONS

1. If Justin could evaluate only three possible applications of Plastiwear, how should he choose them?

2. If Justin could apply only three criteria in doing these evaluations, which three should they be? Why?

3. What is the difference between using present value analysis as a strategy tool and using it as a financial tool?

4. What is the value of using alliances, including joint ventures, to explore new and uncertain business opportunities?

5. What are some of the organizational and management challenges of using an international joint venture to launch a new product, or a new portfolio of products?

6. What concrete actions can Justin take to work more effectively with Vivek and Livia?

— 10 —

A FITTING TEST

"Dr. Campbell, it's good to see you again. And so soon."

Harriet obviously remembered me from my recent visit to the R&D center. Vivek gave me a confused look.

"Dr. Campbell?"

"It's a long story." Turning my attention to Harriet, I responded, "Good morning, Harriet. We're here to see Leonard Kibrick."

"Oh, yes. He's expecting you. I'll call him." As she dialed the number, she turned to me with a question.

"By the way, what's your colleague's name? I'll need to get him a visitor's badge."

Vivek introduced himself as Harriet prepared our tags. "Hi, I'm Vivek Chatterjee."

"You boys here for the burn test? Should be very interesting. Have a nice day, you hear?"

"Thanks, Harriet." I put my badge on my jacket. Not surprisingly, it read "Dr. Justin Campbell, PhD." Vivek's read only "Vivek Chatterjee." It slowly dawned that Harriet was playing with me.

Vivek looked concerned. "How does this woman know about the lab's research schedule?"

A man I took to be Leonard Kibrick approached. I reached out my hand in greeting.

"Leonard Kibrick? Hi, my name is Justin Campbell, and this is Vivek Chatterjee."

"Dr. Campbell, Mr. Chatterjee, it's good to meet you."

"It's not Dr. Campbell. I don't have a PhD."

"An easy mistake to make around here. May I call you Justin?"

"Certainly."

"And you can call me Vivek, although I do have a PhD," Vivek interjected.

Kibrick seemed intrigued. "In what field?"

"Chemical engineering, UC Berkeley. Finished a couple of years ago. I've been consulting since then."

"Ever thought about going into research or industry?"

"I try to keep my options open," was Vivek's noncommittal reply.

With introductions complete, Kibrick turned and motioned us to follow him. He was a nondescript man—around five feet ten, maybe two hundred pounds, with dark hair parted on the side and only the slightest hint of gray at the temples, dark horn-rimmed glasses on a handsome but slightly pudgy face. He was wearing khaki pants and a white shirt, covered by a white lab coat with his name embroidered over the left pocket. And yes, there was a pocket protector and a collection of at least fifteen pens in his pocket. Overall, he looked like what the Professor on *Gilligan's Island* would have looked like at age fifty-two.

"My office is back here."

We passed through yet another set of glass doors and turned right down a corridor. Kibrick directed us into a small office—about half the size of Tucker's office—that was dominated by a desk piled high with papers and a whiteboard covered with a variety of equations and diagrams. Except for his appearance and the size of this room, Kibrick reminded me a lot of Tucker. I worried that we would be in for another "imagine your own world" kind of rant—another complete waste of time.

"Please, sit down. Make yourselves comfortable. Would you like something—coffee or water?"

"Water would be good." After the long cab ride, I was parched.

Vivek demurred. "I don't care for anything, thanks."

Kibrick reached under his desk, opened a small hidden refrigerator, and pulled out a cold bottle of water.

"Here you are." Kibrick handed me the water. "Once I heard you guys were coming, I pulled together some of our latest findings about Plastiwear."

Kibrick handed me a report, about a half inch thick, in a three-ring binder. I put the water down on the floor, near my chair, and took the report.

"I had only one copy made."

Vivek apologized. "Yes, that's fine. I didn't know until very recently that I was going to be able to attend this meeting. I'll just share with Justin."

"Great," Kibrick continued. "That report has two parts. In part one, I summarize the chemical structure of Plastiwear. This, of course, is all company-confidential, right?"

Vivek answered for both of us. "Nondisclosures are in place."

"Good. Well, in part one, I summarize the chemical structure of Plastiwear. Vivek, I'm sure you'll see the importance of what we've got here. The guys downtown, they've been focusing on shirts and what-not. I guess that's what they've got to do, for the business and every-thing. But this technology is actually very cool. I think we've stumbled onto something that is unique, chemically speaking. We're just begin-ning to understand the implications of the chemistry we've got here. For example, look at the structure of the molecule . . . "

At that point, Kibrick's lecture exceeded the limits of my chemistry knowledge, but he and Vivek were engaged in deep conversation. As an observer, all I was required to do was, every once in a while, nod or say something like "that's very interesting" out loud—to give the appear-ance that I knew what they were talking about. In fact, I had no idea what they were saying—except that Kibrick was suggesting that the chemistry underlying Plastiwear was an entirely new approach in the fiber and fabric business, fundamentally different from the chemistry of nylon, rayon, and the other miracle fibers of last century. He was also arguing that this approach could end up generating an entirely new family of fibers and fabrics, not just Plastiwear.

Finally, after almost thirty minutes of this technical conversation, I saw an opening for a more businesslike question.

"So, how did HGS happen to develop Plastiwear?"

Kibrick seemed surprised I was still in the room. "Well, to tell you the truth, we were lucky. Some R&D guys were working on some packaging technologies. We were conducting experiments on a new kind of plastic for toy packaging, and we tried a different approach to making the plastic. The results—at a chemical level—were quite surprising. At first, its commercial potential was not at all obvious. It just sat there in the flask—looked like white glue. But we began playing with it, found that we could get it formed into fibers. Going from fibers to fabric was simple. But then we made a big mistake."

"What was that?" I asked.

"We took the fabric and made it into a nice men's dress shirt. We thought this would get people's attention. And now for three years, some people can't stop talking about HGS going into the white shirt industry! That shirt turned attention away from this really cool technology. There is so much more here, technically speaking, that hasn't been considered."

"Have you had a chance to examine other commercial possibilities?" Vivek asked.

"That's what's in part two of this report. But I want to emphasize that this is a very tentative and, we're sure, very incomplete list. When you understand the full technical specs on this stuff, when you recognize that it can take the form of a liquid, a solid, can be made into fibers and weaved into cloth, that we have even begun experimenting with an aerosol version, when you really understand its chemical properties . . . white shirts! That's crazy!"

Kibrick took a quick breath and continued. "For example, did you know that Plastiwear is virtually unchanged by heat? It doesn't burn or melt. As a fabric, this has incredible potential in clothing and furniture. We're also looking into building materials—using Plastiwear fabric instead of paper as the outside layer of wallboard—you know, the stuff they use for interior walls in homes. It can be made as stiff and strong as paper, but stops fire from spreading. We're just now testing this application, and it's very exciting."

"No one has mentioned this to us before." I glanced over to Vivek, and he concurred.

"That's because no one outside this building has heard about it yet. We're in the early development phase. But, let me put it this way. Every

142

time I sit down with my people to discuss possible Plastiwear applications, we come up with another ten or fifteen ideas. We have far more ideas than manpower to test them. There are only five people on the Plastiwear team—five people exploring the most important technology HGS has ever developed! Can you believe it? And then I hear that the whole project may get canceled because someone thinks the white shirt market is too competitive." He cleared his throat and reached for his water.

At that moment it struck me that maybe some of Plastiwear's potential had leaked out of this building. Maybe that's how MG Management developed an interest in taking advantage of Plastiwear before its true potential was widely known. Maybe I was paranoid, but I wondered if any of the people on this team were in contact with MG Management.

Kibrick continued. "That's why part two of the report is so incomplete. More ideas than people or time. More potential than we can even describe. Why don't you come with me and meet the Plastiwear team?"

With that Kibrick stood up and moved from behind his desk, through the office door, and down to the left. Vivek and I followed.

"We're just about to run a test on the wallboard idea. I asked them to wait until we got there. Here's the lab."

We turned right into a laboratory, about sixty feet wide and a hundred feet long. The room was dominated by four large tables arrayed down the middle. As we stepped into the lab, Kibrick stopped us up short.

"You'll need these."

With that, he pulled two white lab coats from a closet along with three pairs of goggles.

"Put them on, gentlemen. We don't want any accidents here." To emphasize his point, Kibrick put on his own goggles.

Appropriately attired, we moved to the center of the room where a large clear container—maybe five feet square—sat on one of the tables, surrounded by two technicians dressed like us. Inside the container was a device—it looked like a mechanical claw of some sort—that held what before this meeting I would have assumed was a piece of traditional wallboard. It was held vertically by the claw, suspended over what looked like a butane torch. At first, I thought the torch wasn't on, but when I looked closer, I could just see its faint blue flame. It looked like the technicians were conducting a burn test. The flame was just touching the bottom of the wallboard. Next to the flame was a wire thermometer that was, in turn, connected to a monitor outside the clear container.

One of the technicians began by apologizing. "Sorry, Len. We decided to go ahead."

"It's OK. We were discussing some of the technical details of Plastiwear. How's the test going?"

"Going well so far. The temperature at the flame is 1,250 degrees, we have been running this test about fifteen minutes, and there is no noticeable degradation on the Plastiwear wallboard, neither on the Plastiwear cover nor of the material inside. Later on, we'll check this with the microscope, but so far, so good."

Vivek made the next observation. "But don't house fires really feed off the wood used in the frame? I mean, the wood burns, and that's what causes the house to burn, right?"

Kibrick turned to Vivek and smiled. "And you, my friend, have come up with another possible use of Plastiwear. Right now, in that room over there, we have half a dozen different kinds of commercial-grade lumber soaking in the liquid form of Plastiwear. The question is, can we use Plastiwear to make this wood fireproof? We don't know yet, but if I were to make a bet, I'd say yes. Now, how big is that market?"

After watching nothing happen in the test container for another five minutes, Vivek, Kibrick, and I went back to Kibrick's office. We continued talking about Plastiwear and what it would take to realize its full value for another fifteen minutes. At that point, Vivek brought the interview to a conclusion. We were well beyond the half hour I'd requested, and I was far more impressed than I'd expected to be.

"Thank you, Dr. Kibrick. Obviously, this has been very enlightening. Unfortunately, I need to get back downtown for my next appointment. But, again, I want to thank you for meeting us."

"Glad to. I just hope it makes a difference."

Kibrick escorted us to the foyer, and we returned our badges to Harriet. This time she called me John as Vivek and I went outside. The cab that brought us out from downtown was still there, waiting to take us back.

As we got in the back seat, Vivek seemed unusually energized, almost jumpy. He gave directions to the taxi driver, then turned to me. "So, Justin, what do you think?"

I tried to keep my cool. I wasn't going to get swept up in Kibrick's enthusiasm. Don't believe everything you hear. That's what Ken had told me. "I thought it was interesting. Lots of potential. What did you think?"

Vivek paused before he answered. When he spoke, he did so deliberately, thoughtfully. "I believe we may have caught a glimpse of the potential source of this firm's next core competence."

"What do you mean when you say 'core competence'?" I asked Vivek as our cab sat, barely crawling, in one of Chicago's continuous traffic snarls.

The term *core competence* was thrown around so much in business school that, to me, it had almost no meaning. I once heard a student saying that doing financial calculations was her "core competence." I heard a CEO of a very large company argue that his firm's culture was its "core competence." A professor told me about a CEO who announced to his division managers that if they couldn't show how their divisions contributed to the corporation's core competence, he would sell off or close their divisions. After six months, division managers identified, on average, over five hundred ways that they contributed to the corporation's core competence! In other words, for this, and so many companies, the term *core competence* had ceased to have any real meaning.

This was ironic because I thought I was now beginning to understand what having a core competence really meant—activities in the value chain that created economic value, that were rare among a firm's competitors, and that competitors found difficult to imitate. So, I was very interested in Vivek's answer to my question—what did he mean by core competence?

Ever the scientist, Vivek started from the beginning. "When the term was coined, it referred to value-creating activities that are unique to a particular firm, which other firms find difficult or impossible to duplicate.

145

Usually, these activities cut across multiple businesses or industries. When the firm is able to leverage these activities and processes at a best-in-class level to create and capture distinctive value, they are the firm's core competencies."

I nodded in agreement. In fact, Vivek's definition—not surprisingly—was very consistent with mine, even though I hadn't specifically thought about core competence activities cutting across multiple businesses.

Vivek eyed the taxi driver and continued. "Now, of course, 'P' is not an activity, it's a technology. Technologies, by themselves, are not core competencies. But actions firms take to exploit these technologies—if they are, what did you say in your notes from yesterday, rare and hard to imitate—can be core competencies. And they can sometimes be a source of sustained advantage."

"But we don't know, for sure, if exploiting P"—I adopted Vivek's shorthand to avoid saying the word *Plastiwear* in front of the cabbie—"will be valuable in these markets, and we don't know for sure that it will be rare and hard to imitate even if it is valuable."

"That's correct. That's why I said that we *might* be witnessing the emergence of a core competence. But, at this point, I am cautiously optimistic."

"Why do you say that?"

"Well, this morning, it became clear that if P delivers on its technical promise—and that is a big if—but if it delivers, it would be a significant improvement over products currently sold in multiple markets. And activities designed to exploit P have many attributes that may make them difficult for competitors to imitate."

"Such as?"

"Here, let me show you."

At this point, Vivek reached into his briefcase and pulled out a yellow legal pad. He began writing. "There are a number of reasons why it may be difficult for one firm to imitate the strategy of another firm." Vivek paused after he'd filled about half the page. "I'm sure you could derive a good list if we left you alone for a while, but let's use this one that's pretty standard in Business 101." He read down the pad quickly. "Team-based skills, legal restrictions on imitation, reputation, brand, switching costs, search costs, and application experience. These are the kinds of things that make it very difficult to imitate another firm's strategies."

"Do any of these apply to our client's situation?" I asked.

"Some of them might. For example, the client has a patent on P. That fits under legal restrictions on imitation."

"But will they be willing to spend the time and money required to enforce the patent?"

"If the technology is valuable enough, of course. At least they have that option since their patent controls a very specific molecule." Vivek tapped his legal pad. "Besides that, if the client decides to invest in an intense and extensive branding campaign for P—with an appropriate and better name—it will be even more difficult to imitate. Competitors would not only have to come up with a substitute technology—a fabric that was technically as good and that didn't violate patents—but would also have to invest in their own brand to compete head to head with P's branded offering, or enter the market unbranded at a lower price point."

Vivek put a check mark next to each attribute that seemed likely to apply to Plastiwear.

"Any others?"

"In some applications, P may be able to set the stage for high customer switching costs."

"What do you mean?"

"For example, in the bullet-resistant shirt market, if P catches on in areas where the threat from non–combat zone injuries is high and rising,

Vivek's notes on why a strategy may be difficult to imitate

1. Legal restrictions	4. Customer switching/search costs ✓
a. Patents ✓	5. Team skills ✓
b. Trademarks	6. Unique experience over time ✓
c. Copyrights	
2. Trade secrets	
3. Reputation and brand image ✓	

it could become the de facto standard for protective clothing—like Kleenex in tissues or Xerox in copies. Once P becomes the standard, it's easier for its customers—the DoD or police departments—to stay with it. The hassle of switching specifications and suppliers would have to be motivated by the perception of serious cost savings or aggressive competitive marketing by substitutes."

"That sounds promising, but goes way beyond just entering the protective clothing market."

Vivek nodded. "Obviously we want to prioritize and recommend where the client should compete—which markets and products. But we need a complete strategy—not just a market focus. That means we also need to recommend a set of decisions that support a successful entry and ensure the client's position will be defensible and profitable in those markets."

I'd been so caught up, first in whether or not to produce shirts, and next in determining which of the Plastiwear-based products might be most attractive, that I appreciated the reminder of what our broader mandate really was. Before I could comment, Vivek returned to his analysis.

Tapping his pad, he continued, "Their combination of team-based skills and experience with the technology could be really powerful. I was really impressed with the teamwork in the R&D center—and obviously they have in-depth experience with the technology and its various applications, which are growing daily. Those scientists are on a mission! Another firm might have some difficulty duplicating that kind of effort. At the very least, it would take some time to catch up to this firm's experience with this molecule."

"So, on balance, you think that P may be difficult for other firms to imitate," I said. Vivek's enthusiasm was measured, but undeniably contagious. Still, I didn't want to get accused of "drinking the Kool-Aid" of the R&D guys. Sure, it didn't burn—but would it sell? So my next comment was cautious. "Well, to me, it seems a bit early to say that we have a new core competence here. So far, the only product prototype we've seen is the white shirt. And entering that market seems very complicated."

"You're right on that point. It's going to take a great deal of work to realize P's potential. Lots of tough strategic decisions have to be made and implemented. Many activities and incentives will need to align.

Only time will tell." Vivek made some more notes as we rode in silence. After a few minutes he looked up from his pad.

"You know, that teamwork argument may cut both ways."

"What do you mean?"

"Well, in general, teamwork within a firm—like what we saw in the R&D lab—is costly to imitate. But lack of teamwork can prevent a technology like P from being exploited. So far, I haven't seen much effective teamwork among the top managers. Have you?" Now Vivek was deep in thought, and his voice trailed off.

This time I broke the silence. "Without unified senior management support, can P still give rise to a new core competence?"

"It will be tough. Management will have to agree on a number of critical issues, including how much they are willing to invest and how much risk they will tolerate. How long they'll wait for payback and how they'll organize to exploit Plastiwear will also be critical."

Our conversation was interrupted by the formalities of paying the cab and passing through security back at HGS headquarters. Vivek paid again—I didn't offer, since I hadn't actually received a paycheck yet. We headed back up to the team room together.

Livia was gone, so Vivek took on the role of making assignments. "So, why don't you synthesize our notes from that interview and our discussions?"

"Given how little I understood the chemistry . . ."

"That's right." Vivek shook his head and cut me off. "I'll go ahead and do the write-up. You can continue to push the analysis. Obviously, there is a lot of work to be done there."

Vivek and I each immediately dove into our respective workstreams. But as I was checking facts about the earthquake construction market, I couldn't help but reflect on my conversation with Vivek in the cab. If Vivek was right, this was a singular moment in the history of HGS. If and how Carl and his top management team developed Plastiwear's potential would go a long way toward determining the future of this company for the next decade, or even beyond. Thousands, maybe tens of thousands, of jobs were on the line, along with whatever benefits the broad application of Plastiwear might generate for consumers around the world.

Suddenly, it struck me that I wasn't just trying to "crack the case." I was actually helping to shape the future of a corporation—and all those who depended, or who might depend, on it and its products.

Completing the opportunity scan worksheet suddenly took on a whole new meaning. What we were doing in that room wasn't just an exercise. Especially if taking advantage of Plastiwear contributed to a new competence for HGS. It could actually make a real difference.

REFLECTION QUESTIONS

1. Is there a difference between a technology that has several product uses and a core competence? Explain your answer.

2. How do you think senior managers at HGS would respond to Vivek's use of a "Business 101" checklist?

3. Should HGS increase the Plastiwear R&D staff? If yes, when, and how significantly?

4. What are some likely barriers to effective top management teamwork at HGS?

5. Do you think Justin's hunch about an information leak has any foundation in reality?

6. How do you expect Justin's realization that his work might "make a real difference" will impact his behavior on the strategy team?

— 11 —

A GOOD CALL

Vivek and I worked on the interview notes and opportunity analyses through dinner, until almost 9:00 p.m. At that point, I was fried. Vivek, of course, was going strong. But I needed a break.

"Vivek. Listen, I need a short break. I told Ken that I would call him. I think I'll do that now."

"Thanks for letting me know. I'll keep working."

Geez, that's all Vivek ever does—he keeps working. Not only was I impressed by Vivek's intelligence and time management skills—which were awesome—I was blown away by his stamina. I wondered if I would ever be able to work that hard.

Probably not.

I stepped into the hallway so I wouldn't disturb Vivek. Also, given my last phone call with Ken—when was that? Oh yeah, yesterday! But given that call, I thought a little privacy was a good idea, in case it didn't go well. Also, before I called, I wanted to review what I wanted to say to Ken—my talking points for this phone call.

So, I found a comfortable seat next to a floor-to-ceiling window overlooking Lake Michigan and Lake Shore Drive. Usually, I pretend not to notice the view. But tonight, sitting by myself, I began to gaze out the window. I suddenly thought of my bumpy plane ride on Sunday. Like that night, I could see cars and people, all hurrying to go somewhere. They say that New York never sleeps. Neither, apparently, does Chicago.

It was only five days ago that turbulence had disturbed my flight into Chicago and led me to question whether I'd over-reached in taking this job. After all, if I was honest with myself, I didn't really know much. What I knew, every good MBA student and plenty of practicing managers in the world know. How could I tell clients what to do when, really, I didn't know much myself?

What was becoming clearer to me now was that the value I was adding as a consultant was not that I knew more than anyone else. I definitely didn't. I may know some different things, but the people inside HGS would always know more than I would about HGS and its products, customers, and employees. My value-add was that I could evaluate business alternatives independently and objectively, that I worked with a team of extremely smart people who could get access to a great deal of good information, and that we had the time to focus on the future of this company rather than being caught up in the day-to-day responsibilities of running it.

Our objective third-party perspective was particularly important. We needed to steer clear of historical biases, unfounded assumptions, and political influence inside HGS and conduct a thorough and useful analysis.

I knew Ken didn't need a play-by-play of my contributions to the analysis so far. He kept abreast of the project's progress via Vivek's frequent reports and my not-so-frequent postings. I wanted to use this call to let him know that I now more clearly understood my role on the strategy team.

Looking at the streets below, I wondered how these people, these millions of people, would respond if HGS really took advantage of Plastiwear. Would it change their lives? Would it save lives and property? How many jobs would it create? And what if HGS didn't exploit Plastiwear? Would anyone know? Would they care? Would HGS remain an independent company? Would it grow and provide a secure source of income for its employees?

My dad was laid off from his factory job when I was ten years old. I never found out the details, but I remember the look on his face when I came home from school that day. He looked like he had failed all of us. It didn't last long—that look of failure. He started up his own feed store shortly afterward, and it's grown into the biggest feed and ranch products store in the county. But for the first few weeks after he was laid off, my dad thought he was a failure.

I must be tired. I hadn't thought about these feelings in years. Time to call Ken. I reached into my pocket and punched his cell number into my mobile. After three rings, he answered.

"Hello, Ken McCombs."

"Hi, Ken. It's Justin Campbell."

"Hi, Justin."

"Is this a good time to talk? I thought I might bring you up to date on the project."

"Yes, I have a couple of minutes. Go ahead."

"First, I wanted to thank you for the feedback you gave me last night. It wasn't fun, but I needed to hear it."

"Good, I'm glad you've got that attitude toward feedback, Justin. In this business, the ability to receive and process feedback is critical to your team and to your professional growth."

"Well, it gave me a lot to think about. Speaking of which, I think we've made good progress on the engagement."

"I spoke to Livia earlier tonight. She told me about the analysis you did on your own. She appreciated how you worked with her and Vivek to integrate your work and theirs. Getting multiple perspectives on this data is very important." He paused, and I thought he said something to someone else; then he continued, "She seemed to think you preferred to alternate between working alone and with the team, so it also sounds like you're getting to know your own work style as well."

I let that comment slide, although it wasn't really accurate. Livia was within her rights to spin things a bit. Instead, I focused on the analysis. "When we brought the analyses together, it became clear where we had to get more data, what our priorities need to be. I had tended to focus on growth projections, while they fleshed out obstacles on the cost side more fully."

"I also understand that you and Vivek went on an interview this afternoon."

"Yes, and a good thing he was there. Our appointment was with the chemist in charge of exploring product options with Plastiwear. To tell you the truth, most of the chemistry was way over my head. But Vivek was eating it up."

"It's good to be surrounded, and not intimidated, by really smart people, like Vivek. He is a well-rounded consultant, but he also has depth in one field—in his case it's chemistry. That's something you'll need to do, continue to be well rounded, but figure out where your unique area of strength is. Every successful consultant I know has a world-class spike of expertise in some area."

I could hear more voices in the background when Ken paused.

"It's probably too early to figure out where that spike is for me, but I see why it's important."

"Good. So, give me the one-line summary of what you learned from the chemist."

"Well," I had to give credit where it was due, "Vivek thinks that HGS's ability to exploit Plastiwear may actually be the source of a new core competence for them. We discussed that possibility in the cab on the way back to HGS."

"Good. I'll look forward to reading your notes later. Have you had a chance to reflect on what we talked about last night?"

I'd been dreading this question. I knew it was coming, but really didn't want to get into it. All I could say was what I had just thought of, about ten minutes before, as I was looking out the window. "Well, I think I've figured out a couple of things. First, I'll never know as much about HGS and Plastiwear as the people inside HGS. So, what a consultant like me brings to the discussion is not this depth of knowledge—although I do have to get up to speed to some extent and evaluate information in an objective and independent way. Where I can add value is in separating the politics and process of decision making from the content and logic of decision making."

"Good; anything else?" Ken sounded busy, but he kept asking me questions.

"Yes, one other thing. I thought this job was kind of like 'me against the problem.' It isn't. What became clear today is that while each of us works a lot on our own, the real value is created when we figure out how to take this individual work and bring it together, integrate it. This is something that managers at HGS—because of day-to-day demands on their time, incentives to focus on short-term metrics, competition for internal resources, and their own and their divisions' agendas—have a harder time doing. But it's something that our team should excel at."

"Justin, those are some useful insights. Sounds like you've had a productive day. Get some rest and let's see what you come up with tomorrow."

"Thanks, Ken."

"OK, Justin. I'll talk with you soon."

———————

The phone call with Ken was a great improvement. "Sounds like you've had a productive day" wasn't the most effusive feedback I'd ever received, but it was positive. Of course, compared to the last call, any positive feedback was a great improvement.

After finishing up with Ken, I went back to the team room, and Vivek and I continued working on the opportunity matrix. Around 11:00, we shifted our attention to updating the work plan. We now knew most of the information we needed to get and how it would be integrated into our final analysis. There was still a lot of work to do, including issues we had barely even considered. For instance, how would the fiber and fabric be made? How would it be sold and distributed? How would the Plastiwear business be organized and managed? Who would lead the Plastiwear launch? How much investment would be needed to succeed in this business? Many of the answers to our questions raised additional questions, and the costs, risks, and feasibility of our strategic options were all important, but difficult to assess. We were continuously prioritizing our work to focus on where the key insights were most likely to be found. There was no way we were going to answer every question—and it would be crazy to try.

Vivek encouraged me to group the questions logically, rather than just make longer and longer lists. I had to admit, I appreciated his ability to drive the analysis forward while simultaneously considering our future audience and their particular concerns. In the team room, Vivek and I weren't constantly interacting, but we'd share insights as we came up with them, and share problems as well for a quick huddle. We—well, I—avoided quite a bit of unnecessary and redundant work by touching base frequently and informally. It may have slowed the "iron man" down, but working this way was surprisingly efficient for me.

By 1:00 a.m., I felt I had done all I could do that day. Of course, Vivek was still going strong, but I had hit a wall. I excused myself and headed back to my hotel room. Chicago, at least this part of Chicago, had finally settled down. There were only a couple of cabs circulating the streets as I crossed from the HGS building to my hotel. I could see no one else on the block or two that separated these two buildings. In the dark, in the midst of this quiet Chicago scene, I suddenly felt a pang of intense loneliness, like I was all alone in the world.

Here I was, working upwards of eighteen hours a day, mostly by myself. My only connections with other human beings were with Vivek and Bill, every once in a while with Livia and a disembodied Ken on the phone, and with the people we interviewed. Gordon hadn't even checked in the past day or so. I spent most of my time talking to people I don't know about business opportunities I don't fully understand. Either that or reading reports written by experts and other consultants, people who have also been working eighteen-hour days for who knows how long. Sure, my conversation with Ken tonight had been a boost, but was that really enough to justify the intellectual and emotional commitment I had made to this job and this client? I had been on this assignment for four days. How could I possibly have burned out already?

I entered the lobby of my hotel. When I first arrived here, I thought of this hotel as a virtual palace. Now, I barely noticed the floors, the woodwork, the chandeliers. It was just a place to sleep. Burned out, cynical, and spoiled, all in less than ninety-six hours. What would I be like after several years on this job?

The elevator took me swiftly to my floor. Normally, the classical music playing softly throughout the public spaces in the hotel soothed me. Tonight, Vivaldi in the elevators was just too much.

Finally, my floor. The elevator door opened to an almost eerie silence. Vivaldi was replaced by the sound of my blood rushing through my veins. After a second, I realized it wasn't my blood—it was the smooth whisper of the air conditioning.

I decided I was tired.

I fumbled with my electronic key, hoping it still worked. They sometimes lose their magnetic charge after a few days, especially when in close contact with cell phones and BlackBerries, and have to be recharged. Tonight, I wanted to get into my room with no difficulties, no hassles. The little green light on the lock illuminated, and I gratefully opened the door and entered. To drown out the silence of my room, I turned on the television—CNN, of course.

I was changing into my pajamas when the phone rang—a startling electronic screech at one in the morning. I immediately thought that it must be bad news. No one calls this late unless it's bad news—someone is sick, been in an accident, died. As I made my way to the phone, I realized that in this bizarre consulting world, a 1:00 a.m. phone call would not be that unusual. It could be Vivek with some questions, or one of the experts I had e-mailed answering a question.

"Hello, this is Justin Campbell." I answered the phone with the demeanor expected of a strategy professional about to provide some profound insights to a colleague. Instead of Vivek's or a stranger's voice, I heard a woman speak.

"Hi, Justin. It's me, Jackie."

Suddenly, all my loneliness fell away. My spirits lifted. I was still tired, but now I was tired and happy.

"Boy, it's great to hear your voice."

"I hope it's not too late."

"No, no. It's not too late. I'm just getting back to my room, just now."

"I didn't want to interrupt you with a cell call, so I've been calling your room about every thirty minutes since eleven your time." Jackie sounded curious and ventured playfully, "Coming in late after a wild night on the town?"

"I wish. More like another boring night in the team room."

"How did it go today?"

"Pretty well, I think." I gave Jackie some observations on Vivek, the "iron man," and some highlights of my recent adventures.

"Any more conversations with your boss—what's his name?"

"Ken. Yeah, we spoke this evening. But, this time, it went well. I told him some things that I had learned."

"About the client or about yourself?"

"A little of both." I quickly summarized my conversation with Ken.

"How did he react to what you said?"

"He said that it sounded like I had had a productive day—high praise from him, I think. Maybe I'm beginning to sound like a real strategy professional."

She chuckled a bit. "What does that mean?"

"Oh, you know. A real know-it-all attitude, arrogant, cynical," I joked.

"Yep, that's you all right."

"Seriously, I could see that type of attitude being an occupational hazard."

"That will never happen to you."

"Why not?"

"I won't let it. I won't let you become all high and mighty and self-important."

"How can you stop me?"

"Oh, I don't know. Maybe by forcing you to tell me how you feel about me, instead of about your fancy job." She was teasing, and I joined in.

"How I feel about you? I haven't even had time to think about you!"

"Well, that's not very nice." She actually sounded hurt.

"I will tell you this, though, Jackie. Tonight, I don't know. Maybe it's because I'm tired. Maybe it's just a let-down after my talk with Ken. Maybe it's just this job—too much work, too much pressure. Whatever, I was pretty down when I came back to my room tonight. When the phone rang, I assumed it was a member of the team, asking me a question."

"They would do that at 1:00 a.m.?"

"They haven't yet. But it wouldn't surprise me. Anyway, I was really down. And then when I picked up the phone and heard your voice . . . well, it was really nice. It changed everything. I was so glad it was you."

"You know why, don't you?"

"Why?"

"Because you love me."

"You're right about that."

REFLECTION QUESTIONS

1. How do you think Justin's new perspective on the consultant's role will influence his work going forward?

2. Why did Livia "spin" her report to Ken about Justin's "lone ranger" approach to working? What other options did she likely consider?

3. Is Justin's emotional state a problem for the strategy team? Why or why not?

4. If you were in Jackie's position, would a long-term relationship with Justin seem viable? Why or why not?

5. How do you think Justin's new perspective on this engagement—that it could actually affect people's lives—will influence his work going forward?

— 12 —

A CONSTRUCTIVE
MEETING

Fortified with some sleep and the reassuring knowledge that there was still life outside HGS, I rejoined Vivek and Livia the next morning. For much of the next two days we focused on analyzing potential Plastiwear opportunities in different product segments. Bill also provided us with some helpful insights, especially about HGS. Even Gordon was finally able to break away from his other obligations. Normally we wouldn't work through the weekend. But because of the time crunch, we had no choice.

After a brief conversation, the strategy team—including Bill—decided that it made sense to try out our recommendations on Walter Albright, the VP of R&D. He was more knowledgeable about Plastiwear than anyone else on the top management team, so his feedback would be helpful. Besides, I thought that if there was going to be a major investment in Plastiwear, he'd probably be the one to lead it. Might as well get him on board sooner rather than later.

Livia asked me to arrange a time on Monday afternoon for the strategy team to meet with Albright. He was available at 3:30, so we had until then to finish the first draft of the slides that would summarize our work to date.

I had used the term "first draft" in describing our objective for the weekend in front of Livia. Her response was pointed.

"This will not be a first draft. It will be complete and rigorous. Our conversation with Albright on Monday will probably generate some additional ideas that will require new analyses that we may decide to incorporate into further versions of the presentation. But there will be nothing 'drafty' about what we pull together."

So the bar was set pretty high. But it had to be high. Our final presentation to the CEO and the top management team was going to be at 4:00 p.m. on Wednesday, just two days after our internal presentation to Albright. To be ready Wednesday, we needed to be in good shape Monday.

After the first three days of the project, when I worked alone, I found the days working with the strategy team enjoyable. They were professional, thorough, intelligent, and incredibly focused.

On Friday afternoon, I remembered how I had once speculated about a possible romantic relationship between Livia and Ken. Of course, that idea came just after a tough phone call with Ken, when I was mad at both of them. But any doubts I had had about Livia's motives or abilities were more than put to rest after working closely with her. Truth be told, I had a lot to learn from both Livia and Vivek, and not just about this project, but about strategic analysis and management consulting in general.

Bill was amazing, too. He didn't have the same quantitative and analytical skills as our team, but his in-depth understanding of HGS was invaluable. Several times in our discussion, his knowledge was critical in making sure that the team's analysis passed an "HGS commonsense test." Any reservations I had about trusting him—"Carl's spy"—evaporated as I watched him pitch in with no holds barred.

Before we could flesh out the "deck"—the PowerPoint slides for our presentation—the team had to discuss the set of feasible strategic alternatives that HGS faced with Plastiwear. Livia led that discussion Friday evening.

––––––––

Livia began the meeting by referring to some handwritten notes. She started down her list. "So, fairly quickly we can get to the point that the Plastiwear opportunity has relatively little to do with white shirts." We all nodded in agreement.

Gordon summarized the group's conclusions. "It may turn out that white shirts are an important use of Plastiwear, but they're certainly

A CONSTRUCTIVE MEETING

Livia's notes for the Friday night team briefing

Team meeting

1. Review due diligence on white shirts
2. Revisit value capture options re: Plastiwear

   a. Sale of technology
   b. License of technology
   c. Deployment of technology internally

3. Consider downstream opportunities (Plastiwear-based products)

   a. Manufacture Plastiwear-based products
   b. Retail Plastiwear-based products to consumers

4. Explore upstream opportunities (fiber and/or fabric)

   a. Make—HGS to manufacture
   b. Buy—contract with manufacturer(s)
   c. Ally—partner with manufacturer(s)

5. Identify customer segments

   a. Agree on evaluative criteria

6. Consider governance of Plastiwear

   a. Part of oil and gas BU
   b. Part of packaging BU
   c. Freestanding BU

not its most critical strategic application. Most of the work in HGS focused only on white shirts and really missed this point."

"It did take us off on a wild goose chase," I observed, remembering my early interviews with some chagrin.

"So," Livia continued, "let's look at HGS's options with Plastiwear. Rather than debate the potential of its various applications right now, let's start by assuming that it will deliver on its technical promises in at least some market segments. Fundamentally, HGS needs to choose how it wants to extract value from this new technology. For example, the company could sell Plastiwear outright, for a lump sum, or license the rights to use it in exchange for an ongoing revenue stream."

"That's what the private equity firm would probably do," interrupted Gordon.

"Perhaps," Livia continued, "but Vivek and I have done some analysis that suggests that HGS will probably want to deploy Plastiwear itself." She nodded, and Vivek took the floor.

Vivek began by passing out some pages that synthesized his analysis. "As you can see from the first page, an outright sale of Plastiwear might be possible. We developed a list of potential buyers. But the problem here is getting a good price for such an untested technology. Also, if HGS sells the technology now, it loses any real options that might be embedded in a Plastiwear initiative—the buyer gets all the upside. Our guess is that Carl has already come to this conclusion, which is why he turned away at least one overture from a potential buyer."

I was stunned. I hadn't heard that there was anyone interested in buying Plastiwear. Early in the engagement, I had fallen behind reading the notes and documents posted by the rest of the team, but in the last forty-eight hours I thought I had caught up, and no one had mentioned a possible sale of Plastiwear.

Gordon leaned over, recognizing my distressed look, and winked. "Hey, Justin, don't worry. This part of the engagement was shared strictly on a 'need to know' basis. HGS just isn't that good at maintaining confidentiality, so we had to be more careful than usual."

Vivek continued. "You can see on the next two slides that licensing presents similar problems. We've worked up a range of estimates, along with some potential licensees, but in the most realistic scenarios, attractive returns just aren't likely. So, I agree with Livia. We should be able to focus pretty quickly on how HGS should deploy Plastiwear itself."

Livia took over. "Thanks, Vivek. Any questions?"

Livia looked around the room. Everyone seemed satisfied with Vivek's logic. I was still getting used to the idea that there were some important facts about this engagement I didn't know. But I needed to concentrate on the issues at hand and decided to do a Scarlett O'Hara—I would think about that tomorrow.

Livia continued. "OK. Vivek and I will button up this analysis and get it in the deck."

Livia ticked off a line on her notes and began again. "Now, let's look at Plastiwear's value chain and see where HGS might develop and sustain a competitive advantage. Let's start downstream, with making consumer products and retail sales. Does HGS have distinctly valuable and hard-to-imitate skills in these stages of the value chain?"

I knew a lot about HGS's skill base—or lack of skill base—in these stages of the value chain, so was the first to answer. "I just don't see it. Whether we're talking about tents, construction materials, shirts, or whatever, HGS has no experience in most of these markets—it doesn't currently manufacture these kinds of products and has no experience whatsoever in retail sales. No distinctive value here, and nothing difficult to imitate. These customers are mostly unfamiliar to HGS, and the inventory management and other skills the company would need to operate in this space are really different from the expertise in the oil and gas and packaging divisions. Jumping into any of these markets is just an extension of the kind of 'white shirt' logic we've already rejected." I was pleased—and a bit relieved—when I realized that we might be able to use some of the work we had done on white shirts to help show that HGS shouldn't go into consumer product manufacturing or retail sales.

Gordon agreed with my summary and added, "Of course, that doesn't mean that HGS should sell Plastiwear to any downstream company that wants to use it in their products. If HGS wants to brand Plastiwear as, what was it—the miracle fiber of the twenty-first century—it's going to need to restrict the use of Plastiwear to higher-end products, products that help differentiate Plastiwear in the consumer's mind."

Bill observed, "Most people we talked to seemed to support the idea of branding Plastiwear, but no one really talked about how to do this or, as important, the implications of this branding strategy for the kinds of Plastiwear products HGS should explore."

"Great point, Bill." Livia seemed very impressed by Bill's observations. "We can't lose track of this, even though our recommendation is probably going to be that they don't move downstream, toward their ultimate consumers. Can you run through the deck and amplify this message where you think it would make sense?"

Bill looked directly at Livia as he considered her request. "Of course."

"You know, Livia," I wondered aloud, "it might be necessary for HGS to manufacture some Plastiwear products itself. Maybe not at scale, but more than just as prototypes, to create some buzz about the technology. Didn't the guys who invented nylon start by making their own nylon stockings?"

"I don't know about nylon, but there are other examples where breaking into new markets required extensive sampling," was Livia's reply. "Justin, it should be easy for you to get some facts on how other 'miracle fabrics' managed their market entry strategies. Just make sure you choose some that make sense in today's environment." She didn't wait for me to agree to the assignment before she moved on.

"That leads us to the next item." Livia was very task-oriented today. "Upstream manufacturing options. Vivek, I know you've thought a great deal about this."

Vivek stood up and went to the whiteboard. "Thanks, Livia. So, based on what we've said here, let's assume we can rule out retailing—selling directly to customers—and we also can rule out downstream manufacturing, like shirts." He began drawing a diagram on the board while he talked. "Now let's summarize the upstream manufacturing options for Plastiwear."

"There are three basic ways to participate in manufacturing—make, buy, or ally. Make means HGS builds its own plant for Plastiwear production or uses excess plant capacity that's already available within HGS to make Plastiwear. Buy means it outsources and relies on outside firms to make Plastiwear. Ally is the blended option where it works closely with one or more manufacturing firms in an alliance or a joint venture to make Plastiwear. And then, each of these options needs to be evaluated relative to both fiber manufacture and fabric manufacture."

The result of Vivek's minilecture on manufacturing Plastiwear was a simple two-by-three matrix.

"Good; thanks, Vivek." Livia moved the discussion forward. "So, what are the advantages and disadvantages of each of these options?"

Gordon answered this question with another question. "Are there any advantages, from a manufacturing point of view, to having the fiber and fabric operations co-located? For example, is it hard to transport the fiber? Does there have to be continuous feedback between fabric and fiber operations—you know, to ensure the quality of the fiber being produced, control inventories, and so forth?"

Vivek's matrix of upstream manufacturing options

	Make	Buy	Ally
Fiber			
Fabric			

I knew part of the answer to that question. "Nothing major. Currently, HGS makes small amounts of the fiber at its packaging division plant. Weaving is outsourced to a small firm working at arm's length. Of course, none of this is done at scale, so we don't know if there would be advantages to physically linking, or co-locating, these two stages of the value chain at scale."

Bill asked the next question. "Do we know if other fiber and fabric firms co-locate these operations?"

He looked around the room at blank stares for only a couple seconds before Livia spoke. "OK, that's something we'll need to know. Justin, get us comparables on that before tomorrow, will you?"

I nodded, and Vivek took the floor again. "I agree that the links between fiber and fabric manufacturing are important issues. But strategically, I think the advantages and disadvantages of these different approaches to manufacturing—make, buy, or ally—are similar for both fiber and fabric products."

Livia responded, "Say more, Vivek."

"Well, how manufacturing is organized could potentially have three important effects on HGS. First, it may have an impact on the quality and the cost of the Plastiwear that is produced. Second, it may have an impact on HGS's ability to continue to learn about new Plastiwear uses. Finally, it may have an impact on HGS's ability to retain control of its Plastiwear intellectual property."

I was confused. It almost sounded like Vivek was arguing for making Plastiwear in-house. That's not what he—or Livia—seemed to suggest earlier in the week. So, I asked, "Are you arguing for producing Plastiwear in-house?"

"Not necessarily," Vivek replied. "It seems to me that HGS could get high-quality, low-cost fabric by outsourcing manufacturing and still position itself to explore new uses of this technology. In fact, outsourcing manufacturing might help—if HGS works with high-volume fiber/fabric manufacturing firms, their contractors may do a better job making Plastiwear than HGS could. This would let HGS focus on finding new uses for Plastiwear and working with downstream firms to develop those uses into products. No, I'm mostly worried about the impact of outsourcing manufacturing on HGS's IP, at least until the company is able to brand Plastiwear."

Gordon didn't seem convinced. "I agree with you about the intellectual property, but if you outsource manufacturing, especially internationally, don't you risk losing control of costs and quality?"

Vivek did seem convinced. "Competition across multiple potential suppliers, contracts, and working closely with selected outside suppliers can provide the same level of control as manufacturing in-house. Look, if this stuff does turn out to be the 'miracle fiber of the twenty-first century,' then HGS won't have problems finding firms willing to invest to make high-quality/low-cost Plastiwear. The problem is that HGS simply hasn't developed the skills to manufacture high-quality/low-cost Plastiwear at scale. You saw Justin's notes on the current manufacturing operations—they're laboratory experiments, not real manufacturing. And manufacturing fibers and fabrics are really different from their other businesses."

"So," Gordon continued in his devil's advocate role, "how can they outsource manufacturing and not lose control of their IP? They would have to reveal all their secrets to any firms that manufactured Plastiwear—both in making Plastiwear and in exploring its possible uses. Even with a patent, these firms could build on HGS's work and come out with their own new fibers and fabrics. Heck, HGS is just barely able to keep this stuff confidential as it is. Share the technology with these suppliers—it would soon be all over the Web."

Now Bill chimed in. "In fact, this may already be happening. Have you heard of Zwanziger Fabrics—an Israeli firm that makes industrial specialty textiles?" No one in the room had.

"Well," Bill continued, "I just found out today that they have introduced a new fabric product that—they claim—has many of the same attributes as Plastiwear. They don't name Plastiwear directly, but . . . "

I was shocked to hear this news. Had HGS been trumped? Had this company—Zwanziger Fabrics—impinged on HGS's patent? I wondered—did this new development undermine our entire strategic analysis?

Livia was calmer. "Really appreciate that information, Bill. Justin, will you follow up on this company and see what's going on."

I agreed to look into this bombshell, although no one else seemed as panicked as I felt.

Gordon wasn't panicked, but he did sound concerned. "Let's make sure we've really done our due diligence on competitors—both copycats and innovators with their own technologies." Then he turned back to Vivek. "Look, we've convinced ourselves that Plastiwear is headed toward a profitable market space; obviously other firms might come to a similar conclusion."

"That's why maintaining control of this technology is so important." Now Vivek began to turn the conversation back to upstream manufacturing. "If HGS outsources manufacturing, it could be giving away this control. Personally, I think it might make sense for HGS to form some sorts of alliances or joint ventures with manufacturing firms. Maybe these alliances could be constructed to protect HGS's IP while still getting access to low-cost/high-quality manufacturing. It's at least worth exploring. Besides, there's another reason to explore this option."

Vivek continued. "Suppose HGS formed a joint venture with a firm in, say, Mexico or Costa Rica or some other low-cost location. This could be a fifty-fifty joint venture—and this is important—where HGS maintains the right to buy out its partner, depending on the performance of the venture, for some period of time, say three years. This partner brings manufacturing expertise to the table, expertise in fiber and fabrics manufacturing. The JV jointly invests in a factory just big enough to realize economies of scale. Let's say half the capital is put up by HGS, half by the partner. This limits HGS's downside risk—not as much as outsourcing would, but still quite a bit. It also enables HGS to control its intellectual property—not as well as vertical integration might, but still pretty well. If Plastiwear turns out to be a great product, then HGS can decide whether to fully vertically integrate or fully outsource. If it decides to make fibers and fabric, HGS buys out its partner. If Plastiwear runs into serious obstacles, you close or repurpose the factory, and HGS is only partially liable. This kind of JV creates real options for HGS—the option to expand and the option to exit—in the Plastiwear market."

It looked like Gordon was beginning to come around, but he had one more question. "Do we know if there are any potential alliance partners in this space?"

Bill nodded and slowly replied, "I don't see that as being a problem."

Livia seemed skeptical. "With a number of my clients, finding JV partners—especially capable, trustworthy ones—was often a big problem."

"Well, in Mexico, we worked closely with several firms, a couple of which have fiber and fabric operations. If Plastiwear is as exciting as we think it is, I have contacts who might be interested in beginning a conversation about a JV. They might go for it."

"Can you create some materials describing those possibilities?" Livia asked, and moved on almost before Bill's quick affirmative nod. She then continued. "OK, it seems we're getting closer to a recommendation on this topic area. Vivek, I would like you and Bill, after we're done here, to work on fleshing out those arguments, including some estimates on cost, risk, and timing."

Vivek made some notes on the whiteboard. "No problem, Livia. You up for that, Bill?"

"Absolutely."

Now I added my two cents. "But what about the excess capacity in packaging?"

Vivek had obviously thought of this already. "If there was a compelling reason to vertically integrate the production of Plastiwear, it would make sense to at least consider the use of this extra capacity. But, if there isn't a compelling reason to vertically integrate, in general, then there also isn't a compelling reason to vertically integrate into the packaging division.

Even if it is beneficial for the packaging division, if it doesn't help Plastiwear achieve its potential, then I wouldn't really consider that option. Just because you can do it, doesn't mean you should."

I briefly wondered if Vivek had learned that phrase from *his* mother.

"OK." Livia wasn't slowing her pace at all. "We've estimated the profit potential of different Plastiwear applications. My sense is that we know something about four or five potential applications in three important segments—clothing, construction, and recreation."

Gordon responded, "We know something, but we really aren't in a position yet to do any detailed analysis of the cash flows associated with specific applications within these segments, like earthquake fabric for office buildings versus fireproof residential wallboard wrappings."

Everyone nodded in agreement. Despite the hours we had put in, we really hadn't gone beyond a first cut on Plastiwear applications in these—or any other—segments, and to do a good job on estimating the potential of new products in new markets would require significant additional work.

Livia continued. "Although we can't do detailed cash flow analyses, we can still give HGS some sense of the relative size, growth potential, and possible profitability of these market segments. Justin, I want you to work with Gordon to explore the potential profitability of these three markets in a way that will resonate with HGS's managers."

Gordon seemed excited about this possibility. "I've done similar analyses for other clients. We can define the general parameters of the competitive landscape in a segment and estimate a range of demand for Plastiwear in each—high, medium, and low estimates—and then make some simple assumptions about the cost of delivering Plastiwear at different levels of demand. We can then project sales based on high, medium, and low levels of market penetration—multiplied by the size of the market, giving us potential revenues. Then, it's simple arithmetic to get some sense of the range of possible pretax income that Plastiwear might generate in different segments. Justin, your research should help us estimate the costs of developing products, marketing, distribution, and so forth."

Gordon paused for a quick breath before continuing. "We can then present our results in terms of the range of profitability that HGS might be able to expect in both start-up and launch phase, and also in some steady state in the future. We could do a similar kind of exercise for each Plastiwear segment the team has identified. I think we already have most of the data we need to do this."

I wondered where the extra two days to get this done was going to come from, but no one else seemed fazed.

"That would be great." Livia seemed pleased with this approach. "We know there is significant profit potential for Plastiwear under certain assumptions, but your sensitivity analysis will give people an idea of how large or small this potential might be, and what will most influence these outcomes. Our audience is going to be looking for an analysis of how much risk will be associated with launching Plastiwear. Is it a 'bet the company' move, or just another large project? Remember, our audience has a lot to lose if they jeopardize their current operations while trying to get Plastiwear up and running."

"You mean, could it destroy the firm?" I said, and without thinking about the additional work it would create, asked, "Do you want us to model a worst-case scenario?"

"We need to be ready to respond to questions about risk. But I don't expect a doomsday snapshot will make it into our presentation deck." Livia paused and then adopted a more cautious tone. "Just remember, don't overpromise on this analysis. This is still just about identifying future research priorities, not providing any guarantees about future levels of profitability. When we get your slides, we'll circle back to these issues to make sure we've done all we can at this time."

Both Gordon and I nodded. I looked at Gordon and said, "Sounds like fun. I sure wish I knew how to use spreadsheets."

Gordon grimaced at my feeble joke, but I got a quick smile from Bill.

Livia summed up what was beginning to seem like a daunting amount of work very briefly before continuing down her checklist. "All right, Vivek will finish the section on manufacturing—making the case for a joint venture in fiber and/or fabric, and Gordon will lead the work needed to demonstrate the profit potential of three or four possible market segments. Bill and Justin, I think your roles are clear on these and the other, smaller deliverables we've identified. The next question that has come up several times is—assuming it goes forward as a business—how should Plastiwear be organized within HGS? At least three possibilities exist—as a part of the oil and gas products division, as a part of the packaging division, or as a separate business unit reporting to Carl."

"It could also be kept as part of the R&D operation, with no change," observed Vivek.

"Good point. So, Bill, you have the most experience here with HGS. What do you think?"

"Well, when I started with this team, I thought that Plastiwear could be incorporated into one of the current divisions, just as another product line. But I've changed my mind about this, for two reasons. First— and I think Albright talked to Justin about this—the oil and gas and packaging divisions are both good at exploiting current technologies and innovating incrementally, especially the oil and gas division. But Plastiwear is something completely new for our firm. We are going to be exploring new markets, some of which HGS will actually need to create. You put that kind of effort inside a preexisting business unit that specializes in exploiting current markets, and I think you are creating more problems than you're solving."

"What's your second reason?" I asked, hoping he would refer to my work again.

"The second reason is that Plastiwear seems to have potential applications in markets that could extend well beyond our current markets. If we put Plastiwear in oil and gas, they would explore oil and gas applications. There may be some, but that's not only what Plastiwear is about. If we put it in the packaging division, then we would see packaging applications. I guess this is what I mean when I say these two divisions are good at exploiting opportunities in their current markets, but not inclined to look beyond those markets."

Bill was beginning to get comfortable. "In fact, that reminds me of a third reason why we shouldn't fold Plastiwear into current businesses.

Plastiwear will be HGS's entry into the fiber and fabric industry. This industry is really different than the oil and gas and packaging industries—different chemistry, different suppliers, different manufacturing, different customers, different marketing. So, if Plastiwear does realize its full potential—at least as we see it now—managing this business will require different sets of skills than our current businesses need. We have to anticipate that now, early in the evolution of Plastiwear."

"That's interesting, Bill," Livia observed, "especially in light of the private equity pressure HGS is feeling right now. We should include a valuation of Plastiwear as a standalone option, and we'll have to be fully prepared to discuss whether HGS should simply sell it off, in spite of management's predisposition not to. Bill, would you be willing to work with me to develop these arguments for the presentation so we get the tone just right? Gordon, we'd like your input as well."

"I'd be happy to," was Bill's response.

"Sounds great," was Gordon's reply.

"OK." Again, Livia was pressing on. "So, if we're going to recommend creating a new Plastiwear division, then we need to start thinking about the responsibilities of a new division general manager and that group's relationship with the existing businesses."

I thought there was at least one obvious candidate for the job—Walter Albright—but decided not to say anything.

"So," Livia continued, "Bill, with your insights about HGS and its internal processes, I was wondering if you would help me address these issues?"

"I'd be happy to," was Bill's reply.

"Great." Livia was beginning to wrap up the meeting. "Any more questions? I think you all understand your tasks over the next few days and I look forward to hearing from each of you as you make progress."

I felt like that last comment was directed right at me.

REFLECTION QUESTIONS

1. Why do you think HGS rebuffed potential buyers for Plastiwear?

2. With regard to upstream manufacturing, which would you recommend: make, buy, or ally? Why?

3. Do you agree that HGS may have to manufacture limited amounts of some end products to help create "buzz" for Plastiwear? Why or why not?

4. What are the biggest challenges in estimating the market potential of Plastiwear in different product segments?

5. The team emphasized the advantages of organizing Plastiwear in its own division. What are the disadvantages of this approach?

6. Is the team's work being distributed in an equitable way? Efficiently? Is Justin playing an appropriate role?

— 13 —

A SEAMLESS
ARGUMENT

Livia had given each of us our marching orders, and since then we'd been working hard to complete our parts of the overall deck. I had completed most of my individual assignments relatively quickly—I found that while fiber and fabrics could be technically separated, most fiber firms manufactured their own fabric; the first nylon stockings were made and marketed by the company that invented nylon; and Zwanziger Fabrics had introduced a new fabric that sounded like Plastiwear, but that didn't build on the same chemistry and seemed to HGS scientists like more of a marketing campaign than a fundamentally new technology.

Most of my time was spent with Gordon estimating the profitability of Plastiwear in several different product segments under a range of assumptions. I was well into developing a worst-case scenario model to test whether investing too heavily in Plastiwear could bring HGS down. Livia had indicated that this analysis probably wouldn't be in the deck, but would be important backup if this issue arose.

Over these last few days, I had come to appreciate Gordon. OK, he was still a snob, but he really knew what he was doing in quantitative analysis. He kept reminding me that all we were doing was setting some priorities for future research by getting a sense of the upside and downside potential of Plastiwear, but he was terrific at distilling the essential drivers of profitability from the ocean of information I'd been drowning in. He was a real bloodhound when it came to finding data—even better than me, and I thought I was pretty good.

Everyone was coming up with great stuff—Vivek and Bill on Plastiwear manufacturing; Livia, Bill, and Gordon on how the Plastiwear effort should be organized within HGS. The materials they shared clearly laid out the issues and alternatives and made well-supported recommendations. Through an iterative process—we talked through draft slides with each other, took suggestions, revised materials, solicited more feedback and inputs—we kept improving our conclusions. I thought the team was beginning to reach a strong consensus. The presentation began to take on a remarkably simple structure, so simple it could be summarized on a single—albeit crowded—page at the beginning of our deck.

First, HGS must protect and control its critical value drivers: HGS's proprietary knowledge about Plastiwear and its brand identity. Second, HGS should optimize the production of Plastiwear fiber and fabric for sale into selected markets, making investments in learning, quality assurance, and ongoing innovation. Third, to build and manage the mechanisms necessary to protect and focus on Plastiwear's potential, a separate division should be formed.

Of course, underneath each of these general bullets were detailed arguments that outlined why these issues were critical and justified our recommendations. The deck also described alternative solutions, presented their advantages and disadvantages, and made recommendations on certain critical action steps for implementation.

My section of the deck, developed with Gordon, had more than twenty-five slides. I was convinced, by this point, that Plastiwear had the potential to play in a variety of market segments. Overall, our analysis suggested that the profitability of Plastiwear in these segments would range from a couple of million to several hundred million dollars annually, depending on our predictions about manufacturing costs, market share, demand, and competitive behavior—and depending on how we defined the construction, clothing, and recreational segments. Right now, it looked like the construction segment was the most promising option for Plastiwear, at least over the next one to three years.

Livia, Bill, and Gordon's recommendations on how Plastiwear should be managed built closely on HGS's prior success in building a new business unit—the packaging division. Bill analyzed this experience and emphasized HGS's proven track record of success to help his management colleagues see the benefits of organizing the Plastiwear venture in a similar way.

I also found three case studies that described firms that had been unable to realize creative uses for a new technology using their standard organizational structure. I summarized key actions that enabled these firms to reorganize successfully and linked these to the plans that Livia was proposing. While none of these firms was in the fiber or fabric industry, I used only firms with close parallels to HGS.

Livia did a great job of prioritizing the critical decisions in HGS's Plastiwear marketing strategy and identifying the types of marketing plans that would be needed. She favored a high-end strategy—where a branded Plastiwear product would be used only in highly differentiated end user products—but laid out options for both premium branding and high-volume sales. Whoever took over the division manager job could hit the ground running just by "filling in the blanks" on some of the work she produced.

My money was still on Albright as the most likely leader of the Plastiwear division, but we didn't speculate much about this on the team.

We had plenty of work to do before our meeting with the VP of R&D at 3:30. Vivek outlined some critical follow-up work that would be needed, assuming the strategy we were recommending was approved. He focused on two short-term tasks: (1) identifying criteria—like location, size, skills, prior experience with HGS, and reputation—to screen potential joint venture partners to invest in a fiber and fabric facility, and (2) identifying some critical product development, sales, and profitability milestones and metrics for the proposed fiber and fabric division that would support and reinforce entrepreneurial behaviors.

Vivek worked with Bill on the JV issues. Bill's experience in Mexico was extremely helpful—not just in identifying potential partners, but in understanding aspects of HGS's culture and capabilities that might support or hinder the success of such a partnership. Vivek had also vetted our ideas with some JV experts in the firm. Now we really needed to sharpen our thinking around how the JV might actually be structured—the terms of the contract, buy-out clauses, protection of intellectual property rights, and other critical negotiating points.

Bill, Vivek, and I worked through lunch on Monday, pausing only long enough to wolf down some sandwiches and sodas. I got my daily dose of Diet Dr. Pepper and a second wind. By 2:45, the three of us had made considerable progress on our respective assignments when Livia and Gordon came into the room. Livia spoke first.

––––––––––––

"OK, guys. We just reviewed our work with Ken, and he made a few suggestions that we need to incorporate."

I was surprised and said so. "I thought the deck had been put to bed."

Gordon's response built on my metaphor, but he was clearly unfazed. "Ah, the deck never sleeps. Not until it's actually delivered to the client."

Livia continued in the same vein. "Well, let's get the deck out of bed; we need to change a few sheets."

I wondered how long my silly metaphor could be kept going. Fortunately, Vivek spoke up. All business.

"Let me see the changes."

Livia handed Vivek about a dozen pages. "OK. I'll start making these changes on the computer and, Justin, you pull the pages that need to be changed from the hard copies. When I'm done, I'll print the inserts."

I wondered why we didn't discuss the changes as a team, but I followed Livia's lead. So, high-powered strategic analysis had deteriorated, finally, into low-powered paper shuffling. As Vivek and I worked through these last-minute adjustments—none of which seemed significant to me—Livia and Gordon returned to their work. By 3:15, Vivek and I were ready with five hard copies of the modified deck, along with an electronic version we'd saved on a thumb drive. In the meeting room, we found Gordon—standing by the far wall—checking e-mail on his BlackBerry.

"Hey, guys. Listen, the JV attorney just gave me some innovative ideas on how to structure the deal to retain flexibility for HGS, while providing serious upside potential for the right partner."

Vivek responded, "It's probably too late to put them in the deck for this afternoon. But why don't you make a note and give it to Livia. She can ask you to chime in when the JV issues come up."

"Sounds good." Gordon returned his attention to his BlackBerry and Vivek, the PhD engineer, uploaded our PowerPoint file onto the laptop in the room and got the projector started. "Livia won't use it, but it never hurts to have it ready," he commented. I had a chance to take a breather and look at the meeting room where, I hoped, we would begin to convince HGS leaders to support and act on our recommendations.

It was the most boring room I had seen at HGS. Worse than our team room. Four white walls, one covered by a screen pulled down to within three feet of the floor. No artwork, no windows. The white walls were accentuated by white fluorescent lights, the kind that made my mother look ten years older—or so she claimed. In the center of the room was a square wooden table, about eight feet long and four feet wide. Well, not really wood—wood color. It was obviously a cheap veneer over pressed sawdust. Surrounding the table were eight black chairs—not quite folding chairs, but not much better. They were upholstered, and the back reclined a few inches, but the upholstery was worn at the armrests, and the one I was sitting in squeaked every time I shifted my weight.

In other words, a meeting room only engineers could love. I should know. It was the kind of meeting room where I lived in my last job. I changed chairs a couple of times until I found one that didn't squeak. Today, I didn't want to be the squeaky wheel, either literally or figuratively.

After setting up the AV, Vivek headed for the door, with a casual goodbye. "I don't think I need to sit in on this discussion, so take good notes, Justin."

———————

At 3:25, Livia came into the room and stood chatting with Gordon. At 3:32 Walter Albright, VP of R&D, walked into the room. Following Albright was Leonard Kibrick, the R&D guy in charge of developing products with Plastiwear, and Jerry Tucker, the R&D guy who invented Plastiwear.

Albright spoke first.

"Good afternoon, gentlemen." He quickly realized that Livia was in the room and, nodding to her, he added, "And lady. I'm looking forward to hearing what you've prepared today. I hope you don't mind, but I brought two interested parties along."

Albright introduced Kibrick and Tucker. Of course I knew them both. Livia and Gordon had met neither, while Bill knew them all. With the preliminaries out of the way, Albright turned to Livia.

"Great. Why don't we get started? I know this is kind of a sparse room. I've asked my assistant to bring us some water. But she won't interrupt us much if we get started now."

"Yes, thank you." Livia took her place, sitting in the chair at the head of the table next to the screen. As Livia began, I quickly took my seat in the only chair in the room that I knew didn't squeak.

"Thanks for coming this afternoon. First, I wanted to thank you for all the help you've given us on this very tight work schedule. We couldn't have done anything like this without you and your team."

Albright responded for his colleagues. "We were happy to be of assistance."

Livia continued, "As I mentioned to you, Walter, when we talked last week, we didn't want to do a formal presentation today. Instead, I wanted to walk you through our deck to get any reactions or suggestions you might have. It's great that the two of you," she nodded toward Kibrick and Tucker, "were able to join us as well. Please feel free to share your thoughts as we discuss our findings."

Tucker's reply sounded almost ominous. "Don't worry. We will."

"Great." Livia was nonplussed. "OK, then. Let's start."

Livia then began working her way through the deck. She worked off the hard copies, not the screen. I already knew what she was going to say, so I focused on the style and flow of her presentation.

She made it look easy.

She made eye contact and paced the presentation as though she were having a serious conversation with Albright and his colleagues, not making some prepared speech. I noticed that she was wearing a black top and skirt out of some knit material that had slight pink highlights. It was businesslike and yet flattering.

She reviewed our core arguments with only a few interruptions for questions or discussion. Albright asked a question about the size of the clothing segment; Kibrick asked about the risk associated with a manufacturing JV. Tucker expressed some disappointment that we weren't recommending his "ten in ten" plan—but he couldn't have been surprised.

The only tension in the presentation came in the discussion of organizing the fiber and fabric division—what we were now calling the F&F division. Not surprisingly, all the R&D guys agreed a new division was necessary. They weren't 100 percent convinced fiber and fabrics captured the most high-potential applications, including liquid versions of Plastiwear.

"Livia," Albright asked, "has your team given any thought to who might head up the F&F division?"

Livia's response was noncommittal. "Well, we are currently working on a role description to discuss with Carl."

"Do you think we have the skills inside HGS, or do we need to look outside?" Albright continued.

Livia gave the question careful consideration before responding. "Right now, we don't have a strong recommendation either way on that. What we think is most important now is to have a clear conception of the responsibilities and performance targets that this division manager will have."

"Hmmm. OK, thanks." Albright was making a note to himself.

I paid close attention to this exchange. It seemed to me that Albright was positioning himself for this new job, but maybe I was wrong. For sure, Livia was neutral in her responses—no commitments one way or the other.

Livia's presentation took about an hour. She had the same energy at the end as she did in the beginning. As she turned over the last slide in the deck, Livia looked at all of us and asked, "So, gentlemen. This is where we are now. Are there any other questions?"

I couldn't think of anything. She had me at hello.

But Tucker had something else to say. "I'm surprised you didn't mention the MG Management offer to buy HGS."

Livia's response was very careful. "I'm not in a position to comment on the existence of any outside offers at this time."

183

"Come on," Tucker continued, "everyone knows about it. And everyone also knows that this is the only reason that HGS is beginning to take Plastiwear seriously. A foolproof way to get senior managers' attention is to threaten their livelihood."

Livia continued to be cool. "Regardless of the existence—or not—of any external interest in HGS, our analysis of Plastiwear stands on its own merit."

"Come on." Tucker wouldn't give up. "If MG Management retracts its offer, all this effort will be wasted. The conservative culture at HGS will swat this idea down. Don't get me wrong—I love your analysis and your recommendations. If anything, I'd be more aggressive. But I just don't think your ideas have a snowball's chance of getting implemented."

Livia seemed to want to bring this part of the discussion to an end. "Well, I appreciate your point of view, Mr. Tucker. And that is certainly a risk, but I can assure you that the strategy team will be working very hard to build the momentum needed to make sure that—if our recommendations are accepted by senior management and the board—they are actually implemented."

"Well, all I can say is—good luck." Tucker seemed to want to have the last word.

But Albright didn't let him. He glanced from Livia, to Gordon, to me. "I guess I'm not as pessimistic as Jerry. I think the quality of your analysis is outstanding. In fact, it's hard to believe that you've been here only a week. Your analyses were detailed and thorough, and I find your recommendations compelling." Albright paused for a moment. "But it's more our responsibility—my responsibility—than yours to make sure these ideas get executed. If we can pull this off, well, your study may be instrumental in significantly altering the future of our firm—for the better."

At the end of what would be a normal working day for most people, the strategy team got together in the team room for a debrief of the meeting with the R&D folks. Once again, my usual beverage and entrée from the Chinese food menu were brought in. Ken joined us on the phone as Livia began the session.

"So, impressions, everyone."

Gordon went first. "I thought it went very well, both the substance of the discussion and how you led it. Livia, you did a masterful job getting through all that material."

I agreed. "Absolutely top-notch. And a very good analysis. Obviously, we can refine and strengthen it, but I actually think we'll be well-prepared for Wednesday. "

Livia wanted to move forward. "OK, guys; let's not break our arms patting ourselves on the back. What did you think about Tucker's comments at the end of the presentation?" Livia quickly summarized Tucker's comments for Ken.

Gordon replied first. "So, how did Tucker know about the MG Management thing? I thought that was still highly confidential. Hasn't anyone in this firm heard about insider trading?"

Livia turned to Bill and me. "You guys interviewed Tucker. Did anything about MG Management come up?"

I responded for the both of us. "Absolutely not. It's true that Tucker did raise some corporate governance issues during the interview. Clearly, he is very frustrated with the conservative management approach at HGS. But he got his information about MG Management from somewhere else."

"I know," Livia tried to reassure me. "But I had to ask."

Now Vivek joined in the conversation. "Frankly, my experience out at the R&D lab tells me it's an information sieve out there. All the labs are open, security is not very tight—there doesn't seem to be any appreciation of the importance of keeping some things proprietary. That is going to make it harder to implement some of our Plastiwear recommendations. Let me put it this way—I don't know how Tucker got his information, but it wouldn't surprise me at all if MG Management got its information about Plastiwear from someone in the lab."

Ken built on this observation. "We may need to add some recommendations about internal security to our final presentation. Livia, will you see if you can get any information about leaks coming out of the lab—or anywhere else inside HGS for that matter."

"No problem. Justin will help me with that."

I responded the only way I could. "I'll be happy to."

Bill now chimed in. "You know, over and above the insider trading problem created by Tucker, he did have a good point. Today was an easy dress rehearsal in front of a friendly audience. HGS is a very conservative company. It is quite likely our Plastiwear recommendations will have a tough time moving from concept to implementation."

Gordon built on Bill's comments. "I agree. In fact, I think it's worse than just having a 'conservative approach to management.' From my reading of the interview notes, most of the senior managers at HGS have specific reasons to object to our Plastiwear recommendations."

Now it was Livia's turn. "OK. Let's go back to the stakeholder discussion we had in our first team meeting—sorry, Bill. You weren't on the team yet. We knew we'd need to become informed about who might be most interested in this decision and who would be influential in determining the outcome."

I had met with most of these senior managers, so I felt I could comment about what each had at stake if our strategy recommendations were adopted, so I jumped in.

"Well, start with Scott Beckett, VP of oil and gas. First, he may feel that any dollar invested in Plastiwear is a dollar not invested in his division. And, as you've suggested, Ken, Beckett probably sees himself as the next CEO of HGS. If successful, Plastiwear could conceivably rival his division in size and contribution. He has already very publicly come out against Plastiwear in dress shirt applications."

"Go on," Livia encouraged me as she finished her food.

"OK. Robert Hutchins, VP of packaging. He doesn't have the same power as Beckett, and doesn't make the same returns, especially with a half-empty factory, and he wants Plastiwear to fill it up and also to help improve his bottom line. We're not recommending that Plastiwear solve his capacity problems."

I mentally ticked off the key players as I continued. "Shirley Rickert, CFO. She has in her office six present value analyses of Plastiwear, all of which assume that HGS will enter the retail shirt industry to exploit Plastiwear. Our analysis makes all of this work useless and, frankly, a little embarrassing, since they totally missed the boat on the larger opportunities. In fact, the only people I interviewed whose interests are wholly consistent with what we are recommending are the people we talked to today, the R&D folks."

I paused and amended my statement. "And even some of them—like Tucker—object to our plan because it's not aggressive enough."

Ken got us focused on the real problem. "So, the question is, what can we do to turn these people around, make them supporters of our recommended strategy?"

There was a moment of silence. I glanced at Vivek, but he was working head down revising diagrams, so after a few seconds, I decided to venture forward with an idea.

"To me, Beckett is crucial. He runs the largest business unit and I assume has the CEO's ear." I paused, but no one contradicted me, so I went on, "He's a person we really need because he could potentially either block approval or obstruct implementation of our plan."

"Any ideas?" Livia asked.

"Well," Vivek offered, "if Beckett really wants to be the next CEO, we have to link our proposed strategy to his career aspirations. There are at least two useful arguments. First, if HGS doesn't do something about Plastiwear, MG Management—or another firm—will acquire it."

Gordon chimed in emphatically. "Division managers in firms acquired by private equity firms, in general, and by MG Management, in particular, usually do not end up in the CEO's chair."

Vivek acknowledged Gordon with a nod and continued. "Right. Second, Beckett might see that our recommendations are in his best interest because they are conservative in terms of the risk they carry. There are two possible outcomes of the Plastiwear strategy we have proposed, and neither one has a significant downside for him."

Vivek and I had discussed this, so I confidently recapped. "Of course, it could go badly. But, because we have proposed the use of various partners, if Beckett supports these recommendations and things do not go well, the downside risk to HGS of Plastiwear is actually quite small. On the other hand, maybe Plastiwear goes really well, and if Beckett supports it, he can share the glory."

Vivek then summarized. "Bottom line is, by minimizing the downside on Plastiwear, we may be able to get Beckett to a neutral, if not positive, position. Now, if he had to support an investment in shirt making—that would be difficult. He's been so public about his objections there. But he may be able to get behind going into the fiber and fabric industry with the right partners."

"Not bad," observed Gordon. "You two may have a bright future as consultants to Machiavelli. But remember, the JV is not just a financial play. The way they want to structure the deal, the skills and expertise they're hoping to find in a partner, and the challenges of managing strategic alliances all carry different types and amounts of risk."

"Livia, have you been keeping Beckett in the loop? Are these ideas clear in the deck? What's our plan for ensuring Beckett is on board before the meeting?" asked Ken, peppering us with questions.

"We've been in close touch, and we intend to highlight the aspects of our recommendations that align with earlier suggestions from Beckett and other HGS managers," responded Livia calmly. "I think we can do this in a way that doesn't cast the current management team in an unfavorable light."

I continued my argument, now more assertively. "Really, the only person we need to worry about is Beckett. I think he alone could stop this strategy from going forward."

"Right," agreed Gordon. "Hutchins sounds like he needs a separate proposal on how to address his capacity problem. If he could solve that problem he might let go of his ideas about producing Plastiwear. I could pull together a tentative proposal to look at his problem and have a chat with him if that makes sense. Unless that message should come from you, Ken."

"Put the proposal together and send it to me," responded Ken. "Then we'll decide how best to approach Hutchins."

I continued where I left off. "As for Shirley, I think she will go along with what the rest of the group says. She might have a bit of egg on her face after focusing so much on shirt NPVs, but we can give her an easy out by supporting her argument that this is a very different situation from what they've had in the past, so her intention to encourage a firmwide conversation was well founded."

Ken reached out to draw Bill into the conversation. "I would like to hear Bill's take on these ideas. Bill, you know these people well; what will it take to build the support we need, especially from Beckett?"

"I think Justin's evaluation of Beckett is accurate, if a bit too political. He thinks he is the most likely candidate for the CEO position when Carl retires. But while he does have some career-agenda stuff here, he is also intensely loyal to the people in the oil and gas products division. If he perceives Plastiwear as a threat, either to the status of that division within HGS or to the capital that the division needs to continue to grow, I think he will be hard to turn around—especially if you spring your Plastiwear strategy on him at the meeting on Wednesday."

Ken agreed with Bill. "Thanks, Bill. I think you're right. I think we can tell a logical, fact-based story about why Beckett should support our strategy, for both personal and competitive reasons. But it will be difficult for him to change his views in a public setting, if he's hearing the recommendations for the first time. I'd like to talk with him myself. And if we preview Beckett, we will need to preview Hutchins as well."

"I think that's a good idea," Bill replied.

Ken continued. "Livia, I will be coming into Chicago late Tuesday afternoon. If you haven't already, could you set up a meeting—about an hour would be fine—to include Beckett, you, and me on Tuesday evening or Wednesday morning? Once that meeting is set up, do the same with Hutchins. I think that will pretty much cover the critical bases for Wednesday. And Justin, will you work on some talking points that summarize the arguments from this discussion? I'll need them by Tuesday noon."

Vivek quietly pushed a few of his hand-drawn slides over to me. I glanced at them. They captured much of what we had been talking about, so I confidently replied, "No problem, Ken, I'll have something to you shortly," then silently mouthed "Thanks" to Vivek.

"And let's make sure we all circulate details of meetings, outcomes of analyses, and breaking news teamwide," added Livia.

Gordon jumped in. "So that addresses the interests of pretty much everyone who is going to be at the meeting."

"Everyone except one person," Livia added.

We all looked at her with questions on our faces. Whom did we miss? We talked about all the division VPs, most of the critical functional people. Livia waited, but when none of us provided a name, she filled in the blank.

"Why, the CEO, Carl Switzer, of course."

REFLECTION QUESTIONS

1. Do you agree with Justin that Albright is the most likely candidate to run the new Plastiwear division?

2. What are some of the problems associated with having an R&D lab that is an "information sieve"?

3. What is the point of having a formal final presentation if all the major players have previewed the findings?

4. Which of the client managers are most likely to alter their views on Plastiwear based on the strategy team's arguments?

5. What suggestions would you give Livia regarding the team hierarchy and the work processes the team is using?

— 14 —

A TAILORED PRESENTATION

Over the next two days, Bill, Vivek, and I tried to anticipate questions members of the top management team might have about our process or recommendations. We then constructed arguments to counter expected objections. Vivek and I also started modeling some business dynamics in the segments where Plastiwear seemed to have the greatest potential—describing a range of possible competitor reactions to HGS's entry. We were steadily busy, but thought we were in pretty good shape. Livia and Ken, in the meantime, met with Scott Beckett, Bob Hutchins, and Carl Switzer to give each of them a preview of our findings and recommendations. They reported no major problems.

Livia gave us a brief summary. "Beckett and Hutchins asked a couple of tough questions. Hutchins, in particular, didn't like that we rejected the 'I've got the space' argument, but he appreciated the risk-reduction advantages of the joint venture model we were recommending. Beckett was relieved we weren't recommending going into shirt manufacturing or retail. He seemed open to the possibility of selling Plastiwear as a branded technology to be incorporated into high-end branded products."

"Remember," Ken cautioned, "this was the first time these guys were seeing our conclusions. Sometimes, clients are very careful about revealing their reactions to a recommendation, especially when they first hear it. It wouldn't surprise me if they have much stronger reactions on Wednesday, so we've got to be able to nail the 'I've got the space' argument. Beckett is going to be harder to prepare for. At one level, our recommendations are consistent with his earlier arguments—we don't think HGS should manufacture shirts or go into the retail shirt industry. But if his real interest is to try to reduce investment in Plasti-wear so that he can increase investment in the oil and gas products division, or if he has a different assessment of the risk, pessimism about potential partnerships, or concerns about putting in place the right leadership, then he could come back at us on any number of points—or maybe all of them."

Livia then continued, "We left early versions of the deck with both Beckett and Hutchins but were clear that we were still making changes as new information was coming in. I said that I'd be surprised if any of our recommendations changed, but that the data supporting those recommendations might evolve."

"What about Carl?" I asked.

Livia responded. "He is totally on board with our analysis, more than either Beckett or Hutchins. He's most interested in the level and pace of the investment we are recommending, since he's going to need to convince the board to invest millions."

Having the CEO on board gave me confidence. "So, sounds like we've got most of our ducks in a row for the final meeting."

Livia was focused and serious. "We'll see. But I want you two," she pointed to me and Vivek, "to continue working on the core logic of our arguments, both the evidence and the storyline, as if on Wednesday we had to convince these people from scratch. I want to be sure that the recommendations we are making are as good as they can be. Remember, if we are successful, our work will form the backbone of a strategy that will be shared throughout HGS."

We both nodded, and assured her that that was what we were doing: building the best fact-based case for our recommendations that we possibly could, given the time and resources available. And we understood that as data evolved, we'd continue to challenge our conclusions.

We inserted the final changes into the deck at noon on Wednesday, e-mailed it to copier services, and received the hard copies at 2:30. Showtime.

———————————

The plan was for Ken to start the meeting, then turn it over to Livia. Livia's large role in the final presentation seemed to surprise Gordon a bit. But since Livia had been heavily involved in the day-to-day work on this engagement, it made sense to me.

Unlike our practice meeting, Livia would work off the screen for this presentation. She would go through the logic of each of our recommendations, and Bill and Gordon would add comments whenever it seemed appropriate. Vivek and I were to sit in the back and take notes. The only way we were to join the presentation was if Ken, Livia, or Gordon asked us a direct question; if that happened, it would probably be about some details of our work. Vivek and I had each organized our data and notes on our laptops for quick access.

I was excited to attend the meeting, but relieved I wouldn't have to present anything. I know I played a central role in developing the recommendations, but I'd heard that often only the senior team members attended the big meetings. In a real sense, this presentation, the content at least, was mine. And Bill's and Vivek's. And Livia's. And, to a lesser extent, Gordon's.

OK, it was a team effort.

But I had put lots of work into it, and I had an emotional attachment to what was going to be presented. Maybe that was one of the reasons why Ken and Livia decided not to let me make the presentation. That and because I'm a total rookie.

The meeting was to be held in the boardroom at HGS headquarters. It turned out to be much nicer than the meeting room where we presented to the R&D people. I saw it the first time at 3:25 Wednesday afternoon, as Vivek and I arrived to load the slides on the computer and check on the room setup.

About sixty feet long and twenty feet wide, with a ceiling that soared at least twenty feet high, the boardroom was impressive along every dimension. Of course, one wall was glass from floor to ceiling, providing yet another beautiful view of Chicago. The other walls were deeply paneled in dark walnut, with built-in recesses for portraits of people important in the history of HGS. The floor was covered in a neutral-colored thick carpet with HGS logos cut into it every few feet.

The center of the room was dominated by a table running almost its entire length. No pressed sawdust and laminate here; the wood in this table was deep brown, the grain gnarled and twisted. Twenty chairs were arrayed around the table—black high-density mesh stretched onto black metal frames that reached up high on the backs of those lucky enough to sit in them. They were examples of the latest effort to merge technology, art, and comfort in seating.

Cut into the table in front of each of these chairs was a computer screen mounted at an angle underneath the table and covered by glass. Board members could look directly at each other, with papers spread out in front of them on the table, and still examine any figures or files displayed on these computer screens. A wireless mouse was discreetly placed near the screen to give those attending the meeting control of their computers.

Over the center of the table was a modest chandelier—the only thing modest in the room. Press a button on the wall and the chandelier disappeared into the ceiling, replaced by an LCD projector. In addition, a floor-to-ceiling screen unrolled in the front of the room, and sun shades covered the windows—enough to make it easy to see the picture on the screen, but not so dark as to make the room gloomy or cold.

"Wow," I observed, "the only thing missing from this room is a bar."

Vivek responded, offhandedly, "It's in the back; you go through a hidden door, over there."

With the slides loaded on the computer and copies of the deck on the table, we were ready. We each busied ourselves with small things, waiting for the audience to arrive.

Gordon and Bill soon joined Vivek and me in the boardroom. We chatted about the room and sports—turns out that Gordon is a Red Sox fan and I hate the Red Sox. Not much of a surprise there.

Soon after Bill and Gordon arrived, members of the HGS management team began to show up. Our exchanges were less formal than I'd expected.

"You guys don't need much sleep, I guess," was Shirley's hello to me and Vivek. "We've got to stop meeting like this," cracked Albright.

Everyone but Carl, Ken, and Livia was in the boardroom by 4:00. At 4:02, these three arrived, continuing a conversation they seemed to be enjoying. When Carl sat down, the rest of us took our seats, Vivek and me in the back.

Carl began the meeting conversationally, standing behind his chair and speaking just a bit louder than normal.

"Well, I see everyone is here. I want to thank all of you for your contributions to this important work. Ken and Livia have been keeping me up to date on its progress, but I'm sure we're all looking forward to hearing the team's findings and recommendations. So, without further ado, Ken."

Carl motioned Ken's way, and Ken stood and moved to the front of the room. As he began talking, he casually nodded to Vivek who pushed a single button on the console, and the room transformed itself from a setting designed for a discussion to one designed for presentations.

"Justin," Ken spoke to me directly. "Will you distribute copies of the materials?"

I did as requested.

"Most of you," he said, referring to the members of the management team, "have seen at least parts of this deck previously."

While the materials could have been set out ahead of time, or not at all, I figured Ken had his reasons for asking me to hand deliver each deck as he outlined the process we had used to come to our recommendations and reiterated the importance of the strategic decision facing HGS.

"As you will see," Ken continued, "our team has developed specific recommendations concerning Plastiwear and ruled out others."

Ken then put up a slide that broadly summarized our recommendations. "You have a valuable asset here. Plastiwear may be a source of a new core competence for HGS. That's why we recommend, first, that you invest in controlling what you have; second, that you focus on creating value with this asset; and third, that you build a scalable platform for Plastiwear." Ken emphasized each of the key verbs just a bit.

He then began drilling down on each of these three points. "First, to tap the potential of Plastiwear, we think it's very important that HGS maintain full control of this technology."

Final presentation slide recommending HGS control key value drivers

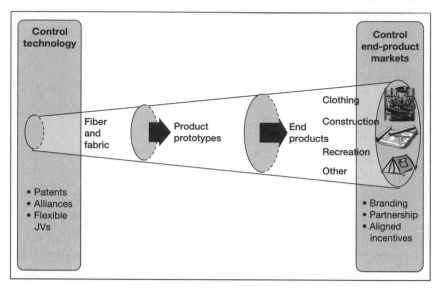

When he said the word *control,* the slide that focused on control was shown on the screen.

Isn't PowerPoint cool?

Ken didn't seem to be impressed. He was looking at the group, not the screen—and I noticed most of them were focused on him, rather than the slides. "Upstream, control means expanding and defending your patent, and working with trusted partners to produce Plastiwear. Downstream, it means controlling Plastiwear's position in end markets, even though we won't be recommending that you actually make these end products—much like an 'Intel inside' or Gore-Tex's strategy. Nevertheless, HGS must protect and control its critical value drivers, including its proprietary knowledge about Plastiwear and its brand identity."

Ken moved to the second point. "Focus is the next imperative."

The screen changed to the slide on focus.

"You'll need to focus not only on what you produce, but also on its quality and market position, to be as competitive as possible in your selected segments. That begins with a strategy to stage investments in Plastiwear over time in a way that will let you monitor the quality of

Final presentation slide recommending a focus on high-value activities

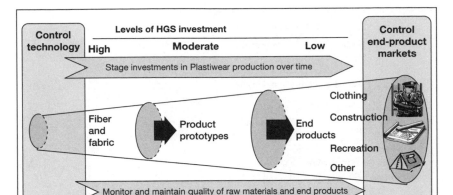

both the Plastiwear that is produced and the products in which it is used. Throughout this effort, HGS will need to gather market intelligence about Plastiwear-based products while simultaneously investigating new applications in the lab. Again, carefully selected strategic partners, both upstream and downstream, will be important to help Plastiwear reach its full potential."

Ken then linked the third key point to the first two. "By controlling and focusing your strategic assets, you will be poised to build."

With this, a third slide came on the screen.

Ken continued, "To build on Plastiwear's considerable potential, we recommend that HGS create a separate division to manage the branding, positioning, partnerships, security policies, performance measurement, and staff development—among other things—necessary to exploit Plastiwear."

Ken spoke deliberately and seemed to connect with the group. I could swear he caught Albright's eye when he mentioned security policies and nodded to Shirley when he mentioned performance measurement.

He continued, "This division will be the scalable platform that brings Plastiwear to the world."

Final presentation slide recommending building the architecture

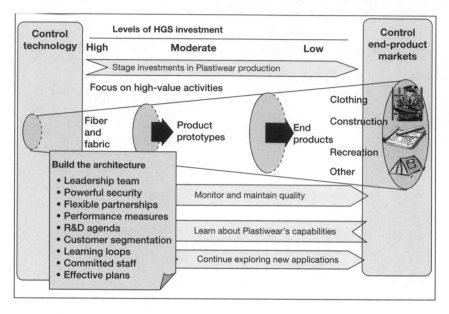

Maybe, I thought, we could stop right here and vote to approve our recommendations. Ken had me totally on board.

"To walk us through the rationale underlying these recommendations, I'd like to turn the podium over to Livia Chambers, who has been leading the work here at HGS. Livia."

Livia took Ken's position, standing at the head of the table, and began talking through the slides. Unlike the meeting with the R&D people, there were lots of questions, interrupting almost every point. Hutchins, the VP of packaging, was first.

"So, why exactly should HGS invest in more manufacturing capacity when we already have excess capacity available? Isn't that a waste of money?"

His predictable but sincere question was followed by Beckett's more difficult question: "How can we know that Plastiwear is a better investment option than, say, investing more money in our current businesses when you haven't evaluated the economic potential of new opportunities in those businesses?"

Even Shirley got into the act. "How can you recommend investing in Plastiwear when you have only the vaguest notion of the kind of cash flow that this investment is likely to generate?" Her gambit was less a real question than an entrée into a discussion she wanted to start about the risks of investing in Plastiwear and the required investment levels. This discussion was quite informative, and Livia stepped back from presenting and encouraged the dialogue.

Later Beckett came back with another tough question. "Based on your recommendations to engage in multiple small experiments to learn more about possible markets and applications, couldn't Plastiwear's managers choose milestones and goals that they can easily reach, but have nothing to do, really, with generating profits?"

The group's comments on milestones and goals suggested some compensation and reporting issues regarding the proposed fiber and fabric division that might warrant later consideration. Then the group circled back to a focus on timing and worst-case thinking. Fortunately, questions like, "How long before we will know if Plastiwear is viable?" and "How and when do we pull the plug if it turns out to be a dog?" were among those we had prepared for.

And so it went—for over two hours. The team had anticipated most of these questions, and Livia was well-briefed and poised; she also didn't hesitate to nod to Ken or Bill for additional information. A few times Ken jumped in to ask the group a clarifying question about their concerns, and he seemed hyperattuned to the body language of each of the listeners.

Eventually Livia got to the last slide. At this point, Ken was at the front of the room with her, Gordon had answered a couple of financial questions, Bill described the potential of his international contacts, and Vivek explained where various data had come from. No one asked me anything. After handing out the materials, I could have vaporized and no one in the meeting would have noticed.

Livia wrapped up and then turned the floor back over to Ken.

"Thank you, Livia, for a complete review of the team's analysis. I would also like to thank HGS management, particularly Bill Dixon, for the time they've devoted to this effort, especially given the extremely short time frame we've been working in. If there are no more questions, let me turn it back over to Carl."

At this point, Ken sat down and Carl stood up.

"Thank you, Ken. And thank you, team. I know you've been burning the midnight oil on this one. Your analysis and insights are provocative; they've given us a lot to think about. Again, thank you very much."

With that, Carl left the room, followed closely by Ken and Livia.

The HGS managers began shuffling their papers and talking among themselves as they moved on to their next meetings or other work obligations. Just another day at the office. I couldn't hear everything they said, but I did hear Shirley say something like, "They must think we're made of money."

I remained seated.

How anticlimactic.

That was it. Ten days of my life, no sleep, brilliant insights, great data, access to incredible minds and reports, and all we got was, "Your analysis is provocative" and "It's given us a lot to think about." What kind of response was that?

My disappointment morphed quickly into anger. "Provocative"? And "lots to think about"? Our report had laid out a new future for this company and completely new businesses that could revolutionize everything HGS was doing. And all we got was "provocative" and "lots to think about"!

No wonder MG Management wants to take over this company and kick these managers out—what a bunch of wimps. Doesn't anybody in this company know how to make a decision? Doesn't anybody have any guts, any vision, any courage?

Vivek leaned over to me. His comments were completely inconsistent with my feelings.

"Well, that went well, don't you think?"

It was all I could do to keep my growing anger in check. I turned to him and said, as calmly as I could, "Well, we didn't get much of a commitment from the CEO about Plastiwear."

Vivek look genuinely surprised. "Did you expect that, in this meeting?"

"Yeah. We laid out our recommendations. They asked their questions, we had answers for all of them. What else is there to do except make a decision?"

"I'm afraid that's a bit simplistic." Vivek shook his head and gathered up his things.

"Why's that? Carl's the CEO, isn't he?"

"Yes, but the CEO won't make this kind of decision quickly, on his own. He will want to confer with his senior managers, to make sure he has their support. I imagine that he has been informally in contact with the board about the potential takeover and everything else going on. Now that he has our recommendations, he has to meet formally with the board of directors. He won't be making or announcing a decision for a while."

"But I thought that HGS needed a response to MG Management about Plastiwear, like, this week."

"He needs it soon, but he can't do anything without communicating with the appropriate players. Besides, he has already decided to invest in Plastiwear. We were here to give him some cover in that decision and to help outline his alternatives in more detail."

I was shocked.

Dumbfounded.

"What do you mean, he has already decided? Have you talked to him?"

"No, no, nothing like that. But just look at the facts. Most of his senior management team—as we saw today—is neutral to negative on Plastiwear. If he wanted to stop Plastiwear, he could do so easily by just agreeing with his management team. So, the easy decision would be to can Plastiwear. But since he doesn't want to do that, he brought us in to give him support for the decision that, strategically, he already wanted to make."

"But our analysis might have gone the other way. I was never biased in favor of investing in Plastiwear. In fact, sometimes I thought it was a terrible idea."

"True. But like most CEOs, he probably has confidence in his ability to make a decision. So, he was probably willing to make the bet that we would identify some settings under which an investment would make sense. Or, even if we had come out negative, he wouldn't be that much worse off. After all, his top management team is already against the investment; adding some consultants against it doesn't make that much difference. He can set up the decision, much like we have recommended, to minimize the downside risk—no factories, no giant organization, and so forth—and go for it. Yes, I'd bet Carl was already predisposed to do Plastiwear in a relatively serious way. The big questions were how and when to do it—and we helped him a lot there. He also wanted help getting his senior managers and the board to support him—where we've also moved the ball forward. That's why I thought the meeting today went pretty well, overall."

My anger was replaced with confusion.

"So, all we did was a study that confirmed what the CEO wanted to do anyway?"

"No, no. We did much more. We probably reinforced some of his thinking, but altered it in other areas. We clarified some of the critical decisions that will need to be made, with regard to both their timing and their importance. We also outlined some fairly specific and feasible strategies to exploit Plastiwear that have a good chance of creating real value for the company. We gave him materials he can use not only to help bring his managers around, but to build excitement and support across the whole organization and with key stakeholders. I think that's pretty good work."

"Suppose he really didn't want to invest in Plastiwear."

"Well, in that case, we would never have been called in, would we? Let's put it this way, Justin. In my experience, I've never seen an externally generated strategy report change the mind of a CEO if his mind was already made up."

At this point, Vivek was halfway out the door of the empty boardroom, and I was close behind.

Vivek continued. "If Carl wanted to do Plastiwear, HGS would do Plastiwear in some form. If he didn't want to do Plastiwear, no report we could have written would have changed his mind. And if he really didn't know what he wanted—well, he wouldn't be much of a CEO then, would he?"

REFLECTION QUESTIONS

1. How helpful were Ken and Livia's meetings with Bob Hutchins, Scott Beckett, and Carl Switzer in getting HGS ready for the changes the strategy team was going to recommend?

2. How important is the CEO's commitment to a strategy for its implementation?

3. Do you think it was appropriate for Livia to lead the bulk of the final presentation?

4. Do you agree with Vivek that Carl had made his decision about Plastiwear before the strategy team began their work?

5. Was Justin's expectation that a decision about Plastiwear would be made in the final presentation meeting unrealistic, or are managers at HGS just unable to make decisions quickly?

6. Based on everything you've read, are there any weaknesses in the strategy team's analysis or recommendations?

A STAFFING QUESTION

One minute, I know exactly what I'm going to do and when I'm going to do it—I have a crystal-clear agenda, a strict work plan, laserlike focus, data to collect, clocks ticking.

And the next minute, I don't. No plan, no agenda, no focus. Instead, I'm waiting. Waiting to find out what's next. Waiting to find out if any-one is interested in working with me again. Just waiting. And sending out my belated thank-yous for my interviews. I even sent a thank-you to Darla for her support.

I'm on the beach. Between studies. Unstaffed. At loose ends.

Oh, Vivek and I had a few things to finish up. We had to break down the team room and get the information we'd collected into a form that could be referenced by the client and any future consultants they engage, shred any printed materials not worth keeping, and delete extraneous files. This largely clerical work was something of a letdown after the heady, adrenalin-filled days when we were trying to figure out how to exploit the "miracle fabric of the twenty-first century."

I think Vivek noticed my lethargy.

"Come on, Justin. We've got to get this done by tomorrow. I have a flight to catch tomorrow afternoon to get to the office on Friday."

"What are you going to do on Friday?"

"Oh, mostly just paperwork, catching up on e-mail, stuff like that. I've also got to drop by my apartment and make some arrangements so I'm ready to leave Sunday night."

"Where are you going Sunday?" So maybe Vivek takes vacations after all!

"I'm staffed on a study for the government of Malawi, something on reforestation and sustainable development."

"Where the heck is Malawi?"

"Southeast Africa. Quite a change from Chicago. But I need to get to Geneva by Monday morning. That's where the team is gathering before we go to Africa. On Tuesday, we have meetings with some World Bank officials who are going to brief us about the situation in Malawi. I believe they are behind the project." Vivek seemed relaxed. Maybe he just didn't get excited about anything. "Where are you headed next?"

I hesitated, a bit embarrassed. "I don't really know. Back to the office on Friday, like you. But after that, I haven't heard anything."

"Don't worry. You won't be on the beach very long. Not with this project under your belt."

"You think I did a good job, Vivek? I don't have anything to compare it to."

"Well, I'm sure it felt like trial by fire, and there were some rough spots early on." He paused and flipped a pile of papers over, smiling. "But that was mostly just your enthusiasm. Once you started working more with the team, I thought things came together fine. And that's what I'm going to say on my peer evaluation. I wouldn't mind working with you again."

"Well, that's nice of you, Vivek. It would be great to work with you again, too." I paused, remembering some of my more difficult conversations with Ken. "Of course, at this point, I'd be glad to work at all."

He didn't laugh, so neither did I. We continued to separate the shredding from the filing until about 6:00 that evening, purging old versions of documents and ".pdfing" the important ones. Then, for the first time since I began working on this project, I actually went home—well, not really home; back to the hotel—at a reasonable hour. After a real dinner and some exercise, I was in my room by 8:30.

It was actually too early to call Jackie, so I set my alarm and watched television. Somehow, it was comforting to find out that television was just as uninteresting now as it had been ten days ago, when I started at HGS. I flipped the channel to a cable station and watched one of the blockbuster movies from the previous summer. Lots of explosions, fistfights between good guys and bad guys that lasted longer than a typical professional heavyweight bout, and one interminable car chase. I turned it off after fifteen minutes.

I don't remember how long I lay there, but I think I fell asleep around 9:00. The next thing I remember was my alarm going off at 6:30. 6:30! That was the latest I had slept since I had started working with HGS. Some sit-ups, some breakfast, and I was back at it in the team room by 8:00. Vivek, of course, was already there.

"Morning, Vivek."

"Good morning. Have you looked at your e-mail yet this morning?"

"No. Didn't think there would be anything too pressing this morning." None of my friends outside the firm had this e-mail, so my BlackBerry vibrated mostly with human resources alerts and "all-office memos."

"Well, there is a meeting of HGS senior managers and the strategy team today at 2:30."

"What's that about?"

"I don't know for sure. Maybe they've made a decision about Plastiwear already. That would be fast, but given the unfriendly takeover possibility, maybe they've needed to move quickly."

"That would be interesting."

"In the meantime," Vivek refocused our conversation on the work at hand, "we need to finish up here."

"You're right."

By lunch, we had made great progress—in spite of the fact that Vivek had some files open on Malawi already and had to take a few calls with his new teammates. I even had time to finish my expense and time sheets. It looked like Vivek and I would both be able to leave that evening, depending on the flight availability. At the very worst, I would be able to leave early in the morning and still get some work in at the office on Friday. That was one advantage of working in Chicago—lots of airline connections.

At 2:15, just as Vivek and I were getting ready to head for the meeting, Livia walked through the door. She was dressed in a dark patterned top and black tailored pants. She was also wearing flat shoes, not heels, so she didn't seem as tall—still very professional looking, but not as formal as I was used to seeing her dress.

"How's it going, guys? Ready to get out of Dodge?"

"Yep. Vivek is flying out first, but I'll be close behind."

"Well," Livia began. She paused, then continued. "Good. Looks like you're ready for the meeting then. Let's head over."

I wanted to ask Livia what the meeting was about. But we didn't really have time, and she was responding to some text messages anyway. A few moments in the elevator and we were back on the seventy-second floor. And there to greet us, as the elevator door opened, was Darla Hood, Carl Switzer's secretary.

"Good afternoon." I thought I detected a slightly friendlier demeanor toward me and wondered if she'd gotten my thank-you note.

Darla led us down the hallway to the same meeting room where we had begun this project, so few and yet so many days earlier. As I walked into the room, I saw that the entire strategy team had assembled—Ken, Livia, Gordon, Bill, Vivek, and me—along with the HGS senior management team—Carl Switzer, Scott Beckett, Walter Albright, Robert Hutchins, and Shirley Rickert. This was the second time in two days all these people had assembled.

Carl called the meeting to order with a friendly, yet businesslike tone. "OK, I see we're all here now. Like everything else on this Plasti-wear project, we've had to move much more quickly than normal. I guess that is one of the benefits of having outside pressure on us. Now we've built some urgency and momentum, not to mention shared enthusiasm." I wondered if this was just a sound bite or if he really believed what he was saying.

No matter his actual motivation, the CEO definitely held the full attention of everyone present.

"As many of you know, I convened an emergency meeting of the board yesterday evening. Ken briefed the board on the final recommendations from the consulting team. Actually, Ken had been keeping them up to date pretty much all along. We then debated those recommendations for some time."

Carl paused for effect and then continued. "Late last night, the board approved, in principle, our proposal to retain and protect our rights to Plastiwear and to invest in developing a portfolio of applications for our Plastiwear technology, with a focus on fibers and specialty fabrics. Obviously, the details of how we'll move ahead require further deliberation. But the board wholeheartedly supported the idea that we would need to create a new division—we have provisionally dubbed it the fiber and fabric division."

My heart was pounding, and I tried to keep a smile from breaking out on my face. I thought it might appear to be unprofessional to high-five Vivek.

"As we create this important new division, it's necessary to carefully select its leadership—including a division general manager who will recruit a management team, prioritize research projects and development opportunities, craft the marketing strategy, and bring alive the full potential of this innovation. While we have a great deal of talent within HGS, the fiber and fabric division will be something very new for us—exploring a new set of technologies and entering unfamiliar markets. So, I decided to go outside the HGS family for a new division GM."

This was surprising. I thought Albright would get the job. As Hutchins had mentioned, maybe there were just too many other R&D projects on the burner for Albright to leave. As I ruminated, Carl continued.

"I've brought you all here to announce that HGS has hired Ms. Livia Chambers as vice president and general manager of HGS's proposed fiber and fabric division." Carl looked around the room and motioned to Bill, continuing, "Mr. William Dixon will join her leadership team full time, as director of strategy and operations, effective immediately. A public announcement is forthcoming, but given the unique circumstances, we convened this group to share this exciting news. Livia, would you like to say a few words?"

I'm sure my mouth was wide open. Livia was leaving the firm to work with HGS—and Bill—full time! I had not seen that coming. I was shocked and leaned in to hear Livia's remarks.

"I know this probably surprises my consulting colleagues. But, during this project, I became convinced that Plastiwear was a technology with tremendous promise and that HGS was a company poised to exploit it. I look forward to working with Bill and my new colleagues in HGS to bring this promise to life." She looked genuinely pleased and made eye contact with Bill as she added, "Oh, yes. One of the first things we'll do in the new division is find a new name for Plastiwear."

Everyone chuckled.

I looked at Ken expecting him to be shocked, angry, or maybe just stoic. He actually looked proud. Pleased, even. I was just confused. I looked around the room at the HGS managers. Some—including Beckett and Hutchins—were nodding in apparent approval of Livia's and Bill's new roles. Shirley was standing next to Bill and patted him on the back. Albright didn't register any discernable response. I wondered whether it was a surprise to them or if they were just far better at concealing their true feelings than I was. After a few seconds, Carl returned to his agenda.

"Obviously, Livia and Bill will be building their team and staffing up the fiber and fabric division over the next several months. But the work of further exploring and exploiting Plastiwear's potential really can't wait. If we're going to successfully implement a Plastiwear strategy, we need to get started on answering some of our outstanding questions and identifying critical milestones and metrics as quickly as possible." Bill nodded emphatically as the CEO gave the floor to him.

Now I noticed Bill's shirt and tie were a notch nicer than anything we'd seen in the team room, and he seemed to have grown a couple of inches. "We've really appreciated the strategy team's outside-in viewpoint and found their rapid data analysis very helpful. Livia and I have agreed with Ken to extend the current consulting contract for another four to six weeks. I hope that Gordon and Justin will be able to continue their excellent work here."

Gordon replied for both of us, "It will be our pleasure."

Bill continued his speech. "Vivek, sorry you'll miss the fun, but I understand you are off to Africa for your next assignment on Sunday."

"That is correct."

"Well, if you need more resources, I'm sure we'll be able to help," Ken offered.

"I look forward to negotiating the details of our engagement," joked Livia, as everyone laughed. Now that she was on the client side, the cost of our work would come out of her budget.

"Great," Carl interjected. "I'd like to propose a little toast."

Right on cue, Darla was at the door with a tray of small plastic cups, each filled with what looked to be champagne.

"Ah, wonderful. Here's Darla."

It took a minute for the cups to be passed around. I was among the last to get one. When we all had a cup, Carl proposed a toast.

"To the rosy future of the substance formerly known as Plastiwear, the success of the fiber and fabric division, and most of all, to Livia Chambers and Bill Dixon. Congratulations and cheers!"

In my mind, I couldn't help adding an addendum to the toast—to Justin Campbell. There were some rough spots, but I guess I didn't do so badly after all. My work made a difference, and I still had a job!

REFLECTION QUESTIONS

1. Is the choice of Livia to lead the new division strategically sound? Organizationally sound?

2. Is Bill a good choice to be director of strategy and operations for fiber and fabrics?

3. What will be some of Livia's most serious challenges in taking up her new role?

4. Do you think Justin did a good job? Explain.

A READING LIST

Each chapter in the novel raises one or more issues that can have an impact on the ability of a firm to develop and execute strategy. These notes identify these issues by chapter and then suggest additional readings that can be helpful in thinking about them. When appropriate, the additional readings include chapters from two strategic management textbooks:

- Barney, J. B. *Gaining and Sustaining Competitive Advantage*. 4th ed. Upper Saddle River, NJ: Pearson, 2011 [referred to as Barney (2011)].

- Barney, J. B., and W. Hesterly. *Strategic Management and Competitive Advantage: Concepts and Cases*. 3rd ed. Upper Saddle River, NJ: Pearson, 2010 [referred to as Barney and Hesterly (2010)].

Barney (2011) is a more advanced textbook, full of graphs, charts, and equations. Barney and Hesterly (2010) is less technical, but covers many of the same topics as Barney (2011).

In addition, some topics discussed in this book are marked as a *core strategy topic*. These are topics that are covered in most strategic management textbooks and widely applied in developing and executing strategy.

PROLOGUE: A LITTLE TURBULENCE

Onboarding in Professional Service Firms

Justin is starting a new job with a consulting firm.

Suggested reading: The human resource challenges associated with managing professional organizations—including challenges associated with onboarding new professionals—are discussed by J. Swait and N. Kinnie and by M. Lengnick-Hall and C. Lengnick-Hall.

- Swait, J., and N. Kinnie. "Organizational Learning, Knowledge Assets, and HR Practices in Professional Service Firms." *Human Resources Management Journal* 20, no. 1 (2010): 64–79.

- Lengnick-Hall, M., and C. Lengnick-Hall. *Human Resource Management in the Knowledge Economy*. San Francisco: Berrett-Koehler, 2003.

In this book: See pages xix–xxiii.

A READING LIST

CHAPTER 1: A SIMPLE PROBLEM

Preparing an Organization for Strategic Change

The strategy team understands how important it is to get HGS ready for any strategic changes it might undertake based on the team's recommendations.

Suggested reading: D. Garvin and R. Michael discuss how conflicts between functions and business units can sometimes inhibit innovation in corporations. D. Garvin and M. Roberto have also commented on the importance of preparing an organization for strategic change. R. Miles; J. Ford and L. Ford; and G. Nelson, K. Martin, and E. Powers have also made important contributions to this conversation.

- Garvin, D., and R. Michael. "What You Don't Know About Making Decisions," *Harvard Business Review,* September 2001, 108–116.

- Garvin, D., and M. Roberto. "Change Through Persuasion." *Harvard Business Review,* February 2005, 104–112.

- Miles, R. H. "Accelerating Corporate Transformations (Don't Lose Your Nerve!)." *Harvard Business Review,* January–February 2010, 68–75.

- Ford, J., and L. Ford. "Decoding Resistance to Change." *Harvard Business Review,* April 2009, 99–103.

- Nelson, G., K. Martin, and E. Powers. "The Secrets to Successful Strategy Execution." *Harvard Business Review,* June 2008, 60–70.

In this book: See pages 1–15.

CEOs/Top Management Teams and the Timing of Strategic Decisions

What Justin describes as a CEO's "biological clock" is known more formally as the "career horizon problem."

Suggested reading: Research on the "career horizon" problem suggests that as CEOs come to the end of their careers, their decision-making incentives may change. Examples of this work include E. Matta and P. Beamish. The behavioral underpinnings of this research are beautifully described in D. Hambrick and G. Fukutomi. C. Gersick suggests why a top management team—like the one that works with Carl—might begin to feel pressure to make bigger strategic decisions about halfway through its tenure. This "half time" effect is also anticipated in Hambrick and Fukutomi.

- Matta, E., and P. Beamish. "The Accentuated CEO Career Horizon Problem: Evidence from International Acquisitions." *Strategic Management Journal* 29, no. 1 (2008): 683–700.

- Hambrick, D., and G. Fukutomi. "The Seasons of a CEO's Tenure." *Academy of Management Review* 16, no. 4 (1991): 719–742.

- Gersick, C. J. G. "Marking Time: Predictable Transitions in Task Groups." *Academy of Management Journal* 32, no. 2 (1989): 274–309.

In this book: See pages 8–12.

The Effects of Private Equity on Managers in Public Firms

Justin's mind begins racing when he hears about MG Management's letter. What will this mean for HGS and the engagement?

Suggested reading: P. Pozen and K. Wruck discuss some of the potential impacts that private equity investors can have on managers in the firms they acquire.

- Pozen, P. "If Private Equity Sized Up Your Business." *Harvard Business Review,* November 2007, 78–87.

- Wruck, K. "Private Equity, Corporate Governance, and the Reinvention of the Market for Corporate Control." *Journal of Applied Corporate Finance* 20, no. 3 (2008): 8–21.

In this book: See pages 13–14.

CHAPTER 2: A NEW SHIRT

The Effects of Private Equity on Corporate Governance

Justin and Gordon discuss the impact of private equity on a firm more generally.

Suggested reading: M. Wright and colleagues discuss the alignment of interests between a firm's managers, stockholders, and private equity investors.

- Wright, M., K. Amess, C. Weir, and S. Girma. "Private Equity and Corporate Governance: Retrospect and Prospects." *Corporate Governance* 17, no. 3 (2009): 353–375.

In this book: See pages 17–18.

Present Value Analysis and Strategic Decision Making (core strategy topic)

Justin discovers that present value analysis has some important limitations.

Suggested reading: A summary of a standard approach to using present value analysis to evaluate product extension strategies can be found in R. Brealey, S. Myers, F. Allen, and G. Geig. Some of the challenges associated with using these techniques to calculate the present value of innovative new products are discussed by P. Bromiley. Brealey et al. also do a good job of laying out the limitations of NPV in a highly innovative setting. Research on the interaction between a manager's present value analyses and his/her personal interests is known as "positive accounting." An excellent review of this work can be found in R. L. Watts and J. L. Zimmerman. Again, Bromiley examines these issues from a more behavioral perspective.

- Brealey, R., S. Myers, F. Allen, and G. Geig. *Principles of Corporate Finance.* New York: McGraw-Hill, 2010.

- Bromiley, P. *The Behavioral Foundations of Strategic Management.* Oxford: Blackwell, 2005.

- Watts, R. L., and J. L. Zimmerman. "Positive Accounting Theory: A Ten Year Perspective." *Accounting Review* 65, no. 1 (1990): 131–156.
- Barney (2011): Chapters 2 and 12.
- Barney and Hesterly (2010): Chapter 8.

In this book: See pages 26–35.

CHAPTER 3: A MOVING TARGET

Role of the CFO

Justin is surprised that the CFO is acting as a facilitator.

Suggested reading: This is actually not uncommon. M. Desai argues that CFOs are often in a good position to help build consensus, especially around controversial strategic choices—like investing in Plastiwear.

- Desai, M. "The Finance Function in a Global Corporation." *Harvard Business Review,* July–August 2008, 108–112.
- Barney (2011): Chapter 12.
- Barney and Hesterly (2010): Chapter 8.

In this book: See pages 38–40.

Five Forces Analysis of Industry Threats (core strategy topic)

Beckett applies the five forces model to show that HGS should not go into the shirt industry.

Suggested reading: The five forces model was first developed by M. Porter. Its limitations are described in Barney (2011) and elsewhere. Despite these limitations, five forces analysis is an important analytical tool that, in our experience, is often used in strategy development, by both managers and consultants.

- Porter, M. "How Competitive Forces Shape Strategy." *Harvard Business Review,* March–April 1979, 137–145.
- Porter, M. *Competitive Strategy.* New York: Free Press, 1980.
- Barney (2011): Chapters 3 and 4.
- Barney and Hesterly (2010): Chapter 2.

In this book: See pages 41–45 and 53–57.

Mentoring in Professional Service Firms

Ken's attempts to mentor Justin may not be having the impact he intends.

Suggested reading: The challenges of mentoring new employees in a professional service firm are discussed by T. DeLong, J. Gabarro, and R. Lees. The seminal work in this area is by K. Kram.

- DeLong, T., J. Gabarro, and R. Lees. "Why Mentoring Matters in a Hypercompetitive World." *Harvard Business Review,* January 2008, 115–121.

- Kram, K. *Mentoring at Work: Developmental Relationships in Organizational Life.* Glenview, IL: Scott Foresman, 1985.

In this book: See pages 52–57 and 83–85.

Capital Rationing

Ken's observation that capital available in a firm is limited and usually fixed every year is called the "capital rationing problem" in finance and is so obvious to managers that it is seldom explicitly discussed.

Suggested reading: If internal capital markets worked perfectly, then capital would not be rationed and Justin would be right—a firm should just fund all positive NPV projects. However, as H. Shin and R. Stulz show, internal capital markets rarely operate perfectly.

- Shin, H., and R. Stulz. "Are Internal Capital Markets Efficient?" *Quarterly Journal of Economics* 113, no. 2 (1998): 531–552.

- Barney (2011): Chapter 11.

- Barney and Hesterly (2010): Chapter 7.

In this book: See pages 54–55.

CHAPTER 4: A WORKING LUNCH

Outsiders on a Team

Bill arrives from outside the strategy team. What impact will that have on team dynamics?

Suggested reading: The impact of the arrival of "outsiders"—like Bill—on a working team is discussed in a classic book by E. Schein. Schein identifies three roles that group newcomers may adopt. At this point, it's not clear what role Bill will play.

- Schein, E. *Process Consultation.* Reading, MA: Addison-Wesley, 1969.

In this book: See page 60.

Related Diversification (core strategy topic)

Hutchins raises the question of related diversification and synergy—at least partly as a way to fill up his half-empty factory.

Suggested reading: The concept of related diversification and synergies across multiple businesses within a diversified firm is discussed in, among other places, R. Rumelt and in D. Collis and C. Montgomery. The analytical tools needed to evaluate whether or not manufacturing and volume purchasing at HGS qualify as potential synergies are discussed in chapter 5 of this book. These readings also describe why it is often difficult to realize these synergies.

- Rumelt, R. *Strategy, Structure, and Economic Performance.* Cambridge: Harvard University Press, 1974.

- Collis, D., and C. Montgomery. *Corporate Strategy: Resources and the Scope of the Firm.* Chicago: Irwin, 1997.

- Barney (2011): Chapter 11.

- Barney and Hesterly (2010): Chapter 7.

In this book: See pages 63–69.

Firm Boundaries and Resource-Based Competitive Advantages (core strategy topic)

One of the reasons Livia cites for not vertically integrating into Plastiwear production has to do with HGS's current manufacturing capabilities.

Suggested reading: The advantages of outsourcing functions where a firm does not have a capability-based competitive advantage are discussed in J. Barney.

- Barney, J. "How a Firm's Capabilities Affect Boundary Decisions." *Sloan Management Review* 40, no. 3 (1999): 137–145.

- Barney (2011): Chapter 10.

- Barney and Hesterly (2010): Chapter 7.

In this book: See pages 69–73.

Transactions Cost Economics (core strategy topic)

Livia's arguments about when to vertically integrate into a business function also build on what is known as transactions cost economics.

Suggested reading: See O. Williamson. In 2009, Professor Williamson won the Nobel Prize in economics for this and related work.

- Williamson, O. *The Economic Institutions of Capitalism.* New York: Free Press, 1985.

- Barney (2011): Chapter 10.

- Barney and Hesterly (2010): Chapter 6.

In this book: See pages 69–73.

Cost Leadership (core strategy topic)

Livia observes that having multiple suppliers of Plastiwear may make it difficult for any one supplier to realize economies of scale. This could increase the cost of producing Plastiwear.

Suggested reading: Cost leadership is one of two generic business-level strategies identified by M. Porter. The other is product differentiation. F. M. Scherer summarizes many sources of cost advantage.

- Porter, M. Competitive Strategy. New York: Free Press, 1980.

- Porter, M. *Competitive Advantage*. New York: Free Press, 1985.

- Scherer, F. M. *Industrial Market Structure and Economic Performance*. Boston: Houghton Mifflin, 1980.

- Barney (2011): Chapters 6 and 7.

- Barney and Hesterly (2010): Chapters 4 and 5.

In this book: See pages 69–73.

CHAPTER 5: A VALUABLE CHAIN

The VRIO Framework for Analyzing Internal Capabilities (core strategy topic)

The framework that Justin applies in the first part of this chapter is derived from what is known as resource-based theory.

Suggested reading: This theory is explained in detail in J. Barney and D. Clark. The economic underpinnings of this theory were articulated first by E. Penrose. The VRIO framework was first presented in J. B. Barney.

- Barney, J. B., and D. Clark. Resource-Based Theory: Creating and Sustaining Competitive Advantage. New York: Oxford University Press, 2007.

- Penrose, E. *The Theory of the Growth of the Firm*. New York: Wiley, 1959.

- Barney, J. B. "Firm Resources and Sustained Competitive Advantage." *Journal of Management* 17, no. 1 (1991): 99–120.

- Barney (2011): Chapter 5.

- Barney and Hesterly (2010): Chapter 3.

In this book: See pages 76–81.

Value Chain Analysis (core strategy topic)

The way Justin identifies potentially valuable strategies is to apply the value chain to the white shirt industry.

Suggested reading: Among the first to use the value chain to describe a firm's business was M. Porter.

- Porter, M. *Competitive Advantage.* New York: Free Press, 1985.

- Barney (2011): Chapter 5.

- Barney and Hesterly (2010): Chapter 3.

In this book: See pages 75–82 and 164–166.

CHAPTER 6: A THOUGHTFUL WORKOUT

Emotional Impact of Strategic Management Process

Justin is having a difficult time, emotionally. This reminds us that strategies are made by human beings and that feelings as well as logic impact both the strategy development process and its outcomes.

Suggested reading: The mourning process that Jackie sees Justin going through was first described by E. Kubler-Ross as comprising five stages: (1) denial, (2) anger, (3) bargaining, (4) depression, and (5) acceptance. This type of analysis was originally applied to responses to very difficult life events, including the death of a loved one. More recently, it has been used to understand responses to other stressful life events, including getting a divorce, losing a job, and performing poorly on the job.

- Kubler-Ross, E. *On Death and Dying.* New York: Routledge, 1973.

In this book: See pages 83–94.

CHAPTER 7: A SWEEPING VISION

Setting Audacious Goals

Tucker has some ambitious goals in mind.

Suggested reading: Some research suggests that setting ambitious goals—like those Tucker has in mind—can help motivate individual employees and improve a firm's performance. It can even be self-motivating. See, for example, E. Locke and G. Latham, as well as J. Collins and J. Porras. On the other hand, overly ambitious goals, or goals without clear approaches to their realization, can be very demotivating.

- Locke, E., and G. Latham. "Building a Practically Useful Theory of Goal Setting and Task Motivation: A 35-Year Odyssey." *American Psychologist* 57, no. 9 (2002): 705–717.

- Collins, J., and J. Porras. *Built to Last.* New York: Harper Collins, 1994.

In this book: See pages 99–104.

Product Differentiation (core strategy topic)

Tucker believes that Plastiwear can be positioned as the "miracle fiber of the twenty-first century"—an example of a product differentiation strategy.

Suggested reading: Product differentiation is the second of the two generic business strategies introduced by M. Porter. A variety of sources of product differentiation have been identified in the literature.

- Porter, M. *Competitive Strategy.* New York: Free Press, 1980.

- Scherer, F. M. *Industrial Market Structure and Economic Performance.* Boston: Houghton Mifflin, 1980.

- Barney (2011): Chapter 7.

- Barney and Hesterly (2010): Chapter 5.

In this book: See pages 99–104 and 142–144.

Agency Theory and Managerial Risk Preferences (core strategy topic)

Tucker believes that managers at HGS are risk averse and that this posture limits their ability to develop an appropriate strategy.

Suggested reading: The risk-averse preferences of managers are described in both finance and strategy literatures. Both literatures focus on the difficulties that managers have in diversifying their firm-specific human capital investments. Such risk aversion is generally seen as an example of agency conflicts between a firm's managers and its shareholders and can lead managers to diversify more broadly than what shareholders would prefer. See also H. Lang and R. Stulz.

- Jensen, M., and W. Meckling. "Theory of the Firm: Managerial Behavior, Agency Costs, and Ownership Structure." *Journal of Financial Economics* 3, no. 4 (1976): 305–360.

- Wang, H., and J. Barney. "Employee Incentives to Make Firm-Specific Investments: Implications for Resource-Based Theories of Corporate Diversification." *Academy of Management Review* 31, no. 2 (2006): 466–476.

- Lang, H., and R. Stulz. "Tobin's Q, Corporate Diversification, and Firm Performance." *Journal of Political Economy* 102, no. 6 (1994): 1248–1280.

- Barney (2011): Chapter 12.

- Barney and Hesterly (2010): Chapter 8.

In this book: See pages 100–101, 183–184, and 185–187.

Mergers and Acquisitions (core strategy topic)

Tucker believes that the market for corporate control is not likely to correct a merely mediocre firm.

Suggested reading: The ability of the market for corporate control to address poor organizational performance has been widely studied. The following sources are particularly insightful:

- Fama, E. "Efficient Capital Markets: A Review of Theory and Empirical Work." *Journal of Finance* 25, no. 2 (1970): 383–417.

- Jensen, M., and R. Ruback. "The Market for Corporate Control: The Scientific Evidence." *Journal of Financial Economics* 11, no. 1–4 (April 1983): 5–50.

- Marquez, R., and B. Yilmaz. "Information and Efficiency in Tender Offers." *Econometrica* 76, no. 5 (2008): 1075–1101.

- Barney (2011): Chapter 14.

- Barney and Hesterly (2010): Chapter 10.

In this book: See pages 105–107 and 169–171.

Conducting Interviews

Justin continues to struggle to structure and conduct useful interviews.

Suggested reading: Appropriate interview techniques for this type of context are described in P. Rosenfeld, J. Edwards, and M. Thomas. The role of these kinds of interviews in helping prepare a firm for significant strategic change is discussed by R. Lines.

- Rosenfeld, P., J. Edwards, and M. Thomas, eds. *Improving Organizational Surveys: New Directions, Methods, and Applications.* Newbury Park, CA: Sage, 1993.

- Lines, R. "Influence of Participation in Strategic Change: Resistance, Organizational Commitment, and Change Goal Achievement." *Journal of Change Management* 4, no. 3 (2004): 193–215.

In this book: See pages 30–34, 107–108, 109–110, and 120–121.

CHAPTER 8: A LONE RANGER

Evaluating Market Entry (core strategy topic)

Albright's implicit criterion for choosing potential markets for Plastiwear seems to be mostly potential sales revenues.

Suggested reading: More sophisticated approaches might look at the overall attractiveness of an industry (e.g., M. Porter) or at the likelihood that a firm will be able to gain and sustain a competitive advantage in an industry (e.g., J. Barney). A closely related approach can be found in G. Day.

- Porter, M. *Competitive Strategy.* New York: Free Press, 1980.

- Barney, J. "Firm Resources and Sustained Competitive Advantage." *Journal of Management* 17, no. 1 (1991): 99–120.

- Day, G. "Is It Real? Can We Win? Is It Worth Doing?" *Harvard Business Review,* December 2007, 110–120.

- Barney (2011): Chapters 3, 4, and 5.

- Barney and Hesterly (2010): Chapters 2 and 3.

In this book: See pages 111–126.

Exploitation Versus Exploration Strategies (core strategy topic)

Albright's distinction between product extensions and product innovations is similar to the distinction in the management literature between exploitation and exploration.

Suggested reading: This distinction was first introduced by J. March and by D. Levinthal and J. March. There is ongoing debate about whether or not a single firm can both exploit and explore. Some have argued that it is possible, although usually firms must create independent organizational units to execute these two strategies simultaneously. See, for example, S. Raisch, J. Birkinshaw, G. Probst, and M. Tushman. Even with independent units, others have argued that it is very difficult for single firms to both exploit and explore. See, for example, C. M. Christensen.

- March, J. "Exploration and Exploitation in Organizational Learning." *Organization Science* 2, no. 1 (1991): 71–87.

- Levinthal, D., and J. March. "The Myopia of Learning." *Strategic Management Journal* 14, special issue (1993): 95–112.

- Raisch, S., J. Birkinshaw, G. Probst, and M. Tushman. "Organizational Ambidexterity: Balancing Exploitation and Exploration for Sustained Advantage." *Organization Science* 20, no. 4 (2009): 685–695.

- Christensen, C. M. *The Innovator's Dilemma.* Boston: Harvard Business School Press, 1997.

- Barney (2011): Chapters 11 and 12.

- Barney and Hesterly (2010): Chapters 7 and 8.

In this book: See pages 113–117.

Alliances (core strategy topic)

Albright raises the possibility of using partnerships with potential customers to help explore uses of Plastiwear.

Suggested reading: There is now a growing understanding of the importance of customer-oriented research and development. See, for example, S. Thomke and E. von Hippel. However, Albright is suggesting the possibility of not learning from customers directly, but rather, working with other firms to identify potential customer needs. The opportunities and challenges associated with these kinds of partnerships have been described in J. Bleeke and D. Ernst; and R. Gulati.

- Thomke, S., and E. von Hippel. "Customers as Innovators: A New Way to Create Value." *Harvard Business Review,* April 2002, 74–81.

- Bleeke, J., and D. Ernst. *Collaborating to Compete.* New York: Wiley, 1993.

- Gulati, R. *Managing Network Resources: Alliances, Affiliations, and Other Relational Assets.* New York: Oxford University Press, 2007.

- Barney (2011): Chapter 13.

- Barney and Hesterly (2010): Chapter 9.

In this book: See pages 100–101, 113–114, 136–137, 166–171, 179–181, and 187–188.

Keeping Corporate Secrets

Justin puts a lot of faith in Plastiwear's patents. Albright is skeptical.

Suggested reading: Research by E. Mansfield, M. Schwartz, and S. Wagner focuses on the costs of imitating patents. They are substantially lower than the cost of innovation. More recent work shows that firms use technological head starts, secrecy, or patents to protect their intellectual property, but of these three, patenting is the least effective overall. See W. Cohen, R. Nelson, and J. Walsh.

- Mansfield, E., M. Schwartz, and S. Wagner. "Imitation Cost and Patents: An Empirical Study." *Economic Journal* 91, no. 364 (1981): 907–918.

- Cohen W., R. Nelson, and J. Walsh. "Protecting Their Intellectual Assets: Appropriability Conditions and Why U.S. Firms Patent (or Not)." NBER working paper no. 7552, 2000.

- Barney (2011): Chapters 3 and 5.

- Barney and Hesterly (2010): Chapters 2 and 3.

In this book: See pages 115–117.

CHAPTER 9: A TEAM EFFORT

The Value of Working with Teams

Justin did not take advantage of opportunities to work with the strategy team early in the engagement.

Suggested reading: Two helpful books that emphasize the importance of working in teams are by L. Gundry and L. LaMantia; and L. Bossidy and R. Charan.

- Gundry, L., and L. LaMantia. *Breakthrough Teams for Breakneck Times.* Chicago: Dearborn, 2001.

- Bossidy, L., and R. Charan. *Execution: The Discipline of Getting Things Done.* New York: Crown, 2002.

- Barney (2011): Chapter 5.

- Barney and Hesterly (2010): Chapter 3.

In this book: See pages 129–137.

Market Segmentation (core strategy topic)

The kind of segmentation analysis proposed by Vivek can be very valuable.

Suggested reading: See, for example, M. Treacy and F. Wiersema; M. McDonald and I. Dunbar; and D. Yankelovich and D. Meer.

- Treacy, M., and F. Wiersema. *The Discipline of Market Leaders: Choose Your Customers, Narrow Your Focus, Dominate Your Market.* Cambridge, MA: Perseus Publishing, 1997.

- McDonald, M., and I. Dunbar. *Market Segmentation.* Burlington, MA: Elsevier Butterworth-Heinemann, 2004.

- Yankelovich, D., and D. Meer. "Rediscovering Market Segmentation." *Harvard Business Review,* February 2006, 122–131.

- Barney (2011): Chapter 7.

- Barney and Hesterly (2010): Chapter 5.

In this book: See pages 131–132.

Decision Making Under Uncertainty

Vivek suggests that sometimes decisions have to be made even if there is not enough information to make a decision in a wholly rational way.

Suggested reading: Making decisions in the face of this level of uncertainty was originally discussed by F. Knight. More recent work on the use of simplifying heuristics to make decisions in these settings—where traditional NPV approaches will fail—includes S. Alvarez and J. Barney; and H. Courtney.

- Knight, F. *Risk, Uncertainty, and Profit.* New York: Houghton Mifflin, 1921.

- Alvarez, S., and J. Barney. "Discovery and Creation: Alternative Theories of Entrepreneurial Action." *Strategic Entrepreneurship Journal* 1, no. 1 (2007): 11–26.

- Courtney, H. *20/20 Foresight: Crafting Strategy in an Uncertain World.* Boston: Harvard Business School Publishing, 2001.

- Barney (2011): Chapter 8.

In this book: See pages 133–134.

Real Options Analysis (core strategy topic)

Justin raises the role that real options can play in choosing to use alliances to pursue an opportunity.

Suggested reading: These ideas were originally developed by B. Kogut. The managerial implications of real options logic is explored in R. McGrath and I. MacMillan. More quantitative approaches to real options analysis can be found in T. Luehrman.

- Kogut, B. "Joint Ventures and the Option to Acquire." *Management Science* 37, no. 1 (1991): 19–33.

- McGrath, R., and I. MacMillan. *The Entrepreneurial Mindset.* Boston: Harvard Business School Publishing, 2000.

- T. Luehrman. "Investment Opportunities as Real Options: Getting Started with the Numbers." *Harvard Business Review,* July–August 1998, 51–67.

- Barney (2011): Chapter 8.

In this book: See pages 134–137.

CHAPTER 10: A FITTING TEST

Serendipity and Innovation

Just like with Plastiwear, serendipity is often a component of successful R&D.

Suggested reading: See, for example, D. Hillis. An economic logic for recognizing the role of luck in gaining competitive advantages is described by J. B. Barney. Earlier arguments for the importance of luck in understanding firm performance can be found in R. Mancke and H. Demsetz.

- Hillis, D. "Stumbling on to Brilliance." *Harvard Business Review,* August 2002, 152.

- Barney, J. B. "Strategic Factor Markets: Expectations, Luck, and the Theory of Business Strategy." *Management Science* 32, no. 10 (1986): 1231–1241.

- Mancke, R. "Causes of Interfirm Profitability Differences: A New Interpretation of the Evidence." *Quarterly Journal of Economics* 88, no. 2 (1974): 181–193.

- Demsetz, H. "Industry Structure, Market Rivalry, and Public Policy." *Journal of Law and Economics* 16, no. 1 (1973): 1–9.

In this book: See pages 141–143.

Core Competencies (core strategy topic)

Vivek suggests that exploiting Plastiwear may be a new core competence for HGS.

Suggested reading: The original work on core competencies was done by C. K. Prahalad and G. Hamel. K. Coyne, S. Hall, and P. Clifford explore ambiguities around defining a firm's core competencies. The list of barriers to imitation that Vivek refers to was originally developed by R. Rumelt.

- Prahalad, C. K., and G. Hamel. "The Core Competence of the Corporation." *Harvard Business Review,* May–June, 1990, 79–93.

- Coyne, K., S. Hall, P. Clifford. "Is Your Core Competence a Mirage?" *The McKinsey Quarterly,* no. 1 (1997): 40–54.

- Rumelt, R. "Toward a Strategic Theory of the Firm." In *Competitive Strategic Management,* edited by R. Lamb, 556–570. Upper Saddle River, NJ: Prentice Hall, 1984.

- Barney (2011): Chapters 5 and 11.

- Barney and Hesterly (2010): Chapters 3 and 7.

In this book: See pages 145–149.

CHAPTER 11: A GOOD CALL

Managing Your Boss

Justin's phone call to Ken is an example of "managing your boss."

Suggested reading: This process is discussed nicely by J. Gabarro and J. Kotter.

- Gabarro, J., and J. Kotter. *Managing Your Boss.* Boston: Harvard Business School Publishing, 2008.

In this book: See pages 153–155 and 158.

Work-Life Balance

Justin's emotional response to Jackie suggests that his work-life balance is off—not surprising, given both the hours he's been working and the way he's been working.

Suggested reading: The long-term impact of such imbalance is discussed by A. McCarthy, C. Darcy, and G. Grady; L. Cohen, J. Duberley, and G. Musson; and K. Borne, F. Wilson, S. Lester, and J. Kickul.

- McCarthy, A., C. Darcy, and G. Grady. "Work-Life Balance Policy and Practice: Understanding Line Managers' Attitudes and Behavior." *Human Resource Management Review* 20, no. 2 (2010): 158–167.

- Cohen, L., J. Duberley, and G. Musson. "Work-Life Balance?" *Journal of Management Inquiry* 18, no. 3 (2009): 229–241.

- Borne, K., F. Wilson, S. Lester, and J. Kickul. "Embracing the Whole Individual: Advantages of a Dual-Centric Perspective of Work and Life." *Business Horizons* 52, no. 9 (2009): 387–398.

In this book: See pages 156–159.

CHAPTER 12: A CONSTRUCTIVE MEETING

Appropriating Value (core strategy topic)

After a brief discussion of white shirts, Livia turns to the question about the best way to appropriate value from the Plastiwear effort.

Suggested reading: The discussion about selling Plastiwear, licensing it, or deploying it within HGS integrates ideas on vertical integration, presented in chapter 4, with the discussion of the market for corporate control in chapter 7.

- Barney (2011): Chapters 10 and 14.

- Barney and Hesterly (2010): Chapters 6 and 10.

In this book: See pages 69–73, 101–102, and 163–166.

Downstream Manufacturing and Retail Sales (core strategy topic)

The third issue on Livia's list.

Suggested reading: The discussions about downstream manufacturing and retail sales both build on the transactions cost and resource-based arguments discussed in chapter 4.

- Barney (2011): Chapter 10.
- Barney and Hesterly (2010): Chapter 6.

In this book: See pages 69–73 and 164–166.

Upstream Manufacturing (core strategy topic)

The fourth issue on Livia's list.

Suggested reading: The discussion about upstream manufacturing also depends on transactions cost and resource-based logic. However, Vivek also introduces the possibility of using a joint venture to help protect HGS's intellectual property and to create some real options for HGS. The opportunities and challenges associated with joint ventures are discussed in chapter 8, and the real options associated with joint ventures are discussed in chapter 9.

- Barney (2011): Chapters 8, 10, and 13.
- Barney and Hesterly (2010): Chapters 6 and 9.

In this book: See pages 136 and 166–171.

Segment Profit Potential (core strategy topic)

The fifth issue on Livia's list.

Suggested reading: The discussion about segmentation analysis first occurs in chapter 9. The discussion about appropriate criteria for entering a new market is first discussed in chapter 8. The limitations of using cash flow–based NPV models in making decisions about entering brand new markets is discussed in chapter 2.

- Barney (2011): Chapters 2, 3, 4, 5, and 7.
- Barney and Hesterly (2010): Chapters 2, 3, and 5.

In this book: See pages 131–132, 165–172, and 177–178.

Organizing to Implement the Plastiwear Strategy (core strategy topic)

The sixth, and final, issue on Livia's list.

Suggested reading: The question of how the Plastiwear initiative should be managed within HGS has been raised before, but gets its first full treatment in this chapter. This type of decision has been discussed by O. Williamson and by J. Brickley, J. Zimmerman, and C. Smith.

- Williamson, O. *Markets and Hierarchies*. New York: Free Press, 1975.

- Brickley, J., J. Zimmerman, and C. Smith. *Managerial Economics and Organizational Architecture*. New York: McGraw-Hill, 2004.

- Barney (2011): Chapters 10 and 11.

- Barney and Hesterly (2010): Chapters 6 and 7.

In this book: See pages 173–174.

CHAPTER 13: A SEAMLESS ARGUMENT

Presentation Style

Livia gives an effective presentation. What makes it so good?

Suggested reading: While everyone needs to develop their own presentation style within the context of the preferred style in their company, some good commonsense suggestions can be found in V. Scudder, S. Williamson, and M. Gelb.

- Scudder, V. "Sound Check: How to Avoid Presentation Dangers." *Public Relations Tactics* 10, no. 10 (2009): 10.

- Williamson, S. "Creating Presentations That Get Results." *Public Relations Tactics* 14, no. 8 (2007): 20.

- Gelb, M. *Present Yourself*. Rolling Hills, CA: Jalmar, 1988.

In this book: See pages 177–190.

Insider Trading

Tucker's knowledge about the MG Management offer shows that HGS inappropriately shares sensitive information.

Suggested reading: If Tucker traded HGS's stock based on this information, or if people Tucker told about this offer traded based on this information, Tucker could be guilty of insider trading. The Security and Exchange Commission's definition of insider trading can be found at http://www.sec.gov/answer/insider.htm.

In this book: See pages 183–184 and 185–186.

Creating the Context for Change

The strategy team returns to a theme from their kickoff meeting (chapter 1)—how do they create conditions at HGS that will be favorable to the changes the team is recommending?

Suggested reading: The approach adopted in this chapter builds on K. Lewin's ideas about creating change, where the likelihood that any social system, including firms, will change depends on the balance between what he calls "driving forces" and "restraining forces." More recent work that develops this approach is by J. Dutton and S. Ashford and their colleagues.

- Lewin, K. *Field Theory in Social Science.* New York: Harper and Row, 1951.
- Dutton, J., S. Ashford, K. Lawrence, and K. Miner-Rubino. "Red Light, Green Light: Making Sense of the Organizational Context for Issue Selling." *Organization Science* 13, no. 4 (2002): 355–369.
- Dutton, J., S. Ashford, R. O'Neil, and K. Lawrence. "Moves That Matter: Issue Selling and Organizational Change." *Academy of Management Journal* 44, no. 4 (2001): 716–736.

In this book: See pages 184–190.

CHAPTER 14: A TAILORED PRESENTATION

Emotional Commitments to a Work Product

Justin has "fallen in love" with the deck. He can't imagine anyone not being completely convinced by it and even wonders why Ken doesn't just leave it alone.

Suggested reading: There is growing recognition of the importance of emotion at work. See, for example, N. Ashkanasy, C. Hartel, and W. Zerbe; and L. Festinger.

- Ashkanasy, N., C. Hartel, and W. Zerbe, eds. *Emotions in the Workplace: Research, Theory, and Practice.* Westport, CT: Quorum, 2005.
- Festinger, L. *A Theory of Cognitive Dissonance.* Palo Alto, CA: Stanford, 1957.

In this book: See pages 193 and 200–202.

Managing the Board

Vivek cautions Justin that Carl needs to build consensus among his management team and with the board before he can announce a decision about Plastiwear.

Suggested reading: The classic statement about managing the board is by J. Lorsch. How these principles can be used in practice is discussed by R. Charan; and P. Terry, J. Rao, S. Ashford, and S. Socolof.

- Lorsch, J. "Empowering the Board." *Harvard Business Review,* January–February 1995, 107–117.
- Charan, R. *Boards at Work.* San Francisco: Jossey-Bass, 1998.
- Terry, P., J. Rao, S. Ashford, and S. Socolof. "Who Can Help the CEO?" *Harvard Business Review,* April 2009, 33–40.
- Barney (2011): Chapter 12.
- Barney and Hesterly (2010): Chapter 8.

In this book: See pages 193–203.

A READING LIST

EPILOGUE: A STAFFING QUESTION

Getting Staffed

Justin is concerned about whether and when he will be staffed on another engagement.

Suggested reading: In many professional service firms, getting staffed is a measure of how much your services are in demand, and staffing impacts and is impacted by various performance metrics—including billable hours. This has been studied the most in law firms. See, for example, A. Likierman; D. Barco, and D. Combs; and E. Poll.

- Likierman, A. "The Five Traps of Performance Measurement." *Harvard Business Review,* October 2009, 96–101.

- Barco, D., and D. Combs. "Calculus of the Damned." *American Lawyer* 31, no. 5 (2009): 22–23.

- Poll, E. *Law Firm Fees and Compensation.* Venice, CA: LawBiz Management Company, 2008.

In this book: See pages 205–211.

Changing Careers

Justin is totally surprised by HGS's decision to hire Livia, and Livia's decision to accept the offer.

Suggested reading: A humorous account of the transition from management consulting to management is given by A. Simonton and G. Kiser. J. Citrin recently wrote a blog about what consultants experience when they become managers (and a second blog about what it takes to work for a manager who was a former consultant).

- Simonton, A., and G. Kiser. *Confessions of a Management Consultant Turned CEO.* Knoxville, TN: SPC Press, 1996.

- Citrin, J. "Transitioning to Top-Level Management," blog post, December 5, 2006, http://finance.yahoo.com/expert/article/leadership/16842; and "Working for an Ex-Management Consultant," blog post December 20, 2006, http://au.pfinance.yahoo.com/b/leadership/26/working-for-an-ex-management-consultant.

In this book: See pages 209–211.

ABOUT THE AUTHORS

JAY B. BARNEY received his BS from Brigham Young University and his master's degree and PhD from Yale University. He served on the faculties at the Anderson Graduate School of Management at UCLA and at the Mays School of Business at Texas A&M, and currently is a professor and holds the Chase Chair in Strategic Management at the Fisher College of Business at The Ohio State University. In addition, he has received two honorary doctorates—from Lund University (Sweden, 2001) and from the Copenhagen Business School (Denmark, 2008)—and has held honorary faculty appointments in China (Peking University, Nankai University, and Sun Yat Sen University), New Zealand (Waikato University), and the United Kingdom (Brunel University).

Jay's research focuses on the relationship between firm resources and capabilities and sustained competitive advantage. He has published over one hundred articles and six books on this topic and was elected as a Fellow of the Academy of Management in 2004 and a Fellow of the Strategic Management Society in 2007. In 2006, he received the Irwin Outstanding Educator Award from the Business Policy and Strategy Division of the Academy of Management. He served as Chair of this division (1996) and currently serves as the President of the Strategic Management Society.

Jay teaches undergraduates, MBAs, and executive MBAs at Ohio State. He has also taught in a variety of executive training programs at Ohio State and other universities (including UCLA, SMU, Michigan, and Bocconi University in Milan) and at several firms (including AEP, AT&T, IBM, Nationwide Insurance, and McKinsey & Company). Jay's consulting work focuses on strategic analysis and organizational change. His clients have included Hewlett-Packard, Texas Instruments, Tenneco, Arco, Koch Industries, Nationwide Insurance, and Columbus Public Schools.

Jay now lives in Ohio with his wife, Kim. They have three married children and eight grandchildren.

TRISH GORMAN CLIFFORD selectively teaches and consults on topics associated with complex managerial challenges. She has taught strategy at the undergraduate, master's, doctoral, and executive levels; presented her research at numerous national and international conferences; and consulted over the past twenty-five years to a mix of Fortune 500 and niche clients in a broad array of industries and geographies. She has published articles in *Harvard Business Review* and the *McKinsey Quarterly* and has conducted hundreds of workshops on strategy development, option generation and evaluation, organizational alignment, and related topics.

Trish is currently an adjunct professor at Columbia University's School of International and Public Affairs and serves as invited Faculty for Executive Education programs at the London Business School, Wharton Graduate School of Business, Duke Corporate Executive Education, and other universities and corporate learning centers. She has held full-time faculty positions at the University of Connecticut and at Columbia University Executive Education, and was Academic Director of the Global Consulting Practicum at Wharton.

Trish worked as a consultant for The LEK Partnership and for McKinsey & Company, and has also served McKinsey as a strategy expert and as Director of Global Strategy Learning. Prior to her academic career, Trish held positions as a vice president at TCG Materials, a general manager at Westex Mills, and an internal consultant at Inland Steel.

Trish earned a BA in the Honors Program in Mathematical Methods in the Social Sciences and Economics from Northwestern University, an MBA from the Anderson School of Management at UCLA, and a PhD in strategy and economics from Case Western Reserve University, where her dissertation on interfirm relationships won support from MIT's International Motor Vehicle Program.

She now lives in Connecticut with her husband, Devereaux, and their three children.